M000159458

Python Data Cleaning Cookbook

Modern techniques and Python tools to detect and remove dirty data and extract key insights

Michael Walker

BIRMINGHAM—MUMBAI

Python Data Cleaning Cookbook

Copyright © 2020 Packt Publishing

All rights reserved. No part of this book may be reproduced, stored in a retrieval system, or transmitted in any form or by any means, without the prior written permission of the publisher, except in the case of brief quotations embedded in critical articles or reviews.

Every effort has been made in the preparation of this book to ensure the accuracy of the information presented. However, the information contained in this book is sold without warranty, either express or implied. Neither the author, nor Packt Publishing or its dealers and distributors, will be held liable for any damages caused or alleged to have been caused directly or indirectly by this book.

Packt Publishing has endeavored to provide trademark information about all of the companies and products mentioned in this book by the appropriate use of capitals. However, Packt Publishing cannot guarantee the accuracy of this information.

Commissioning Editor: Sunith Shetty
Acquisition Editor: Ali Abidi
Senior Editor: Mohammed Yusuf Imaratwale
Content Development Editor: Sean Lobo
Technical Editor: Manikandan Kurup
Copy Editor: Safis Editing
Project Coordinator: Aishwarya Mohan
Proofreader: Safis Editing
Indexer: Tejal Daruwale Soni
Production Designer: Nilesh Mohite

First published: December 2020
Production reference: 1091220

Published by Packt Publishing Ltd.
Livery Place
35 Livery Street
Birmingham
B3 2PB, UK.

ISBN 978-1-80056-566-1

www.packt.com

Packt.com

Subscribe to our online digital library for full access to over 7,000 books and videos, as well as industry leading tools to help you plan your personal development and advance your career. For more information, please visit our website.

Why subscribe?

- Spend less time learning and more time coding with practical eBooks and Videos from over 4,000 industry professionals

- Improve your learning with Skill Plans built especially for you

- Get a free eBook or video every month

- Fully searchable for easy access to vital information

- Copy and paste, print, and bookmark content

Did you know that Packt offers eBook versions of every book published, with PDF and ePub files available? You can upgrade to the eBook version at packt.com and as a print book customer, you are entitled to a discount on the eBook copy. Get in touch with us at customercare@packtpub.com for more details.

At www.packt.com, you can also read a collection of free technical articles, sign up for a range of free newsletters, and receive exclusive discounts and offers on Packt books and eBooks.

Contributors

About the author

Michael Walker has worked as a data analyst for over 30 years at a variety of educational institutions. He has also taught data science, research methods, statistics, and computer programming to undergraduates since 2006. He generates public sector and foundation reports and conducts analyses for publication in academic journals.

About the reviewers

Meng-Chieh Ling has a Ph.D. in theoretical condensed matter physics from Karlsruhe Institute of Technology in Germany. He switched from physics to data science to pursue a successful career. After working for AGT International in Darmstadt for 2 years, he joined CHECK24 Fashion as a data scientist in Düsseldorf. His responsibilities include applying machine learning to improve the efficiency of data cleansing, automatic attributes tagging with deep learning, and developing image-based recommendation systems.

Sébastien Celles is a professor of applied physics at Poitiers Institute of Technology (the thermal science department). He has used Python for numerical simulations, data plotting, data predictions, and various other tasks since the early 2000s. He was a technical reviewer of the books Mastering Python for data science and Julia for Data Science: Explore data science from scratch with Julia

He is also the author of some Python packages available on PyPi, including `openweathermap_requests`, `pandas_degreedays`, `pandas_confusion`, `python-constraint`, `python-server`, and `python-windrose`.

Packt is searching for authors like you

If you're interested in becoming an author for Packt, please visit `authors.packtpub.com` and apply today. We have worked with thousands of developers and tech professionals, just like you, to help them share their insight with the global tech community. You can make a general application, apply for a specific hot topic that we are recruiting an author for, or submit your own idea.

Table of Contents

Preface

1

Anticipating Data Cleaning Issues when Importing Tabular Data into pandas

2

Anticipating Data Cleaning Issues when Importing HTML and JSON into pandas

3

Taking the Measure of Your Data

4
Identifying Missing Values and Outliers in Subsets of Data

5
Using Visualizations for the Identification of Unexpected Values

6

Cleaning and Exploring Data with Series Operations

7

Fixing Messy Data when Aggregating

8

Addressing Data Issues When Combining DataFrames

9

Tidying and Reshaping Data

10

User-Defined Functions and Classes to Automate Data Cleaning

Preface

This book is a practical guide to data cleaning, broadly defined as all tasks necessary to prepare data for analysis. It is organized by the tasks usually completed during the data cleaning process: importing data, viewing data diagnostically, identifying outliers and unexpected values, imputing values, tidying data, and so on. Each recipe walks the reader from raw data through the completion of a specific data cleaning task.

There are already a number of very good pandas books. Unsurprisingly, there is some overlap between those texts and this one. However, the emphasis here is different. I focus as much on the why as on the how in this book.

Since pandas is still relatively new, the lessons I have learned about cleaning data have been shaped by my experiences with other tools. Before settling into my current work routine with Python and R about 8 years ago, I relied mostly on C# and T-SQL in the early 2000s, SAS and Stata in the 90s, and FORTRAN and Pascal in the 80s. Most readers of this text probably have experience with a variety of data cleaning and analysis tools. In many ways the specific tool is less significant than the data preparation task and the attributes of the data. I would have covered pretty much the same topics if I had been asked to write *The SAS Data Cleaning Cookbook* or *The R Data Cleaning Cookbook*. I just take a Python/pandas specific approach to the same data cleaning challenges that analysts have faced for decades.

I start each chapter with how to think about the particular data cleaning task at hand before discussing how to approach it with a tool from the Python ecosystem - pandas, NumPy, matplotlib, SciPy, and so on. This is reinforced in each recipe by a discussion of the implications of what we are uncovering in the data. I try to connect tool to purpose. For example, concepts like skew and kurtosis matter as much for handling outliers as does knowing how to update pandas series values.

Who this book is for

This book is for anyone looking for ways to handle messy, duplicate, and poor data using different Python tools and techniques. The book takes a recipe-based approach to help you to learn how to clean and manage data. Working knowledge of Python programming is all you need to get the most out of the book.

What this book covers

Chapter 1, Anticipating Data Cleaning Issues when Importing Tabular Data into pandas, explores tools for loading CSV files, Excel files, relational database tables, SAS, SPSS, and Stata files, and R files into pandas DataFrames.

Chapter 2, Anticipating Data Cleaning Issues when Importing HTML and JSON into pandas, discusses techniques for reading and normalizing JSON data, and for web scraping.

Chapter 3, Taking the Measure of Your Data, introduces common techniques for navigating around a DataFrame, selecting columns and rows, and generating summary statistics.

Chapter 4, Identifying Missing Values and Outliers in Subsets of Data, explores a wide range of strategies to identify missing values and outliers across a whole DataFrame and by selected groups.

Chapter 5, Using Visualizations for the Identification of Unexpected Values, demonstrates the use of matplotlib and seaborn tools to visualize how key variables are distributed, including with histograms, boxplots, scatter plots, line plots, and violin plots.

Chapter 6, Cleaning and Exploring Data with Series Operations, discusses updating pandas series with scalars, arithmetic operations, and conditional statements based on the values of one or more series.

Chapter 7, Fixing Messy Data when Aggregating, demonstrates multiple approaches to aggregating data by group, and discusses when to choose one approach over the others.

Chapter 8, Addressing Data Issues when Combining DataFrames, examines different strategies for concatenating and merging data, and how to anticipate common data challenges when combining data.

Chapter 9, Tidying and Reshaping Data, introduces several strategies for de-duplicating, stacking, melting, and pivoting data.

Chapter 10, User-Defined Functions and Classes to Automate Data Cleaning, examines how to turn many of the techniques from the first nine chapters into reusable code.

To get the most out of this book

Working knowledge of Python programming is all you need to get the most out of this book. System requirements are mentioned in the following table. Alternatively, you can use Google Colab as well.

Software/Hardware covered in the book	OS Requirements
Python 3.6 +	Windows, Mac OS X, and Linux (Any)
1 TB space, 8 GB RAM, i5 processor (preferred specs)	
Google Colab	

If you are using the digital version of this book, we advise you to type the code yourself or access the code via the GitHub repository (link available in the next section). Doing so will help you avoid any potential errors related to the copying and pasting of code.

Download the example code files

You can download the example code files for this book from GitHub at `https://github.com/PacktPublishing/Python-Data-Cleaning-Cookbook`. In case there's an update to the code, it will be updated on the existing GitHub repository.

We also have other code bundles from our rich catalog of books and videos available at `https://github.com/PacktPublishing/`. Check them out!

Download the color images

We also provide a PDF file that has color images of the screenshots/diagrams used in this book. You can download it here: `https://static.packt-cdn.com/downloads/9781800565661_ColorImages.pdf`.

Conventions used

There are a number of text conventions used throughout this book.

`Code in text`: Indicates code words in text, database table names, folder names, filenames, file extensions, pathnames, dummy URLs, user input, and Twitter handles. Here is an example: "Define a `getcases` function that returns a series for `total_cases_pm` for the countries of a region."

A block of code is set as follows:

```
>>> import pandas as pd
>>> import matplotlib.pyplot as plt
>>> import statsmodels.api as sm
```

Any command-line input or output is written as follows:

```
$ pip install pyarrow
```

Bold: Indicates a new term, an important word, or words that you see onscreen. For example, words in menus or dialog boxes appear in the text like this. Here is an example: "We will work with cumulative data on coronavirus cases and deaths by country, and the **National Longitudinal Survey (NLS)** data."

> **Tips or important notes**
> Appear like this.

Sections

In this book, you will find several headings that appear frequently (*Getting ready*, *How to do it...*, *How it works...*, *There's more...*, and *See also*).

To give clear instructions on how to complete a recipe, use these sections as follows:

Getting ready

This section tells you what to expect in the recipe and describes how to set up any software or any preliminary settings required for the recipe.

How to do it...

This section contains the steps required to follow the recipe.

How it works...

This section usually consists of a detailed explanation of what happened in the previous section.

There's more...

This section consists of additional information about the recipe in order to make you more knowledgeable about the recipe.

See also

This section provides helpful links to other useful information for the recipe.

Get in touch

Feedback from our readers is always welcome.

General feedback: If you have questions about any aspect of this book, mention the book title in the subject of your message and email us at customercare@packtpub.com.

Errata: Although we have taken every care to ensure the accuracy of our content, mistakes do happen. If you have found a mistake in this book, we would be grateful if you would report this to us. Please visit www.packtpub.com/support/errata, selecting your book, clicking on the Errata Submission Form link, and entering the details.

Piracy: If you come across any illegal copies of our works in any form on the Internet, we would be grateful if you would provide us with the location address or website name. Please contact us at copyright@packt.com with a link to the material.

If you are interested in becoming an author: If there is a topic that you have expertise in and you are interested in either writing or contributing to a book, please visit authors.packtpub.com.

Reviews

Please leave a review. Once you have read and used this book, why not leave a review on the site that you purchased it from? Potential readers can then see and use your unbiased opinion to make purchase decisions, we at Packt can understand what you think about our products, and our authors can see your feedback on their book. Thank you!

For more information about Packt, please visit packt.com.

1
Anticipating Data Cleaning Issues when Importing Tabular Data into pandas

Scientific distributions of **Python** (Anaconda, WinPython, Canopy, and so on) provide analysts with an impressive range of data manipulation, exploration, and visualization tools. One important tool is pandas. Developed by Wes McKinney in 2008, but really gaining in popularity after 2012, pandas is now an essential library for data analysis in Python. We work with pandas extensively in this book, along with popular packages such as `numpy`, `matplotlib`, and `scipy`.

A key pandas object is the data frame, which represents data as a tabular structure, with rows and columns. In this way, it is similar to the other data stores we discuss in this chapter. However, a pandas data frame also has indexing functionality that makes selecting, combining, and transforming data relatively straightforward, as the recipes in this book will demonstrate.

Before we can make use of this great functionality, we have to get our data into pandas. Data comes to us in a wide variety of formats: as CSV or Excel files, as tables from SQL databases, from statistical analysis packages such as SPSS, Stata, SAS, or R, from non-tabular sources such as JSON, and from web pages.

We examine tools for importing tabular data in this recipe. Specifically, we cover the following topics:

- Importing CSV files
- Importing Excel files
- Importing data from SQL databases
- Importing SPSS, Stata, and SAS data
- Importing R data
- Persisting tabular data

Technical requirements

The code and notebooks for this chapter are available on GitHub at `https://github.com/PacktPublishing/Python-Data-Cleaning-Cookbook`

Importing CSV files

The `read_csv` method of the `pandas` library can be used to read a file with **comma separated values** (CSV) and load it into memory as a pandas data frame. In this recipe, we read a CSV file and address some common issues: creating column names that make sense to us, parsing dates, and dropping rows with critical missing data.

Raw data is often stored as CSV files. These files have a carriage return at the end of each line of data to demarcate a row, and a comma between each data value to delineate columns. Something other than a comma can be used as the delimiter, such as a tab. Quotation marks may be placed around values, which can be helpful when the delimiter occurs naturally within certain values, which sometimes happens with commas.

All data in a CSV file are characters, regardless of the logical data type. This is why it is easy to view a CSV file, presuming it is not too large, in a text editor. The pandas `read_csv` method will make an educated guess about the data type of each column, but you will need to help it along to ensure that these guesses are on the mark.

Getting ready

Create a folder for this chapter and create a new Python script or **Jupyter Notebook** file in that folder. Create a data subfolder and place the landtempssample.csv file in that subfolder. Alternatively, you could retrieve all of the files from the GitHub repository. Here is a code sample from the beginning of the CSV file:

```
locationid,year,month,temp,latitude,longitude,stnelev,station,
countryid,country
USS0010K01S,2000,4,5.27,39.9,-110.75,2773.7,INDIAN_
CANYON,US,United States
CI000085406,1940,5,18.04,-18.35,-70.333,58.0,ARICA,CI,Chile
USC00036376,2013,12,6.22,34.3703,-91.1242,61.0,SAINT_
CHARLES,US,United States
ASN00024002,1963,2,22.93,-34.2833,140.6,65.5,BERRI_
IRRIGATION,AS,Australia
ASN00028007,2001,11,,-14.7803,143.5036,79.4,MUSGRAVE,AS,Austra
lia
```

> **Note**
>
> This dataset, taken from the Global Historical Climatology Network integrated database, is made available for public use by the United States National Oceanic and Atmospheric Administration at https://www.ncdc.noaa.gov/data-access/land-based-station-data/land-based-datasets/global-historical-climatology-network-monthly-version-4. This is just a 100,000-row sample of the full dataset, which is also available in the repository.

How to do it...

We will import a CSV file into pandas, taking advantage of some very useful read_csv options:

1. Import the pandas library and set up the environment to make viewing the output easier:

    ```
    >>> import pandas as pd
    >>> pd.options.display.float_format = '{:,.2f}'.format
    >>> pd.set_option('display.width', 85)
    >>> pd.set_option('display.max_columns', 8)
    ```

2. Read the data file, set new names for the headings, and parse the date column.

    Pass an argument of 1 to the skiprows parameter to skip the first row, pass a list of columns to parse_dates to create a pandas datetime column from those columns, and set low_memory to False to reduce the usage of memory during the import process:

    ```
    >>> landtemps = pd.read_csv('data/landtempssample.csv',
    ...   names=['stationid','year','month','avgtemp','latitude',
    ...   'longitude','elevation','station','countryid','country'],
    ...       skiprows=1,
    ...       parse_dates=[['month','year']],
    ...       low_memory=False)

    >>> type(landtemps)
    <class 'pandas.core.frame.DataFrame'>
    ```

3. Get a quick glimpse of the data.

    View the first few rows. Show the data type for all columns, as well as the number of rows and columns:

    ```
    >>> landtemps.head(7)
       month_year    stationid   ...  countryid          country
    0  2000-04-01  USS0010K01S   ...         US    United States
    1  1940-05-01  CI000085406   ...         CI            Chile
    2  2013-12-01  USC00036376   ...         US    United States
    3  1963-02-01  ASN00024002   ...         AS        Australia
    4  2001-11-01  ASN00028007   ...         AS        Australia
    5  1991-04-01  USW00024151   ...         US    United States
    6  1993-12-01  RSM00022641   ...         RS           Russia

    [7 rows x 9 columns]
    >>> landtemps.dtypes
    month_year      datetime64[ns]
    stationid               object
    avgtemp                float64
    ```

```
latitude            float64
longitude           float64
elevation           float64
station             object
countryid           object
country             object
dtype: object
>>> landtemps.shape
(100000, 9)
```

4. Give the date column a better name and view the summary statistics for average monthly temperature:

```
>>> landtemps.rename(columns={'month_
year':'measuredate'}, inplace=True)
>>> landtemps.dtypes
measuredate     datetime64[ns]
stationid           object
avgtemp             float64
latitude            float64
longitude           float64
elevation           float64
station             object
countryid           object
country             object
dtype: object
>>> landtemps.avgtemp.describe()
count    85,554.00
mean        10.92
std         11.52
min        -70.70
25%          3.46
50%         12.22
75%         19.57
max         39.95
Name: avgtemp, dtype: float64
```

5. Look for missing values for each column.

Use `isnull`, which returns `True` for each value that is missing for each column, and `False` when not missing. Chain this with `sum` to count the missings for each column. (When working with Boolean values, `sum` treats `True` as `1` and `False` as `0`. I will discuss method chaining in the *There's more...* section of this recipe):

```
>>> landtemps.isnull().sum()
measuredate           0
stationid             0
avgtemp           14446
latitude              0
longitude             0
elevation             0
station               0
countryid             0
country               5
dtype: int64
```

6. Remove rows with missing data for `avgtemp`.

    Use the `subset` parameter to tell `dropna` to drop rows where `avgtemp` is missing. Set `inplace` to `True`. Leaving `inplace` at its default value of `False` would display the data frame, but the changes we have made would not be retained. Use the `shape` attribute of the data frame to get the number of rows and columns:

```
>>> landtemps.dropna(subset=['avgtemp'], inplace=True)
>>> landtemps.shape
(85554, 9)
```

That's it! Importing CSV files into pandas is as simple as that.

How it works...

Almost all of the recipes in this book use the `pandas` library. We refer to it as `pd` to make it easier to reference later. This is customary. We also use `float_format` to display float values in a readable way and `set_option` to make the terminal output wide enough to accommodate the number of variables.

Much of the work is done by the first line in *step 2*. We use read_csv to load a pandas data frame in memory and call it landtemps. In addition to passing a filename, we set the names parameter to a list of our preferred column headings. We also tell read_csv to skip the first row, by setting skiprows to 1, since the original column headings are in the first row of the CSV file. If we do not tell it to skip the first row, read_csv will treat the header row in the file as actual data.

read_csv also solves a date conversion issue for us. We use the parse_dates parameter to ask it to convert the month and year columns to a date value.

Step 3 runs through a few standard data checks. We use head(7) to print out all columns for the first 7 rows. We use the dtypes attribute of the data frame to show the data type of all columns. Each column has the expected data type. In pandas, character data has the object data type, a data type that allows for mixed values. shape returns a tuple, whose first element is the number of rows in the data frame (100,000 in this case) and whose second element is the number of columns (9).

When we used read_csv to parse the month and year columns, it gave the resulting column the name month_year. We use the rename method in *step 4* to give that column a better name. We need to specify inplace=True to replace the old column name with the new column name in memory. The describe method provides summary statistics on the avgtemp column.

Notice that the count for avgtemp indicates that there are 85,554 rows that have valid values for avgtemp. This is out of 100,000 rows for the whole data frame, as provided by the shape attribute. The listing of missing values for each column in *step 5* (landtemps.isnull().sum()) confirms this: *100,000 – 85,554 = 14,446.*

Step 6 drops all rows where avgtemp is NaN. (The NaN value, not a number, is the pandas representation of missing values.) subset is used to indicate which column to check for missings. The shape attribute for landtemps now indicates that there are 85,554 rows, which is what we would expect given the previous count from describe.

There's more...

If the file you are reading uses a delimiter other than a comma, such as a tab, this can be specified in the sep parameter of read_csv. When creating the pandas data frame, an index was also created. The numbers to the far left of the output when head and sample were run are index values. Any number of rows can be specified for head or sample. The default value is 5.

Setting `low_memory` to `False` causes `read_csv` to parse data in chunks. This is easier on systems with lower memory when working with larger files. However, the full data frame will still be loaded into memory once `read_csv` completes successfully.

The `landtemps.isnull().sum()` statement is an example of chaining methods. First, `isnull` returns a data frame of `True` and `False` values, resulting from testing whether each column value is `null`. `sum` takes that data frame and sums the `True` values for each column, interpreting the `True` values as `1` and the `False` values as `0`. We would have obtained the same result if we had used the following two steps:

```
>>> checknull = landtemps.isnull()
>>> checknull.sum()
```

There is no hard and fast rule for when to chain methods and when not to. I find it helpful to chain when I really think of something I am doing as being a single step, but only two or more steps, mechanically speaking. Chaining also has the side benefit of not creating extra objects that I might not need.

The dataset used in this recipe is just a sample from the full land temperatures database with almost 17 million records. You can run the larger file if your machine can handle it, with the following code:

```
>>> landtemps = pd.read_csv('data/landtemps.zip',
compression='zip',
...        names=['stationid','year','month','avgtemp','latitude',
...
'longitude','elevation','station','countryid','country'],
...        skiprows=1,
...        parse_dates=[['month','year']],
...        low_memory=False)
```

`read_csv` can read a compressed ZIP file. We get it to do this by passing the name of the ZIP file and the type of compression.

See also

Subsequent recipes in this chapter, and in other chapters, set indexes to improve navigation over rows and merging.

A significant amount of reshaping of the Global Historical Climatology Network raw data was done before using it in this recipe. We demonstrate this in *Chapter 8, Addressing Data Issues when Combining DataFrames*. That recipe also shows how to read a text file that is not delimited, one that is fixed, by using `read_fwf`.

Importing Excel files

The `read_excel` method of the `pandas` library can be used to import data from an Excel file and load it into memory as a pandas data frame. In this recipe, we import an Excel file and handle some common issues when working with Excel files: extraneous header and footer information, selecting specific columns, removing rows with no data, and connecting to particular sheets.

Despite the tabular structure of Excel, which invites the organization of data into rows and columns, spreadsheets are not datasets and do not require people to store data in that way. Even when some data conforms to those expectations, there is often additional information in rows or columns before or after the data to be imported. Data types are not always as clear as they are to the person who created the spreadsheet. This will be all too familiar to anyone who has ever battled with importing leading zeros. Moreover, Excel does not insist that all data in a column be of the same type, or that column headings be appropriate for use with a programming language such as Python.

Fortunately, `read_excel` has a number of options for handling messiness in Excel data. These options make it relatively easy to skip rows and select particular columns, and to pull data from a particular sheet or sheets.

Getting ready

You can download the GDPpercapita.xlsx file, as well as the code for this recipe, from the GitHub repository for this book. The code assumes that the Excel file is in a data subfolder. Here is a view of the beginning of the file:

Dataset: Metropolitan areas							
Variables GDP per capita (USD), constant prices, constant PPP, base year 2015							
Unit US Dollar							
Year	2001	2002	2003	2004	2005	2006	2007
Metropolitan areas							
AUS: Australia							
AUS01: Greater Sydney	43313	44008	45424	45837	45423	45547	45880
AUS02: Greater Melbourne	40125	40894	41602	42188	41484	41589	42316
AUS03: Greater Brisbane	37580	37564	39080	40762	42976	44475	44635

Figure 1.1 – View of the dataset

And here is a view of the end of the file:

USA162: Tuscaloosa	35370	36593	38907	41846	44774	44298	46190
USA164: Linn	53047	51761	54894	58660	60195	58244	61742
USA165: Lafayette (IN)	38057	38723	39173	40412	40285	40879	41717
USA167: Weber	34592	34997	35587	35776	37613	41213	41554
USA169: Cass	44597	46856	49043	49134	49584	50417	51596
USA170: Benton (AR)	41988	44687	45296	47799	49260	47329	45503
Data extracted on 05 May 2020 10:55 UTC (GMT) from OECD.Stat							

Figure 1.2 – View of the dataset

> **Note**
>
> This dataset, from the Organisation for Economic Co-operation and Development, is available for public use at `https://stats.oecd.org/`.

How to do it...

We import an Excel file into pandas and do some initial data cleaning:

1. Import the `pandas` library:

    ```
    >>> import pandas as pd
    ```

2. Read the Excel per capita GDP data.

    Select the sheet with the data we need, but skip the columns and rows that we do not want. Use the `sheet_name` parameter to specify the sheet. Set `skiprows` to 4 and `skipfooter` to 1 to skip the first four rows (the first row is hidden) and the last row. We provide values for `usecols` to get data from column A and columns C through T (column B is blank). Use `head` to view the first few rows:

    ```
    >>> percapitaGDP = pd.read_excel("data/GDPpercapita.
    xlsx",
    ...      sheet_name="OECD.Stat export",
    ...      skiprows=4,
    ...      skipfooter=1,
    ...      usecols="A,C:T")

    >>> percapitaGDP.head()
                          Year   2001  ...    2017   2018
    0       Metropolitan areas    NaN  ...     NaN    NaN
    1           AUS: Australia     ..  ...      ..     ..
    2    AUS01: Greater Sydney  43313  ...   50578  49860
    3  AUS02: Greater Melbourne  40125  ...   43025  42674
    4   AUS03: Greater Brisbane  37580  ...   46876  46640

    [5 rows x 19 columns]
    ```

3. Use the `info` method of the data frame to view data types and the `non-null` count:

    ```
    >>> percapitaGDP.info()
    <class 'pandas.core.frame.DataFrame'>
    ```

```
RangeIndex: 702 entries, 0 to 701
Data columns (total 19 columns):
 #   Column  Non-Null Count   Dtype
---  ------  --------------   -----
 0   Year    702 non-null     object
 1   2001    701 non-null     object
 2   2002    701 non-null     object
 3   2003    701 non-null     object
 4   2004    701 non-null     object
 5   2005    701 non-null     object
 6   2006    701 non-null     object
 7   2007    701 non-null     object
 8   2008    701 non-null     object
 9   2009    701 non-null     object
 10  2010    701 non-null     object
 11  2011    701 non-null     object
 12  2012    701 non-null     object
 13  2013    701 non-null     object
 14  2014    701 non-null     object
 15  2015    701 non-null     object
 16  2016    701 non-null     object
 17  2017    701 non-null     object
 18  2018    701 non-null     object
dtypes: object(19)
memory usage: 104.3+ KB
```

4. Rename the `Year` column to `metro` and remove the leading spaces.

Give an appropriate name to the metropolitan area column. There are extra spaces before the metro values in some cases, and extra spaces after the metro values in others. We can test for leading spaces with `startswith(' ')` and then use `any` to establish whether there are one or more occasions when the first character is blank. We can use `endswith(' ')` to examine trailing spaces. We use `strip` to remove both leading and trailing spaces:

```
>>> percapitaGDP.rename(columns={'Year':'metro'},
inplace=True)
>>> percapitaGDP.metro.str.startswith(' ').any()
True
```

```
>>> percapitaGDP.metro.str.endswith(' ').any()
True
>>> percapitaGDP.metro = percapitaGDP.metro.str.strip()
```

5. Convert the data columns to numeric.

    Iterate over all of the GDP year columns (2001-2018) and convert the data type
    from `object` to `float`. Coerce the conversion even when there is character data
    – the .. in this example. We want character values in those columns to become
    missing, which is what happens. Rename the year columns to better reflect the data
    in those columns:

```
>>> for col in percapitaGDP.columns[1:]:
...     percapitaGDP[col] = pd.to_numeric(percapitaGDP[col],
errors='coerce')
...     percapitaGDP.rename(columns={col:'pcGDP'+col},
inplace=True)
...
>>> percapitaGDP.head()
                       metro  pcGDP2001  ...  pcGDP2017
pcGDP2018
0         Metropolitan areas        nan  ...        nan
nan
1              AUS: Australia        nan  ...        nan
nan
2       AUS01: Greater Sydney      43313  ...      50578
49860
3    AUS02: Greater Melbourne      40125  ...      43025
42674
4    AUS03: Greater Brisbane      37580  ...      46876
46640

>>> percapitaGDP.dtypes
metro          object
pcGDP2001      float64
pcGDP2002      float64

abbreviated to save space
```

```
pcGDP2017      float64
pcGDP2018      float64
dtype: object
```

6. Use the `describe` method to generate summary statistics for all numeric data in the data frame:

```
>>> percapitaGDP.describe()
       pcGDP2001   pcGDP2002    ...   pcGDP2017   pcGDP2018
count        424         440    ...         445         441
mean       41264       41015    ...       47489       48033
std        11878       12537    ...       15464       15720
min        10988       11435    ...        2745        2832
25%        33139       32636    ...       37316       37908
50%        39544       39684    ...       45385       46057
75%        47972       48611    ...       56023       56638
max        91488       93566    ...      122242      127468

[8 rows x 18 columns]
```

7. Remove rows where all of the per capita GDP values are missing.

   Use the `subset` parameter of `dropna` to inspect all columns, starting with the second column (it is zero-based) through the last column. Use `how` to specify that we want to drop rows only if all of the columns specified in `subset` are missing. Use `shape` to show the number of rows and columns in the resulting data frame:

```
>>> percapitaGDP.dropna(subset=percapitaGDP.columns[1:],
how="all", inplace=True)

>>> percapitaGDP.describe()
       pcGDP2001   pcGDP2002    ...   pcGDP2017   pcGDP2018
count        424         440    ...         445         441
mean       41264       41015    ...       47489       48033
std        11878       12537    ...       15464       15720
min        10988       11435    ...        2745        2832
25%        33139       32636    ...       37316       37908
50%        39544       39684    ...       45385       46057
75%        47972       48611    ...       56023       56638
```

```
max          91488       93566   ...     122242       127468


[8 rows x 18 columns]


>>> percapitaGDP.head()
                      metro   pcGDP2001  ...   pcGDP2017
pcGDP2018
2       AUS01: Greater Sydney      43313  ...        50578
49860
3    AUS02: Greater Melbourne      40125  ...        43025
42674
4    AUS03: Greater Brisbane       37580  ...        46876
46640
5        AUS04: Greater Perth      45713  ...        66424
70390
6    AUS05: Greater Adelaide       36505  ...        40115
39924


[5 rows x 19 columns]


>>> percapitaGDP.shape
(480, 19)
```

8. Set the index for the data frame using the metropolitan area column.

   Confirm that there are 480 valid values for `metro` and that there are 480 unique values, before setting the index:

```
>>> percapitaGDP.metro.count()
480
>>> percapitaGDP.metro.nunique()
480
>>> percapitaGDP.set_index('metro', inplace=True)
>>> percapitaGDP.head()
                       pcGDP2001  pcGDP2002  ...   pcGDP2017
pcGDP2018
metro                                                  ...
AUS01: Greater Sydney      43313      44008  ...        50578
49860
```

```
AUS02: Greater Melbourne 40125      40894  ...      43025
42674

AUS03: Greater Brisbane  37580      37564  ...      46876
46640

AUS04: Greater Perth     45713      47371  ...      66424
70390

AUS05: Greater Adelaide  36505      37194  ...      40115
39924


[5 rows x 18 columns]

>>> percapitaGDP.loc['AUS02: Greater Melbourne']
pcGDP2001    40125
pcGDP2002    40894
...
pcGDP2017    43025
pcGDP2018    42674
Name: AUS02: Greater Melbourne, dtype: float64
```

We have now imported the Excel data into a pandas data frame and cleaned up some of the messiness in the spreadsheet.

How it works...

We mostly manage to get the data we want in *step 2* by skipping rows and columns we do not want, but there are still a number of issues: read_excel interprets all of the GDP data as character data, many rows are loaded with no useful data, and the column names do not represent the data well. In addition, the metropolitan area column might be useful as an index, but there are leading and trailing blanks and there may be missing or duplicated values.

read_excel interprets Year as the column name for the metropolitan area data because it looks for a header above the data for that Excel column and finds Year there. We rename that column metro in *step 4*. We also use strip to fix the problem with leading and trailing blanks. If there had only been leading blanks, we could have used lstrip, or rstrip if there had only been trailing blanks. It is a good idea to assume that there might be leading or trailing blanks in any character data and clean that data shortly after the initial import.

The spreadsheet authors used `..` to represent missing data. Since this is actually valid character data, those columns get the object data type (how pandas treats columns with character or mixed data). We coerce a conversion to numeric in *step 5*. This also results in the original values of `..` being replaced with `NaN` (not a number), pandas' value for missing numbers. This is what we want.

We can fix all of the per capita GDP columns with just a few lines because pandas makes it easy to iterate over the columns of a data frame. By specifying `[1:]`, we iterate from the second column to the last column. We can then change those columns to numeric and rename them to something more appropriate.

There are several reasons why it is a good idea to clean up the column headings for the annual GDP columns: it helps us to remember what the data actually is; if we merge it with other data by metropolitan area, we will not have to worry about conflicting variable names; and we can use attribute access to work with pandas series based on those columns, which I will discuss in more detail in the *There's more...* section of this recipe.

`describe` in *step 6* shows us that only between 420 and 480 rows have valid data for per capita GDP. When we drop all rows that have missing values for all per capita GDP columns in *step 7*, we end up with 480 rows in the data frame, which is what we expected.

There's more...

Once we have a pandas data frame, we have the ability to treat columns as more than just columns. We can use attribute access (such as `percapitaGPA.metro`) or bracket notation (`percapitaGPA['metro']`) to get the functionality of a pandas data series. Either method makes it possible to use data series string-inspecting methods such as `str.startswith`, and counting methods such as `nunique`. Note that the original column names of `20##` did not allow for attribute access because they started with a number, so `percapitaGDP.pcGDP2001.count()` works, but `percapitaGDP.2001.count()` returns a syntax error because `2001` is not a valid Python identifier (since it starts with a number).

Pandas is rich with features for string manipulation and for data series operations. We will try many of them out in subsequent recipes. This recipe showed those I find most useful when importing Excel data.

See also

There are good reasons to consider reshaping this data. Instead of 18 columns of GDP per capita data for each metropolitan area, we should have 18 rows of data for each metropolitan area, with columns for year and GDP per capita. Recipes for reshaping data can be found in *Chapter 9, Tidying and Reshaping Data*.

Importing data from SQL databases

In this recipe, we will use pymssql and mysql apis to read data from **Microsoft SQL Server** and **MySQL** (now owned by **Oracle**) databases, respectively. Data from sources such as these tends to be well structured since it is designed to facilitate simultaneous transactions by members of organizations, and those who interact with them. Each transaction is also likely related to some other organizational transaction.

This means that although data tables from enterprise systems are more reliably structured than data from CSV files and Excel files, their logic is less likely to be self-contained. You need to know how the data from one table relates to data from another table to understand its full meaning. These relationships need to be preserved, including the integrity of primary and foreign keys, when pulling data. Moreover, well-structured data tables are not necessarily uncomplicated data tables. There are often sophisticated coding schemes that determine data values, and these coding schemes can change over time. For example, codes for staff ethnicity at a retail store chain might be different in 1998 than they are in 2020. Similarly, frequently there are codes for missing values, such as 99999, that pandas will understand as valid values.

Since much of this logic is business logic, and implemented in stored procedures or other applications, it is lost when pulled out of this larger system. Some of what is lost will eventually have to be reconstructed when preparing data for analysis. This almost always involves combining data from multiple tables, so it is important to preserve the ability to do that. But it also may involve adding some of the coding logic back after loading the SQL table into a pandas data frame. We explore how to do that in this recipe.

Getting ready

This recipe assumes you have the pymssql and mysql APIs installed. If you do not, it is relatively straightforward to install them with pip. From the terminal, or PowerShell (in Windows), enter pip install pymssql or pip install mysql-connector-python.

> **Note**
> The dataset used in this recipe is available for public use at
> https://archive.ics.uci.edu/ml/machine-learning-databases/00320/.

How to do it...

We import SQL Server and MySQL data tables into a pandas data frame as follows:

1. Import `pandas`, `numpy`, `pymssql`, and `mysql`.

    This step assumes that you have installed the `pymssql` and `mysql` APIs:

    ```
    >>> import pandas as pd
    >>> import numpy as np
    >>> import pymssql
    >>> import mysql.connector
    ```

2. Use the `pymssql` API and `read_sql` to retrieve and load data from a SQL Server instance.

    Select the columns we want from the SQL Server data and use SQL aliases to improve column names (for example, `fedu AS fathereducation`). Create a connection to the SQL Server data by passing database credentials to the `pymssql` connect function. Create a pandas data frame by passing the `select` statement and `connection` object to `read_sql`. Close the connection to return it to the pool on the server:

    ```
    >>> query = "SELECT studentid, school, sex, age,
    famsize,\
    ...    medu AS mothereducation, fedu AS fathereducation,\
    ...    traveltime, studytime, failures, famrel, freetime,\
    ...    goout, g1 AS gradeperiod1, g2 AS gradeperiod2,\
    ...    g3 AS gradeperiod3 From studentmath"
    >>>
    >>> server = "pdcc.c9sqqzd5fulv.us-west-2.rds.amazonaws.
    com"
    >>> user = "pdccuser"
    >>> password = "pdccpass"
    >>> database = "pdcctest"
    >>>
    >>> conn = pymssql.connect(server=server,
    ...    user=user, password=password, database=database)
    >>>
    >>> studentmath = pd.read_sql(query,conn)
    >>> conn.close()
    ```

3. Check the data types and the first few rows:

```
>>> studentmath.dtypes
studentid           object
school              object
sex                 object
age                  int64
famsize             object
mothereducation      int64
fathereducation      int64
traveltime           int64
studytime            int64
failures             int64
famrel               int64
freetime             int64
goout                int64
gradeperiod1         int64
gradeperiod2         int64
gradeperiod3         int64
dtype: object

>>> studentmath.head()
   studentid school  ... gradeperiod2  gradeperiod3
0        001     GP  ...            6             6
1        002     GP  ...            5             6
2        003     GP  ...            8            10
3        004     GP  ...           14            15
4        005     GP  ...           10            10

[5 rows x 16 columns]
```

4. (Alternative) Use the mysql connector and read_sql to get data from MySQL.

Create a connection to the mysql data and pass that connection to read_sql to retrieve the data and load it into a pandas data frame. (The same data file on student math scores was uploaded to SQL Server and MySQL, so we can use the same SQL SELECT statement we used in the previous step.):

```
>>> host = "pdccmysql.c9sqqzd5fulv.us-west-2.rds.
amazonaws.com"
```

```
>>> user = "pdccuser"
>>> password = "pdccpass"
>>> database = "pdccschema"

>>> connmysql = mysql.connector.connect(host=host,
...    database=database,user=user,password=password)

>>> studentmath = pd.read_sql(sqlselect,connmysql)
>>> connmysql.close()
```

5. Rearrange the columns, set an index, and check for missing values.

   Move the grade data to the left of the data frame, just after studentid. Also move the freetime column to the right after traveltime and studytime. Confirm that each row has an ID and that the IDs are unique, and set studentid as the index:

```
>>> newcolorder = ['studentid', 'gradeperiod1',
'gradeperiod2',
...    'gradeperiod3', 'school', 'sex', 'age', 'famsize',
...    'mothereducation', 'fathereducation', 'traveltime',
...    'studytime', 'freetime', 'failures', 'famrel',
...    'goout']
>>> studentmath = studentmath[newcolorder]
>>> studentmath.studentid.count()
395
>>> studentmath.studentid.nunique()
395
>>> studentmath.set_index('studentid', inplace=True)
```

6. Use the data frame's count function to check for missing values:

```
>>> studentmath.count()
gradeperiod1      395
gradeperiod2      395
gradeperiod3      395
school            395
sex               395
age               395
```

famsize	395
mothereducation	395
fathereducation	395
traveltime	395
studytime	395
freetime	395
failures	395
famrel	395
goout	395
dtype: int64	

7. Replace coded data values with more informative values.

Create a dictionary with the replacement values for the columns, and then use `replace` to set those values:

```
>>> setvalues={"famrel":{1:"1:very
bad",2:"2:bad",3:"3:neutral",
...      4:"4:good",5:"5:excellent"},
...    "freetime":{1:"1:very low",2:"2:low",3:"3:neutral",
...      4:"4:high",5:"5:very high"},
...    "goout":{1:"1:very low",2:"2:low",3:"3:neutral",
...      4:"4:high",5:"5:very high"},
...    "mothereducation":{0:np.nan,1:"1:k-4",2:"2:5-9",
...      3:"3:secondary ed",4:"4:higher ed"},
...    "fathereducation":{0:np.nan,1:"1:k-4",2:"2:5-9",
...      3:"3:secondary ed",4:"4:higher ed"}}

>>> studentmath.replace(setvalues, inplace=True)
>>> setvalueskeys = [k for k in setvalues]
```

8. Change the type for columns with the changed data to `category`.

Check for any changes in memory usage:

```
>>> studentmath[setvalueskeys].memory_usage(index=False)
```

famrel	3160
freetime	3160
goout	3160
mothereducation	3160

```
fathereducation     3160
dtype: int64


>>> for col in studentmath[setvalueskeys].columns:
...     studentmath[col] = studentmath[col].
astype('category')
...
>>> studentmath[setvalueskeys].memory_usage(index=False)
famrel            595
freetime          595
goout             595
mothereducation   587
fathereducation   587
dtype: int64
```

9. Calculate percentages for values in the `famrel` column.

    Run `value_counts` and set `normalize` to `True` to generate percentages:

    ```
    >>> studentmath['famrel'].value_counts(sort=False,
    normalize=True)
    1:very bad     0.02
    2:bad          0.05
    3:neutral      0.17
    4:good         0.49
    5:excellent    0.27
    Name: famrel, dtype: float64
    ```

10. Use `apply` to calculate percentages for multiple columns:

    ```
    >>> studentmath[['freetime','goout']].\
    ...     apply(pd.Series.value_counts, sort=False,
    normalize=True)
                  freetime  goout
    1:very low      0.05    0.06
    2:low           0.16    0.26
    3:neutral       0.40    0.33
    4:high          0.29    0.22
    5:very high     0.10    0.13
    ```

```
>>>
>>> studentmath[['mothereducation','fathereducation']].\
...    apply(pd.Series.value_counts, sort=False,
normalize=True)
                 mothereducation   fathereducation
1:k-4                       0.15              0.21
2:5-9                       0.26              0.29
3:secondary ed              0.25              0.25
4:higher ed                 0.33              0.24
```

The preceding steps retrieved a data table from a SQL database, loaded that data into pandas, and did some initial data checking and cleaning.

How it works...

Since data from enterprise systems is typically better structured than CSV or Excel files, we do not need to do things such as skip rows or deal with different logical data types in a column. But some massaging is still usually required before we can begin exploratory analysis. There are often more columns than we need, and some column names are not intuitive or not ordered in the best way for analysis. The meaningfulness of many data values is not stored in the data table, to avoid entry errors and save on storage space. For example, 3 is stored for mother's education rather than secondary education. It is a good idea to reconstruct that coding as early in the cleaning process as possible.

To pull data from a SQL database server, we need a connection object to authenticate us on the server, and a SQL select string. These can be passed to read_sql to retrieve the data and load it into a pandas data frame. I usually use the SQL SELECT statement to do a bit of cleanup of column names at this point. I sometimes also reorder columns, but I do that later in this recipe.

We set the index in *step 5*, first confirming that every row has a value for studentid and that it is unique. This is often more important when working with enterprise data because we will almost always need to merge the retrieved data with other data files on the system. Although an index is not required for this merging, the discipline of setting one prepares us for the tricky business of merging data down the road. It will also likely improve the speed of the merge.

We use the data frame's count function to check for missing values and there are no missing values – non-missing values is 395 (the number of rows) for every column. This is almost too good to be true. There may be values that are logically missing; that is, valid numbers that nonetheless connote missing values, such as -1, 0, 9, or 99. We address this possibility in the next step.

Step 7 demonstrates a useful technique for replacing data values for multiple columns. We create a dictionary to map original values to new values for each column, and then run it using `replace`. To reduce the amount of storage space taken up by the new verbose values, we convert the data type of those columns to `category`. We do this by generating a list of the keys of our `setvalues` dictionary – `setvalueskeys = [k for k in setvalues]` generates [`famrel`, `freetime`, `goout`, `mothereducation`, and `fathereducation`]. We then iterate over those five columns and use the `astype` method to change the data type to `category`. Notice that the memory usage for those columns is reduced substantially.

Finally, we check the assignment of new values by using `value_counts` to view relative frequencies. We use `apply` because we want to run `value_counts` on multiple columns. To avoid `value_counts` sorting by frequency, we set sort to `False`.

The data frame `replace` method is also a handy tool for dealing with logical missing values that will not be recognized as missing when retrieved by `read_sql`. 0 values for `mothereducation` and `fathereducation` seem to fall into that category. We fix this problem in the `setvalues` dictionary by indicating that 0 values for `mothereducation` and `fathereducation` should be replaced with `NaN`. It is important to address these kinds of missing values shortly after the initial import because they are not always obvious and can significantly impact all subsequent work.

Users of packages such as *SPPS*, *SAS*, and *R* will notice the difference between this approach and value labels in SPSS and R, and `proc format` in SAS. In pandas, we need to change the actual data to get more informative values. However, we reduce how much data is actually stored by giving the column a category data type, similar to factors in R.

There's more...

I moved the grade data to near the beginning of the data frame. I find it helpful to have potential target or dependent variables in the leftmost columns, to keep them at the forefront of my thinking. It is also helpful to keep similar columns together. In this example, personal demographic variables (sex, age) are next to one another, as are family variables (`mothereducation`, `fathereducation`), and how students spend their time (`traveltime`, `studytime`, and `freetime`).

You could have used map instead of `replace` in *step 7*. Prior to version 19.2 of pandas, map was significantly more efficient. Since then, the difference in efficiency has been much smaller. If you are working with a very large dataset, the difference may still be enough to consider using map.

See also

The recipes in *Chapter 8, Addressing Data Issues when Combining DataFrames*, go into detail on merging data. We will take a closer look at bivariate and multivariate relationships between variables in *Chapter 4, Identifying Missing Values and Outliers in Subsets of Data*. We demonstrate how to use some of these same approaches in packages such as SPSS, SAS, and R in subsequent recipes in this chapter.

Importing SPSS, Stata, and SAS data

We will use `pyreadstat` to read data from three popular statistical packages into pandas. The key advantage of `pyreadstat` is that it allows data analysts to import data from these packages without losing metadata, such as variable and value labels.

The SPSS, Stata, and SAS data files we receive often come to us with the data issues of CSV and Excel files and SQL databases having been resolved. We do not typically have the invalid column names, changes in data types, and unclear missing values that we can get with CSV or Excel files, nor do we usually get the detachment of data from business logic, such as the meaning of data codes, that we often get with SQL data. When someone or some organization shares a data file from one of these packages with us, they have often added variable labels and value labels for categorical data. For example, a hypothetical data column called `presentsat` has the variable label `overall satisfaction with presentation` and value labels 1-5, with 1 being not at all satisfied and 5 being highly satisfied.

The challenge is retaining that metadata when importing data from those systems into pandas. There is no precise equivalent to variable and value labels in pandas, and built-in tools for importing SAS, Stata, and SAS data lose the metadata. In this recipe, we will use `pyreadstat` to load variable and value label information and use a couple of techniques for representing that information in pandas.

Getting ready

This recipe assumes you have installed the `pyreadstat` package. If it is not installed, you can install it with `pip`. From the terminal, or PowerShell (in Windows), enter `pip install pyreadstat`. You will need the SPSS, Stata, and SAS data files for this recipe to run the code.

We will work with data from the **United States National Longitudinal Survey of Youth (NLS)**.

> **Note**
>
> The National Longitudinal Survey of Youth is conducted by the United States Bureau of Labor Statistics. This survey started with a cohort of individuals in 1997 who were born between 1980 and 1985, with annual follow-ups each year through 2017. For this recipe, I pulled 42 variables on grades, employment, income, and attitudes toward government, from the hundreds of data items on the survey. Separate files for SPSS, Stata, and SAS can be downloaded from the repository. NLS data can be downloaded from `https://www.nlsinfo.org/investigator/pages/search`.

How to do it...

We will import data from SPSS, Stata, and SAS, retaining metadata such as value labels:

1. Import `pandas`, `numpy`, and `pyreadstat`.

   This step assumes that you have installed `pyreadstat`:

   ```
   >>> import pandas as pd
   >>> import numpy as np
   >>> import pyreadstat
   ```

2. Retrieve the SPSS data.

   Pass a path and filename to the `read_sav` method of `pyreadstat`. Display the first few rows and a frequency distribution. Notice that the column names and value labels are non-descriptive, and that `read_sav` creates both a pandas data frame and a meta object:

   ```
   >>> nls97spss, metaspss = pyreadstat.read_sav('data/
   nls97.sav')
   >>> nls97spss.dtypes
   R0000100      float64
   R0536300      float64
   R0536401      float64
   ...
   U2962900      float64
   U2963000      float64
   Z9063900      float64
   dtype: object
   ```

```
>>> nls97spss.head()
   R0000100   R0536300  ...   U2963000   Z9063900
0         1          2  ...        nan         52
1         2          1  ...          6          0
2         3          2  ...          6          0
3         4          2  ...          6          4
4         5          1  ...          5         12

[5 rows x 42 columns]
>>> nls97spss['R0536300'].value_counts(normalize=True)
1.00    0.51
2.00    0.49
Name: R0536300, dtype: float64
```

3. Grab the metadata to improve column labels and value labels.

   The metaspss object created when we called read_sav has the column labels and the value labels from the SPSS file. Use the variable_value_labels dictionary to map values to value labels for one column (R0536300). (This does not change the data. It only improves our display when we run value_counts.) Use the set_value_labels method to actually apply the value labels to the data frame:

```
>>> metaspss.variable_value_labels['R0536300']
{0.0: 'No Information', 1.0: 'Male', 2.0: 'Female'}

>>> nls97spss['R0536300'].\
...     map(metaspss.variable_value_labels['R0536300']).\
...     value_counts(normalize=True)
Male      0.51
Female    0.49
Name: R0536300, dtype: float64

>>> nls97spss = pyreadstat.set_value_labels(nls97spss,
metaspss, formats_as_category=True)
```

4. Use column labels in the metadata to rename the columns.

To use the column labels from `metaspss` in our data frame, we can simply assign the column labels in `metaspss` to our data frame's column names. Clean up the column names a bit by changing them to lowercase, changing spaces to underscores, and removing all remaining non-alphanumeric characters:

```
>>> nls97spss.columns = metaspss.column_labels
```

```
>>> nls97spss['KEY!SEX (SYMBOL) 1997'].value_
counts(normalize=True)
Male      0.51
Female    0.49
Name: KEY!SEX (SYMBOL) 1997, dtype: float64
```

```
>>> nls97spss.dtypes
PUBID - YTH ID CODE 1997                       float64
KEY!SEX (SYMBOL) 1997                         category
KEY!BDATE M/Y (SYMBOL) 1997                    float64
KEY!BDATE M/Y (SYMBOL) 1997                    float64
CV_SAMPLE_TYPE 1997                           category
KEY!RACE_ETHNICITY (SYMBOL) 1997              category
...
HRS/WK R WATCHES TELEVISION 2017              category
HRS/NIGHT R SLEEPS 2017                        float64
CVC_WKSWK_YR_ALL L99                           float64
dtype: object
```

```
>>> nls97spss.columns = nls97spss.columns.\
...        str.lower().\
...        str.replace(' ','_').\
...        str.replace('[^a-z0-9_]', '')
>>> nls97spss.set_index('pubid__yth_id_code_1997',
inplace=True)
```

5. Simplify the process by applying the value labels from the beginning.

The data values can actually be applied in the initial call to `read_sav` by setting `apply_value_formats` to `True`. This eliminates the need to call the `set_value_labels` function later:

```
>>> nls97spss, metaspss = pyreadstat.read_sav('data/
nls97.sav', apply_value_formats=True, formats_as_
category=True)
>>> nls97spss.columns = metaspss.column_labels
>>> nls97spss.columns = nls97spss.columns.\
...     str.lower().\
...     str.replace(' ','_').\
...     str.replace('[^a-z0-9_]', '')
```

6. Show the columns and a few rows:

```
>>> nls97spss.dtypes
pubid__yth_id_code_1997                    float64
keysex_symbol_1997                         category
keybdate_my_symbol_1997                    float64
keybdate_my_symbol_1997                    float64
...
hrsnight_r_sleeps_2017                     float64
cvc_wkswk_yr_all_199                       float64
dtype: object


>>> nls97spss.head()
    pubid__yth_id_code_1997 keysex_symbol_1997  ...  \
0                         1             Female  ...
1                         2               Male  ...
2                         3             Female  ...
3                         4             Female  ...
4                         5               Male  ...


    hrsnight_r_sleeps_2017  cvc_wkswk_yr_all_199
0                      nan                    52
1                        6                     0
2                        6                     0
```

| 3 | 6 | 4 |
| 4 | 5 | 12 |

```
[5 rows x 42 columns]
```

7. Run `frequencies` on one of the columns and set the index:

```
>>> nls97spss.govt_responsibility__provide_jobs_2006.\
...     value_counts(sort=False)
Definitely should be          454
Definitely should not be      300
Probably should be            617
Probably should not be        462
Name: govt_responsibility__provide_jobs_2006, dtype:
int64
```

```
>>> nls97spss.set_index('pubid__yth_id_code_1997',
inplace=True)
```

8. Import the Stata data, apply value labels, and improve the column headings.

   Use the same methods for the Stata data that we use for the SPSS data:

```
>>> nls97stata, metastata = pyreadstat.read_dta('data/
nls97.dta', apply_value_formats=True, formats_as_
category=True)
>>> nls97stata.columns = metastata.column_labels
>>> nls97stata.columns = nls97stata.columns.\
...     str.lower().\
...     str.replace(' ','_').\
...     str.replace('[^a-z0-9_]', '')
>>> nls97stata.dtypes
pubid__yth_id_code_1997                float64
keysex_symbol_1997                     category
keybdate_my_symbol_1997                float64
keybdate_my_symbol_1997                float64
...
hrsnight_r_sleeps_2017                 float64
cvc_wkswk_yr_all_199                   float64
dtype: object
```

9. View a few rows of the data and run `frequency`:

```
>>> nls97stata.head()
    pubid__yth_id_code_1997 keysex_symbol_1997   ...   \
0                         1             Female   ...
1                         2               Male   ...
2                         3             Female   ...
3                         4             Female   ...
4                         5               Male   ...


    hrsnight_r_sleeps_2017   cvc_wkswk_yr_all_199
0                       -5                     52
1                        6                      0
2                        6                      0
3                        6                      4
4                        5                     12


[5 rows x 42 columns]
>>> nls97stata.govt_responsibility__provide_jobs_2006.\
...     value_counts(sort=False)
-5.0                         1425
-4.0                         5665
-2.0                           56
-1.0                            5
Definitely should be          454
Definitely should not be      300
Probably should be            617
Probably should not be        462
Name: govt_responsibility__provide_jobs_2006, dtype:
int64
```

10. Fix the logical missing values that show up with the Stata data and set an index:

```
>>> nls97stata.min()
pubid__yth_id_code_1997              1
keysex_symbol_1997             Female
keybdate_my_symbol_1997             1
keybdate_my_symbol_1997         1,980
```

```
. . .
cv_bio_child_hh_2017                          -5
cv_bio_child_nr_2017                          -5
hrsnight_r_sleeps_2017                        -5
cvc_wkswk_yr_all_199                          -4
dtype: object


>>> nls97stata.replace(list(range(-9,0)), np.nan,
inplace=True)


>>> nls97stata.min()
pubid__yth_id_code_1997                        1
keysex_symbol_1997                        Female
keybdate_my_symbol_1997                        1
keybdate_my_symbol_1997                    1,980
. . .
cv_bio_child_hh_2017                           0
cv_bio_child_nr_2017                           0
hrsnight_r_sleeps_2017                         0
cvc_wkswk_yr_all_199                           0
dtype: object
>>> nls97stata.set_index('pubid__yth_id_code_1997',
inplace=True)
```

11. Retrieve the SAS data, using the SAS catalog file for value labels:

    The data values for SAS are stored in a catalog file. Setting the catalog file path and filename retrieves the value labels and applies them:

    ```
    >>> nls97sas, metasas = pyreadstat.read_sas7bdat('data/
    nls97.sas7bdat', catalog_file='data/nlsformats3.
    sas7bcat', formats_as_category=True)
    >>> nls97sas.columns = metasas.column_labels
    >>>
    >>> nls97sas.columns = nls97sas.columns.\
    ...      str.lower().\
    ...      str.replace(' ','_').\
    ...      str.replace('[^a-z0-9_]', '')
    >>>
    ```

```
>>> nls97sas.head()
    pubid__yth_id_code_1997 keysex_symbol_1997  ...  \
0                         1            Female   ...
1                         2              Male   ...
2                         3            Female   ...
3                         4            Female   ...
4                         5              Male   ...


    hrsnight_r_sleeps_2017   cvc_wkswk_yr_all_199
0                      nan                     52
1                        6                      0
2                        6                      0
3                        6                      4
4                        5                     12

[5 rows x 42 columns]
>>> nls97sas.keysex_symbol_1997.value_counts()
Male      4599
Female    4385
Name: keysex_symbol_1997, dtype: int64
>>> nls97sas.set_index('pubid__yth_id_code_1997',
inplace=True)
```

This demonstrates how to import SPSS, SAS, and Stata data without losing important metadata.

How it works...

The `read_sav`, `read_dta`, and `read_sas7bdat` methods of `pyreadstat`, for SPSS, Stata, and SAS data files, respectively, work in a similar manner. Value labels can be applied when reading in the data by setting `apply_value_formats` to `True` for SPSS and Stata files (*steps 5 and 8*), or by providing a catalog file path and filename for SAS (*step 11*). We can set `formats_as_category` to `True` to change the data type to `category` for those columns where the data values will change. The meta object has the column names and the column labels from the statistical package, so metadata column labels can be assigned to pandas data frame column names at any point (`nls97spss.columns = metaspss.column_labels`). We can even revert to the original column headings after assigning meta column labels to them by setting pandas column names to the metadata column names (`nls97spss.columns = metaspss.column_names`).

In *step 3*, we read the SPSS data without applying value labels. We looked at the dictionary for one variable (`metaspss.variable_value_labels['R0536300']`), but we could have viewed it for all variables (`metaspss.variable_value_labels`). When we are satisfied that the labels make sense, we can set them by calling the `set_value_labels` function. This is a good approach when you do not know the data well and want to inspect the labels before applying them.

The column labels from the meta object are often a better choice than the original column headings. Column headings can be quite cryptic, particularly when the SPSS, Stata, or SAS file is based on a large survey, as in this example. But the labels are not usually ideal for column headings either. They sometimes have spaces, capitalization that is not helpful, and non-alphanumeric characters. We chain some string operations to switch to lowercase, replace spaces with underscores, and remove non-alphanumeric characters.

Handling missing values is not always straightforward with these data files, since there are often many reasons why data is missing. If the file is from a survey, the missing value may be because of a survey skip pattern, or a respondent failed to respond, or the response was invalid, and so on. The NLS has 9 possible values for missing, from -1 to -9. The SPSS import automatically set those values to NaN, while the Stata import retained the original values. (We could have gotten the SPSS import to retain those values by setting `user_missing` to True.) For the Stata data, we need to tell it to replace all values from -1 to -9 with NaN. We do this by using the data frame's `replace` function and passing it a list of integers from -9 to -1 (`list(range(-9,0))`).

There's more...

You may have noticed similarities between this recipe and the previous one in terms of how value labels are set. The `set_value_labels` function is like the data frame `replace` operation we used to set value labels in that recipe. We passed a dictionary to `replace` that mapped columns to value labels. The `set_value_labels` function in this recipe essentially does the same thing, using the `variable_value_labels` property of the meta object as the dictionary.

Data from statistical packages is often not as well structured as SQL databases tend to be in one significant way. Since they are designed to facilitate analysis, they often violate database normalization rules. There is often an implied relational structure that might have to be *unflattened* at some point. For example, the data combines individual and event level data – person and hospital visits, brown bear and date emerged from hibernation. Often, this data will need to be reshaped for some aspects of the analysis.

See also

The `pyreadstat` package is nicely documented at `https://github.com/Roche/pyreadstat`. The package has many useful options for selecting columns and handling missing data that space did not permit me to demonstrate in this recipe.

Importing R data

We will use `pyreadr` to read an R data file into pandas. Since `pyreadr` cannot capture the metadata, we will write code to reconstruct value labels (analogous to R factors) and column headings. This is similar to what we did in the *Importing data from SQL databases* recipe.

The R statistical package is, in many ways, similar to the combination of Python and pandas, at least in its scope. Both have strong tools across a range of data preparation and data analysis tasks. Some data scientists work with both R and Python, perhaps doing data manipulation in Python and statistical analysis in R, or vice-versa, depending on their preferred packages. But there is currently a scarcity of tools for reading data saved in R, as `rds` or `rdata` files, into Python. The analyst often saves the data as a CSV file first, and then loads the CSV file into Python. We will use `pyreadr`, from the same author as `pyreadstat`, because it does not require an installation of R.

When we receive an R file, or work with one we have created ourselves, we can count on it being fairly well structured, at least compared to CSV or Excel files. Each column will have only one data type, column headings will have appropriate names for Python variables, and all rows will have the same structure. However, we may need to restore some of the coding logic, as we did when working with SQL data.

Getting ready

This recipe assumes you have installed the `pyreadr` package. If it is not installed, you can install it with `pip`. From the terminal, or `powershell` (in Windows), enter `pip install pyreadr`. You will need the R `rds` file for this recipe in order to run the code.

We will again work with the National Longitudinal Survey in this recipe.

How to do it...

We will import data from R without losing important metadata:

1. Load `pandas`, `numpy`, `pprint`, and the `pyreadr` package:

```
>>> import pandas as pd
>>> import numpy as np
>>> import pyreadr
>>> import pprint
```

2. Get the R data.

   Pass the path and filename to the `read_r` method to retrieve the R data and load it into memory as a pandas data frame. `read_r` can return one or more objects. When reading an `rds` file (as opposed to an `rdata` file), it will return one object, having the key `None`. We indicate `None` to get the pandas data frame:

```
>>> nls97r = pyreadr.read_r('data/nls97.rds')[None]
>>> nls97r.dtypes
R0000100        int32
R0536300        int32
...
U2962800        int32
U2962900        int32
U2963000        int32
Z9063900        int32
dtype: object

>>> nls97r.head(10)
     R0000100  R0536300  R0536401  ...  U2962900  U2963000
Z9063900
0           1         2         9  ...        -5        -5
52
1           2         1         7  ...         2         6
0
2           3         2         9  ...         2         6
0
3           4         2         2  ...         2         6
4
```

```
4         5          1        10  ...        2          5
12
5         6          2         1  ...        2          6
6
6         7          1         4  ...       -5         -5
0
7         8          2         6  ...       -5         -5
39
8         9          1        10  ...        2          4
0
9        10          1         3  ...        2          6
0

[10 rows x 42 columns]
```

3. Set up dictionaries for value labels and column headings.

Load a dictionary that maps columns to the value labels and create a list of preferred column names as follows:

```
>>> with open('data/nlscodes.txt', 'r') as reader:
...         setvalues = eval(reader.read())
...
>>> pprint.pprint(setvalues)
{'R0536300': {0.0: 'No Information', 1.0: 'Male', 2.0:
'Female'},
 'R1235800': {0.0: 'Oversample', 1.0: 'Cross-sectional'},
 'S8646900': {1.0: '1. Definitely',
              2.0: '2. Probably ',
              3.0: '3. Probably not',
              4.0: '4. Definitely not'}}
...
>>> newcols =
['personid','gender','birthmonth','birthyear',
...    'sampletype',  'category','satverbal','satmath',
...
'gpaoverall','gpaeng','gpamath','gpascience','govjobs',
...
'govprices','govhealth','goveld','govind','govunemp',
```

```
...      'govinc','govcollege','govhousing','govenvironment',
...
'bacredits','coltype1','coltype2','coltype3','coltype4',
...
'coltype5','coltype6','highestgrade','maritalstatus',
...      'childnumhome','childnumaway','degreecol1',
...      'degreecol2','degreecol3','degreecol4','wageincome',
...      'weeklyhrscomputer','weeklyhrstv',
...      'nightlyhrssleep','weeksworkedlastyear']
```

4. Set value labels and missing values, and change selected columns to category data type.

   Use the `setvalues` dictionary to replace existing values with value labels. Replace all values from -9 to -1 with NaN:

```
>>> nls97r.replace(setvalues, inplace=True)
>>> nls97r.head()
   R0000100 R0536300  ...  U2963000 Z9063900
0         1   Female  ...        -5       52
1         2     Male  ...         6        0
2         3   Female  ...         6        0
3         4   Female  ...         6        4
4         5     Male  ...         5       12

[5 rows x 42 columns]

>>> nls97r.replace(list(range(-9,0)), np.nan,
inplace=True)

>>> for col in nls97r[[k for k in setvalues]].columns:
...     nls97r[col] = nls97r[col].astype('category')
...
>>> nls97r.dtypes
R0000100          int64
R0536300       category
R0536401          int64
R0536402          int64
R1235800       category
```

	. . .
U2857300	category
U2962800	category
U2962900	category
U2963000	float64
Z9063900	float64
Length: 42, dtype: object	

5. Set meaningful column headings:

```
>>> nls97r.columns = newcols
```

```
>>> nls97r.dtypes
```

personid	int64
gender	category
birthmonth	int64
birthyear	int64
sampletype	category
	. . .
wageincome	category
weeklyhrscomputer	category
weeklyhrstv	category
nightlyhrssleep	float64
weeksworkedlastyear	float64
Length: 42, dtype: object	

This shows how R data files can be imported into pandas and value labels assigned.

How it works...

Reading R data into pandas with `pyreadr` is fairly straightforward. Passing a filename to the `read_r` function is all that is required. Since `read_r` can return multiple objects with one call, we need to specify which object. When reading an `rds` file (as opposed to an `rdata` file), only one object is returned. It has the key `None`.

In *step 3*, we load a dictionary that maps our variables to value labels, and a list for our preferred column headings. In *step 4* we apply the value labels. We also change the data type to `category` for the columns where we applied the values. We do this by generating a list of the keys of our `setvalues` dictionary with `[k for k in setvalues]` and then iterating over those columns.

We change the column headings in *step 5* to ones that are more intuitive. Note that the order matters here. We need to set the value labels before changing the column names, since the `setvalues` dictionary is based on the original column headings.

The main advantage of using `pyreadr` to read R files directly into pandas is that we do not have to convert the R data into a CSV file first. Once we have written our Python code to read the file, we can just rerun it whenever the R data changes. This is particularly helpful when we do not have R on the machine where we are working.

There's more...

`pyreadr` is able to return multiple data frames. This is useful when we save several data objects in R as an `rdata` file. We can return all of them with one call.

`print` is a handy tool for improving the display of Python dictionaries.

See also

Clear instructions and examples for `pyreadr` are available at `https://github.com/ofajardo/pyreadr`.

Feather files, a relatively new format, can be read by both R and Python. I discuss those files in the next recipe.

We could have used `rpy2` instead of `pyreadr` to import R data. `rpy2` requires that R also be installed, but it is more powerful than `pyreadr`. It will read R factors and automatically set them to pandas data frame values. See the following code:

```
>>> import rpy2.robjects as robjects
>>> from rpy2.robjects import pandas2ri
>>> pandas2ri.activate()
>>> readRDS = robjects.r['readRDS']
>>> nls97withvalues = readRDS('data/nls97withvalues.rds')

>>> nls97withvalues
R0000100 R0536300   R0536401   ...                 U2962900
U2963000
1     1    Female       9  ...                         NaN
-2147483648
2     2     Male        7  ...    3 to 10 hours a week
6
```

3 6	3	Female	9	...	3 to 10 hours a week
4 6	4	Female	2	...	3 to 10 hours a week
5 5	5	Male	10	...	3 to 10 hours a week
... ...	...	...	...	...	...
8980 4	9018	Female	3	...	3 to 10 hours a week
8981 6	9019	Male	9	...	3 to 10 hours a week
8982 -2147483648	9020	Male	7	...	NaN
8983 7	9021	Male	7	...	3 to 10 hours a week
8984 7	9022	Female	1	...	Less than 2 hours per week

```
[8984 rows x 42 columns]
```

This generates an unusual *-2147483648* values. This is what happened when readRDS interpreted missing data in numeric columns. A global replace of that number with NaN, after confirming that that is not a valid value, would be a good next step.

Persisting tabular data

We persist data, copy it from memory to local or remote storage, for several reasons: to be able to access the data without having to repeat the steps we used to generate it; to share the data with others; or to make it available for use with different software. In this recipe, we save data that we have loaded into a pandas data frame as different file types (CSV, Excel, pickle, and feather).

Another important, but sometimes overlooked, reason to persist data is to preserve some segment of our data that needs to be examined more closely; perhaps it needs to be scrutinized by others before our analysis can be completed. For analysts who work with operational data in medium- to large-sized organizations, this process is part of the daily data cleaning workflow.

In addition to these reasons for persisting data, our decisions about when and how to serialize data are shaped by several other factors: where we are in terms of our data analysis projects, the hardware and software resources of the machine(s) saving and reloading the data, and the size of our dataset. Analysts end up having to be much more intentional when saving data than they are when pressing *Ctrl + S* in their word processing applications.

Once we persist data, it is stored separately from the logic that we used to create it. I find this to be one of the most important threats to the integrity of our analysis. Often, we end up loading data that we saved some time in the past (a week ago? a month ago? a year ago?) and forget how a variable was defined and how it relates to other variables. If we are in the middle of a data cleaning task, it is best not to persist our data, so long as our workstation and network can easily handle the burden of regenerating the data. It is a good idea to persist data only once we have reached milestones in our work.

Beyond the question of *when* to persist data, there is the question of *how*. If we are persisting it for our own reuse with the same software, it is best to save it in a binary format native to that software. That is pretty straightforward for tools such as SPSS, SAS, Stata, and R, but not so much for pandas. But that is good news in a way. We have lots of choices, from CSV and Excel to pickle and feather. We save to all these file types in this recipe.

Getting ready

You will need to install feather if you do not have it on your system. You can do that by entering `pip install pyarrow` in a terminal window or `powershell` (in Windows). If you do not already have a subfolder named *Views* in your `chapter 1` folder, you will need to create it in order to run the code for this recipe.

> **Note**
>
> This dataset, taken from the Global Historical Climatology Network integrated database, is made available for public use by the United States National Oceanic and Atmospheric Administration at `https://www.ncdc.noaa.gov/data-access/land-based-station-data/land-based-datasets/global-historical-climatology-network-monthly-version-4`. This is just a 100,000-row sample of the full dataset, which is also available in the repository.

How to do it...

We will load a CSV file into pandas and then save it as a pickle file and as a feather file. We will also save subsets of the data in CSV and Excel formats:

1. Import pandas and pyarrow and adjust the display.

    Pyarrow needs to be imported in order to save pandas to feather:

    ```
    >>> import pandas as pd
    >>> import pyarrow
    ```

2. Load the land temperatures CSV file into pandas, drop rows with missing data, and set an index:

    ```
    >>> landtemps = pd.read_csv('data/landtempssample.csv',
    ...
    names=['stationid','year','month','avgtemp','latitude',
    ...
    'longitude','elevation','station','countryid','country'],
    ...       skiprows=1,
    ...       parse_dates=[['month','year']],
    ...       low_memory=False)
    >>>
    >>> landtemps.rename(columns={'month_
    year':'measuredate'}, inplace=True)
    >>> landtemps.dropna(subset=['avgtemp'], inplace=True)

    >>> landtemps.dtypes
    measuredate        datetime64[ns]
    stationid                  object
    avgtemp                   float64
    latitude                  float64
    longitude                 float64
    elevation                 float64
    station                    object
    countryid                  object
    country                    object
    dtype: object

    >>> landtemps.set_index(['measuredate','stationid'],
    inplace=True)
    ```

3. Write extreme values for temperature to CSV and Excel files.

    Use the `quantile` method to select outlier rows, those at the 1-in-1,000 level at each end of the distribution:

```
>>> extremevals = landtemps[(landtemps.avgtemp <
landtemps.avgtemp.quantile(.001)) | (landtemps.avgtemp >
landtemps.avgtemp.quantile(.999))]
>>> extremevals.shape
(171, 7)
>>> extremevals.sample(7)
                            avgtemp   ...     country
measuredate  stationid                ...
2013-08-01   QAM00041170      35.30   ...       Qatar
2005-01-01   RSM00024966     -40.09   ...      Russia
1973-03-01   CA002401200     -40.26   ...      Canada
2007-06-01   KU000405820      37.35   ...      Kuwait
1987-07-01   SUM00062700      35.50   ...       Sudan
1998-02-01   RSM00025325     -35.71   ...      Russia
1968-12-01   RSM00024329     -43.20   ...      Russia

[7 rows x 7 columns]

>>> extremevals.to_excel('views/tempext.xlsx')
>>> extremevals.to_csv('views/tempext.csv')
```

4. Save to pickle and feather files.

    The index needs to be reset in order to save a feather file:

```
>>> landtemps.to_pickle('data/landtemps.pkl')
>>> landtemps.reset_index(inplace=True)
>>> landtemps.to_feather("data/landtemps.ftr")
```

5. Load the pickle and feather files we just saved.

    Notice that our index was preserved when saving and loading the pickle file:

```
>>> landtemps = pd.read_pickle('data/landtemps.pkl')
>>> landtemps.head(2).T
measuredate      2000-04-01  1940-05-01
stationid        USS0010K01S CI000085406
```

avgtemp	5.27	18.04
latitude	39.90	-18.35
longitude	-110.75	-70.33
elevation	2,773.70	58.00
station	INDIAN_CANYON	ARICA
countryid	US	CI
country	United States	Chile

```
>>> landtemps = pd.read_feather("data/landtemps.ftr")
>>> landtemps.head(2).T
```

	0	1
measuredate	2000-04-01 00:00:00	1940-05-01 00:00:00
stationid	USS0010K01S	CI000085406
avgtemp	5.27	18.04
latitude	39.90	-18.35
longitude	-110.75	-70.33
elevation	2,773.70	58.00
station	INDIAN_CANYON	ARICA
countryid	US	CI
country	United States	Chile

The previous steps demonstrate how to serialize pandas data frames using two different formats, pickle and feather.

How it works...

Persisting pandas data is fairly straightforward. Data frames have to_csv, to_excel, to_pickle, and to_feather methods. Pickling preserves our index.

There's more...

The advantage of storing data in CSV files is that saving it uses up very little additional memory. The disadvantage is that writing CSV files is quite slow and we lose important metadata, such as data types. (read_csv can often figure out the data type when we reload the file, but not always.) Pickle files keep that data, but can burden a system that is low on resources when serializing. Feather is easier on resources, and can be easily loaded in R as well as Python, but we have to sacrifice our index in order to serialize. Also, the authors of feather make no promises regarding long-term support.

You may have noticed that I do not make a recommendation about what to use for data serialization – other than to limit your persistence of full datasets to project milestones. This is definitely one of those "right tools for the right job" kind of situations. I use CSV or Excel files when I want to share a segment of a file with colleagues for discussion. I use feather for ongoing Python projects, particularly when I am using a machine with sub-par RAM and an outdated chip, and I am also using R. When I am wrapping up a project, I pickle the data frames.

2

Anticipating Data Cleaning Issues when Importing HTML and JSON into pandas

This chapter continues our work on importing data from a variety of sources, and the initial checks we should do on the data after importing it. Gradually, over the last 25 years, data analysts have found that they increasingly need to work with data in non-tabular, semi-structured forms. Sometimes they even create and persist data in those forms themselves. We work with a common alternative to traditional tabular datasets in this chapter, JSON, but the general concepts can be extended to XML and NoSQL data stores such as MongoDB. We also go over common issues that occur when scraping data from websites.

In this chapter, we will work through the following recipes:

- Importing simple JSON data
- Importing more complicated JSON data from an API
- Importing data from web pages
- Persisting JSON data

Technical requirements

The code and notebooks for this chapter are available on GitHub at `https://github.com/PacktPublishing/Python-Data-Cleaning-Cookbook`

Importing simple JSON data

JavaScript Object Notation (**JSON**) has turned out to be an incredibly useful standard for transferring data from one machine, process, or node to another. Often a client sends a data request to a server, upon which that server queries the data in the local storage and then converts it from something like a **SQL Server table** or tables into JSON, which the client can consume. This is sometimes complicated further by the first server (say, a web server) forwarding the request to a database server. JSON facilitates this, as does XML, by doing the following:

- Being readable by humans
- Being consumable by most client devices
- Not being limited in structure

JSON is quite flexible, which means that it can accommodate just about anything. The structure can even change within a JSON file, so different keys might be present at different points. For example, the file might begin with some explanatory keys that have a very different structure than the remaining *data* keys. Or some keys might be present in some cases, but not others. We go over some approaches for dealing with that messiness (uh, I mean flexibility).

Getting ready

We are going to work with data on news stories about political candidates in this recipe. This data is made available for public use at `dataverse.harvard.edu/dataset.xhtml?persistentId=doi:10.7910/DVN/0ZLHOK`. I have combined the JSON files there into one file and randomly selected 60,000 news stories from the combined data. This sample (`allcandidatenewssample.json`) is available in the GitHub repository of this book.

We will do a little work with list and dictionary comprehensions in this recipe. *DataCamp* has good guides to list comprehensions (`https://www.datacamp.com/community/tutorials/python-list-comprehension`) and dictionary comprehensions (`https://www.datacamp.com/community/tutorials/python-dictionary-comprehension`) if you are feeling a little rusty.

How to do it...

We will import a JSON file into pandas after doing some data checking and cleaning:

1. Import the `json` and `pprint` libraries.

    `pprint` improves the display of the lists and dictionaries that are returned when we load JSON data:

    ```
    >>> import pandas as pd
    >>> import numpy as np
    >>> import json
    >>> import pprint
    >>> from collections import Counter
    ```

2. Load the JSON data and look for potential issues.

    Use the `json load` method to return data on news stories about political candidates. `load` returns a list of dictionaries. Use `len` to get the size of the list, which is the total number of news stories in this case. (Each list item is a dictionary with keys for the title, source, and so on, and their respective values.) Use `pprint` to display the first two dictionaries. Get the value from the source key for the first list item:

    ```
    >>> with open('data/allcandidatenewssample.json') as f:
    ...     candidatenews = json.load(f)
    ...
    >>> len(candidatenews)
    60000

    >>> pprint.pprint(candidatenews[0:2])
    [{'date': '2019-12-25 10:00:00',
      'domain': 'www.nbcnews.com',
      'panel_position': 1,
    ```

```
    'query': 'Michael Bloomberg',
    'source': 'NBC News',
    'story_position': 6,
    'time': '18 hours ago',
    'title': 'Bloomberg cuts ties with company using prison
inmates to make '
              'campaign calls',
    'url': 'https://www.nbcnews.com/politics/2020-election/
bloomberg-cuts-ties-company-using-prison-inmates-make-
campaign-calls-n1106971'},
  {'date': '2019-11-09 08:00:00',
    'domain': 'www.townandcountrymag.com',
    'panel_position': 1,
    'query': 'Amy Klobuchar',
    'source': 'Town & Country Magazine',
    'story_position': 3,
    'time': '18 hours ago',
    'title': "Democratic Candidates React to Michael
Bloomberg's Potential Run",
    'url': 'https://www.townandcountrymag.com/society/
politics/a29739854/michael-bloomberg-democratic-
candidates-campaign-reactions/'}]
```

```
>>> pprint.pprint(candidatenews[0]['source'])
'NBC News'
```

3. Check for differences in the structure of the dictionaries.

    Use Counter to check for any dictionaries in the list with fewer than, or more
    than, the nine keys that is normal. Look at a few of the dictionaries with almost no
    data (those with just two keys) before removing them. Confirm that the remaining
    list of dictionaries has the expected length – *60000-2382=57618*:

```
>>> Counter([len(item) for item in candidatenews])
Counter({9: 57202, 2: 2382, 10: 416})
>>> pprint.pprint(next(item for item in candidatenews if
len(item)<9))
{'date': '2019-09-11 18:00:00', 'reason': 'Not
collected'}
```

```
>>> pprint.pprint(next(item for item in candidatenews if
len(item)>9))
{'category': 'Satire',
 'date': '2019-08-21 04:00:00',
 'domain': 'politics.theonion.com',
 'panel_position': 1,
 'query': 'John Hickenlooper',
 'source': 'Politics | The Onion',
 'story_position': 8,
 'time': '4 days ago',
 'title': ''And Then There Were 23,' Says Wayne Messam
Crossing Out '
         'Hickenlooper Photo \n'
         'In Elaborate Grid Of Rivals',
 'url': 'https://politics.theonion.com/and-then-there-
were-23-says-wayne-messam-crossing-ou-1837311060'}
>>> pprint.pprint([item for item in candidatenews if
len(item)==2][0:10])
[{'date': '2019-09-11 18:00:00', 'reason': 'Not
collected'},
 {'date': '2019-07-24 00:00:00', 'reason': 'No Top
stories'},
 ...
 {'date': '2019-01-03 00:00:00', 'reason': 'No Top
stories'}]
>>> candidatenews = [item for item in candidatenews if
len(item)>2]
>>> len(candidatenews)
57618
```

4. Generate counts from the JSON data.

   Get the dictionaries just for *Politico* (a website that covers political news) and display a couple of dictionaries:

```
>>> politico = [item for item in candidatenews if
item["source"] == "Politico"]
>>> len(politico)
2732
>>> pprint.pprint(politico[0:2])
```

```
[{'date': '2019-05-18 18:00:00',
  'domain': 'www.politico.com',
  'panel_position': 1,
  'query': 'Marianne Williamson',
  'source': 'Politico',
  'story_position': 7,
  'time': '1 week ago',
  'title': 'Marianne Williamson reaches donor threshold
for Dem debates',
  'url': 'https://www.politico.com/story/2019/05/09/
marianne-williamson-2020-election-1315133'},
 {'date': '2018-12-27 06:00:00',
  'domain': 'www.politico.com',
  'panel_position': 1,
  'query': 'Julian Castro',
  'source': 'Politico',
  'story_position': 1,
  'time': '1 hour ago',
  'title': "O'Rourke and Castro on collision course in
Texas",
  'url': 'https://www.politico.com/story/2018/12/27/
orourke-julian-castro-collision-texas-election-1073720'}]
```

5. Get the `source` data and confirm that it has the anticipated length.

    Show the first few items in the new `sources` list. Generate a count of news stories by source and display the 10 most popular sources. Notice that stories from *The Hill* can have `TheHill` (without a space) or `The Hill` as the value for `source`:

```
>>> sources = [item.get('source') for item in
candidatenews]
>>> type(sources)
<class 'list'>
>>> len(sources)
57618
>>> sources[0:5]
['NBC News', 'Town & Country Magazine', 'TheHill', 'CNBC.
com', 'Fox News']
```

```
>>> pprint.pprint(Counter(sources).most_common(10))
[('Fox News', 3530),
 ('CNN.com', 2750),
 ('Politico', 2732),
 ('TheHill', 2383),
 ('The New York Times', 1804),
 ('Washington Post', 1770),
 ('Washington Examiner', 1655),
 ('The Hill', 1342),
 ('New York Post', 1275),
 ('Vox', 941)]
```

6. Fix any errors in the values in the dictionary.

Fix the source values for The Hill. Notice that The Hill is now the most frequent source for news stories:

```
>>> for newsdict in candidatenews:
...        newsdict.update((k, "The Hill") for k, v in
newsdict.items()
...        if k == "source" and v == "TheHill")
...
>>> sources = [item.get('source') for item in
candidatenews]

>>> pprint.pprint(Counter(sources).most_common(10))
[('The Hill', 3725),
 ('Fox News', 3530),
 ('CNN.com', 2750),
 ('Politico', 2732),
 ('The New York Times', 1804),
 ('Washington Post', 1770),
 ('Washington Examiner', 1655),
 ('New York Post', 1275),
 ('Vox', 941),
 ('Breitbart', 799)]
```

7. Create a pandas DataFrame.

    Pass the JSON data to the pandas `DataFrame` method. Convert the `date` column to a `datetime` data type:

```
>>> candidatenewsdf = pd.DataFrame(candidatenews)
>>> candidatenewsdf.dtypes
title              object
url                object
source             object
time               object
date               object
query              object
story_position      int64
panel_position     object
domain             object
category           object
dtype: object
```

8. Confirm that we are getting the expected values for `source`.

    Also, rename the `date` column:

```
>>> candidatenewsdf.rename(columns={'date':'storydate'},
inplace=True)
>>> candidatenewsdf.storydate = candidatenewsdf.
storydate.astype('datetime64[ns]')
>>> candidatenewsdf.shape
(57618, 10)
>>> candidatenewsdf.source.value_counts(sort=True).
head(10)
The Hill             3725
Fox News             3530
CNN.com              2750
Politico             2732
The New York Times   1804
Washington Post      1770
Washington Examiner  1655
New York Post        1275
```

```
Vox                     941
Breitbart               799
Name: source, dtype: int64
```

We now have a pandas DataFrame with only the news stories where there is meaningful data, and with the values for `source` fixed.

How it works...

The `json.load` method returns a list of dictionaries. This makes it possible to use a number of familiar tools when working with this data: list methods, slicing, list comprehensions, dictionary updates, and so on. There are times, maybe when you just have to populate a list or count the number of individuals in a given category, when there is no need to use pandas.

In *steps 2 to 6*, we use list methods to do many of the same checks we have done with pandas in previous recipes. In *step 3* we use `Counter` with a list comprehension (`Counter([len(item) for item in candidatenews])`) to get the number of keys in each dictionary. This tells us that there are 2,382 dictionaries with just 2 keys and 416 with 10. We use `next` to look for an example of dictionaries with fewer than 9 keys or more than 9 keys to get a sense of the structure of those items. We use slicing to show 10 dictionaries with 2 keys to see if there is any data in those dictionaries. We then select only those dictionaries with more than 2 keys.

In *step 4* we create a subset of the list of dictionaries, one that just has `source` equal to `Politico`, and take a look at a couple of items. We then create a list with just the source data and use `Counter` to list the 10 most common sources in *step 5*.

Step 6 demonstrates how to replace key values conditionally in a list of dictionaries. In this case, we update the key value to `The Hill` whenever key `(k)` is `source` and `value` `(v)` is `TheHill`. The `for k, v in newsdict.items()` section is the unsung hero of this line. It loops through all key/value pairs for all dictionaries in `candidatenews`.

It is easy to create a pandas DataFrame by passing the list of dictionaries to the pandas `DataFrame` method. We do this in *step 7*. The main complication is that we need to convert the date column from a string to a date, since dates are just strings in JSON.

There's more...

In *steps 5* and *6* we use `item.get('source')` instead of `item['source']`. This is handy when there might be missing keys in a dictionary. `get` returns `None` when the key is missing, but we can use an optional second argument to specify a value to return.

I renamed the `date` column to `storydate` in *step 8*. This is not necessary, but is a good idea. Not only does `date` not tell you anything about what the dates actually represent, it is also so generic a column name that it is bound to cause problems at some point.

The news stories data fits nicely into a tabular structure. It makes sense to represent each list item as one row, and the key/value pairs as columns and column values for that row. There are no significant complications, such as key values that are themselves lists of dictionaries. Imagine an `authors` key for each story with a list item for each author as the key value, and that list item is a dictionary of information about the author. This is not at all unusual when working with JSON data in Python. The next recipe shows how to work with data structured in this way.

Importing more complicated JSON data from an API

In the previous recipe, we discussed one significant advantage (and challenge) of working with JSON data – its flexibility. A JSON file can have just about any structure its authors can imagine. This often means that this data does not have the tabular structure of the data sources we have discussed so far, and that pandas DataFrames have. Often, analysts and application developers use JSON precisely because it does not insist on a tabular structure. I know I do!

Retrieving data from multiple tables often requires us to do a one-to-many merge. Saving that data to one table or file means duplicating data on the "one" side of the one-to-many relationship. For example, student demographic data is merged with data on the courses studied, and the demographic data is repeated for each course. With JSON, duplication is not required to capture these items of data in one file. We can have data on the courses studied nested within the data for each student.

But doing analysis with JSON structured in this way will eventually require us to either: 1) manipulate the data in a very different way than we are used to doing; or 2) convert the JSON to a tabular form. We examine the first approach in the *Classes that handle non-tabular data structures* recipe in *Chapter 10, User-Defined Functions and Classes to Automate Data Cleaning*. This recipe takes the second approach. It uses a very handy tool for converting selected nodes of JSON to a tabular structure – `json_normalize`.

We first use an API to get JSON data because that is how JSON is frequently consumed. One advantage of retrieving the data with an API, rather than working from a file we have saved locally, is that it is easier to rerun our code when the source data is refreshed.

Getting ready

This recipe assumes you have the `requests` and `pprint` libraries already installed. If they are not installed, you can install them with pip. From the terminal (or PowerShell in Windows), enter `pip install requests` and `pip install pprint`.

The following is the structure of the JSON file that is created when using the collections API of the Cleveland Museum of Art. There is a helpful `info` section at the beginning, but we are interested in the `data` section. This data does not fit nicely into a tabular data structure. There may be several `citations` objects and several `creators` objects for each collection object. I have abbreviated the JSON file to save space:

```
{"info": { "total": 778, "parameters": {"african_american_
artists": "" }},
"data": [
{
"id": 165157,
"accession_number": "2007.158",
"title": "Fulton and Nostrand",
"creation_date": "1958",
"citations": [
  {
   "citation": "Annual Exhibition: Sculpture, Paintings...",
   "page_number": "Unpaginated, [8],[12]",
   "url": null
  },
  {
   "citation": "\"Moscow to See Modern U.S. Art,\"<em> New
York...",
   "page_number": "P. 60",
   "url": null
  }]
"creators": [
    {
    "description": "Jacob Lawrence (American, 1917-2000)",
    "extent": null,
    "qualifier": null,
    "role": "artist",
```

```
    "birth_year": "1917",
    "death_year": "2000"
    }
]
}
```

> **Note**
>
> The API used in this recipe is provided by the Cleveland Museum of
> Art. It is available for public use at https://openaccess-api.
> clevelandart.org/.

How to do it...

Create a DataFrame from the museum's collections data with one row for each
citation, and the title and creation_date duplicated:

1. Import the json, requests, and pprint libraries.

    We need the requests library to use an API to retrieve JSON data. pprint
    improves the display of lists and dictionaries:

    ```
    >>> import pandas as pd
    >>> import numpy as np
    >>> import json
    >>> import pprint
    >>> import requests
    ```

2. Use an API to load the JSON data.

    Make a get request to the collections API of the Cleveland Museum of Art. Use
    the query string to indicate that you just want collections from African-American
    artists. Display the first collection item. I have truncated the output for the first item
    to save space:

    ```
    >>> response = requests.get("https://openaccess-api.
    clevelandart.org/api/artworks/?african_american_artists")
    >>> camcollections = json.loads(response.text)
    >>> print(len(camcollections['data']))
    778
    >>> pprint.pprint(camcollections['data'][0])
    {'accession_number': '2007.158',
    ```

```
 'catalogue_raisonne': None,
 'citations': [{'citation': 'Annual Exhibition:
Sculpture...',
                'page_number': 'Unpaginated, [8],[12]',
                'url': None},
               {'citation': '"Moscow to See Modern
U.S....',
                'page_number': 'P. 60',
                'url': None}]
 'collection': 'American - Painting',
 'creation_date': '1958',
 'creators': [{'biography': 'Jacob Lawrence (born
1917)...',
               'birth_year': '1917',
               'description': 'Jacob Lawrence
(American...)',
               'role': 'artist'}],
 'type': 'Painting'}
```

3. Flatten the JSON data.

   Create a DataFrame from the JSON data using the `json_normalize` method.
   Indicate that the number of citations will determine the number of rows, and that
   `accession_number`, `title`, `creation_date`, `collection`, `creators`, and
   `type` will be repeated. Observe that the data has been flattened by displaying the
   first two observations, transposing them with the `.T` option to make it easier to view:

```
>>> camcollectionsdf=pd.json_
normalize(camcollections['data'],/
  'citations',['accession_number','title','creation_
date',/
  'collection','creators','type'])
>>> camcollectionsdf.head(2).T
```

	0	1
citation	Annual Exhibiti...	"Moscow to See Modern...
page_number	Unpaginated,	P. 60
url	None	None

accession_number 2007.158	2007.158	
title No...	Fulton and No...	Fulton and
creation_date 1958	1958	
collection Pa...	American - Pa...	American -
creators 'J...	[{'description': 'J...	[{'description':
type Painting	Painting	

4. Pull the birth_year value from creators:

```
>>> creator = camcollectionsdf[:1].creators[0]
>>> type(creator[0])
<class 'dict'>
>>> pprint.pprint(creator)
[{'biography': 'Jacob Lawrence (born 1917) has been a
prominent art...',
   'birth_year': '1917',
   'death_year': '2000',
   'description': 'Jacob Lawrence (American, 1917-2000)',
   'extent': None,
   'name_in_original_language': None,
   'qualifier': None,
   'role': 'artist'}]
>>> camcollectionsdf['birthyear'] = camcollectionsdf.\
...    creators.apply(lambda x: x[0]['birth_year'])
>>> camcollectionsdf.birthyear.value_counts().\
...    sort_index().head()
1821    18
1886     2
1888     1
1892    13
1899    17
Name: birthyear, dtype: int64
```

This gives us a pandas DataFrame with one row for each `citation` for each collection item, with the collection information (`title`, `creation_date`, and so on) duplicated.

How it works...

We work with a much more *interesting* JSON file in this recipe than in the previous one. Each object in the JSON file is an item in the collection of the Cleveland Museum of Art. Nested within each collection item are one or more citations. The only way to capture this information in a tabular DataFrame is to flatten it. There are also one or more dictionaries for creators of the collection item (the artist or artists). That dictionary (or dictionaries) contains the `birth_year` value that we want.

We want one row for every citation for all collection items. To understand this, imagine that we are working with relational data and have a collections table and a citations table, and that we are doing a one-to-many merge from collections to citations. We do something similar with `json_normalize` by using *citations* as the second parameter. That tells `json_normalize` to create one row for each citation and use the key values in each citation dictionary – for `citation`, `page_number`, and `url` – as data values.

The third parameter in the call to `json_normalize` has the list of column names for the data that will be repeated with each citation. Notice that `access_number`, `title`, `creation_date`, `collection`, `creators`, and `type` are repeated in observations one and two. `Citation` and `page_number` change. (`url` is the same value for the first and second citations. Otherwise, it would also change.)

This still leaves us with the problem of the creators dictionaries (there can be more than one creator). When we ran `json_normalize` it grabbed the value for each key we indicated (in the third parameter) and stored it in the data for that column and row, whether that value was simple text or a list of dictionaries, as is the case for `creators`. We take a look at the first (and in this case, only) `creators` item for the first collections row in *step 10*, naming it `creator`. (Note that the `creators` list is duplicated across all `citations` for a collection item, just as the values for `title`, `creation_date`, and so on are.)

We want the birth year for the first creator for each collection item, which can be found at `creator[0]['birth_year']`. To create a `birthyear` series using this, we use `apply` and a `lambda` function:

```
>>> camcollectionsdf['birthyear'] = camcollectionsdf.\
...    creators.apply(lambda x: x[0]['birth_year'])
```

We take a closer look at lambda functions in *Chapter 6, Cleaning and Exploring Data with Series Operations*. Here, it is helpful to think of the x as representing the `creators` series, so `x[0]` gives us the list item we want, `creators[0]`. We grab the value from the `birth_year` key.

There's more...

You may have noticed that we left out some of the JSON returned by the API in our call to `json_normalize`. The first parameter that we passed to `json_normalize` was `camcollections['data']`. Effectively, we ignore the `info` object at the beginning of the JSON data. The information we want does not start until the `data` object. This is not very different conceptually from the `skiprows` parameter in the second recipe of the previous chapter. There is sometimes metadata like this at the beginning of JSON files.

See also

The preceding recipe demonstrates some useful techniques for doing data integrity checks without pandas, including list operations and comprehensions. Those are all relevant for the data in this recipe as well.

Importing data from web pages

We use **Beautiful Soup** in this recipe to scrape data from a web page and load that data into pandas. **Web scraping** is very useful when there is data at a website that is updated regularly, but there is no API. We can rerun our code to generate new data whenever the page is updated.

Unfortunately, the web scrapers we build can be broken when the structure of the targeted page changes. That is less likely to happen with APIs because they are designed for data exchange, and carefully curated with that end in mind. The priority for most web designers is the quality of the display of information, not the reliability and ease of data exchange. This causes data cleaning challenges unique to web scraping, including HTML elements that house the data being in surprising and changing locations, formatting tags that obfuscate the underlying data, and explanatory text that aid data interpretation being difficult to retrieve. In addition to these challenges, scraping presents data cleaning issues that are familiar, such as changing data types in columns, less than ideal headings, and missing values. We deal with data issues that occur most frequently in this recipe.

Getting ready

You will need Beautiful Soup installed to run the code in this recipe. You can install it with pip by entering `pip install beautifulsoup4` in a terminal window or Windows PowerShell.

We will scrape data from a web page, find the following table in that page, and load it into a pandas DataFrame:

Country	Cases	Deaths	Cases per Million	Deaths per Million	population	population_density	median_age	gdp_per_capita	hospital_beds_per_100k
Algeria	9,394	653	214	15	43,851,043	17	29	13,914	1.9
Austria	16,642	668	1848	74	9,006,400	107	44	45,437	7.4
Bangladesh	47,153	650	286	4	164,689,383	1265	28	3,524	0.8
Belgium	58,381	9467	5037	817	11,589,616	376	42	42,659	5.6
Brazil	514,849	29314	2422	138	212,559,409	25	34	14,103	2.2
Canada	90,936	7295	2409	193	37,742,157	4	41	44,018	2.5

Figure 2.1 – COVID-19 data from six countries

> **Note**
>
> I created this web page, `http://www.alrb.org/datacleaning/covidcaseoutliers.html`, based on COVID-19 data for public use from *Our World in Data*, available at `https://ourworldindata.org/coronavirus-source-data`.

How to do it...

We scrape the COVID data from the website and do some routine data checks:

1. Import the `pprint`, `requests`, and `BeautifulSoup` libraries:

```
>>> import pandas as pd
>>> import numpy as np
>>> import json
>>> import pprint
>>> import requests
>>> from bs4 import BeautifulSoup
```

2. Parse the web page and get the header row of the table.

    Use Beautiful Soup's `find` method to get the table we want and then use `find_all` to retrieve the elements nested within the `th` elements for that table. Create a list of column labels based on the text of the `th` rows:

```
>>> webpage = requests.get("http://www.alrb.org/
datacleaning/covidcaseoutliers.html")
>>> bs = BeautifulSoup(webpage.text, 'html.parser')


>>> theadrows = bs.find('table', {'id':'tblDeaths'}).
thead.find_all('th')
>>> type(theadrows)
<class 'bs4.element.ResultSet'>


>>> labelcols = [j.get_text() for j in theadrows]
>>> labelcols[0] = "rowheadings"
>>> labelcols
['rowheadings', 'Cases', 'Deaths', 'Cases per Million',
'Deaths per Million', 'population', 'population_density',
'median_age', 'gdp_per_capita', 'hospital_beds_per_100k']
```

3. Get the data from the table cells.

    Find all of the table rows for the table we want. For each table row, find the `th` element and retrieve the text. We will use that text for our row labels. Also, for each row, find all the `td` elements (the table cells with the data) and save text from all of them in a list. This gives us `datarows`, which has all the numeric data in the table. (You can confirm that it matches the table from the web page.) We then insert the `labelrows` list (which has the row headings) at the beginning of each list in `datarows`:

```
>>> rows = bs.find('table', {'id':'tblDeaths'}).tbody.
find_all('tr')
>>> datarows = []
>>> labelrows = []
>>> for row in rows:
...     rowlabels = row.find('th').get_text()
...     cells = row.find_all('td', {'class':'data'})
...     if (len(rowlabels)>3):
...         labelrows.append(rowlabels)
```

```
...     if (len(cells)>0):
...         cellvalues = [j.get_text() for j in cells]
...         datarows.append(cellvalues)
...
>>> pprint.pprint(datarows[0:2])
[['9,394', '653', '214', '15', '43,851,043', '17', '29',
'13,914', '1.9'],
 ['16,642', '668', '1848', '74', '9,006,400', '107',
'44', '45,437', '7.4']]
>>> pprint.pprint(labelrows[0:2])
['Algeria', 'Austria']
>>>
>>> for i in range(len(datarows)):
...     datarows[i].insert(0, labelrows[i])
...
>>> pprint.pprint(datarows[0:1])
[['Algeria','9,394','653','214','15','43,851,043','17','2
9','13,914','1.9']]
```

4. Load the data into pandas.

    Pass the datarows list to the DataFrame method of pandas. Notice that all data is read into pandas with the object data type, and that some data has values that cannot be converted into numeric values in their current form (due to the commas):

```
>>> totaldeaths = pd.DataFrame(datarows,
columns=labelcols)
>>> totaldeaths.head()
  rowheadings    Cases Deaths  ... median_age gdp_per_
capita  \
0      Algeria   9,394    653  ...         29
13,914
1      Austria  16,642    668  ...         44
45,437
2  Bangladesh   47,153    650  ...         28
3,524
3      Belgium   58,381   9467  ...         42
42,659
```

```
4        Brazil  514,849  29314  ...         34
14,103
```

```
>>> totaldeaths.dtypes
rowheadings                  object
Cases                        object
Deaths                       object
Cases per Million            object
Deaths per Million           object
population                   object
population_density           object
median_age                   object
gdp_per_capita               object
hospital_beds_per_100k       object
dtype: object
```

5. Fix the column names and convert the data to numeric values.

Remove spaces from column names. Remove all non-numeric data from the first columns with data, including the commas (str.replace("[^0-9]","")). Convert to numeric values, except for the rowheadings column:

```
>>> totaldeaths.columns = totaldeaths.columns.str.
replace(" ", "_").str.lower()
>>> for col in totaldeaths.columns[1:-1]:
...     totaldeaths[col] = totaldeaths[col].\
...         str.replace("[^0-9]","").astype('int64')
...
>>> totaldeaths['hospital_beds_per_100k'] =
totaldeaths['hospital_beds_per_100k'].astype('float')
>>> totaldeaths.head()
   rowheadings    cases   deaths   ...   median_age   gdp_per_
capita  \
0       Algeria    9394      653   ...           29
13914
1       Austria   16642      668   ...           44
45437
2   Bangladesh    47153      650   ...           28
3524
```

```
3        Belgium     58381    9467  ...              42
42659
4        Brazil   514849    29314  ...              34
14103
>>> totaldeaths.dtypes
rowheadings                    object
cases                          int64
deaths                         int64
cases_per_million              int64
deaths_per_million             int64
population                     int64
population_density             int64
median_age                     int64
gdp_per_capita                 int64
hospital_beds_per_100k       float64
dtype: object
```

We have now created a pandas DataFrame from an `html` table.

How it works...

Beautiful Soup is a very useful tool for finding specific HTML elements in a web page and retrieving text from them. You can get one HTML element with `find` and get one or more with `find_all`. The first argument for both `find` and `find_all` is the HTML element to get. The second argument takes a Python dictionary of attributes. You can retrieve text from all of the HTML elements you find with `get_text`.

Some amount of looping is usually necessary to process the elements and text, as with *step 2* and *step 3*. These two statements in *step 2* are fairly typical:

```
>>> theadrows = bs.find('table', {'id':'tblDeaths'}).thead.
find_all('th')
>>> labelcols = [j.get_text() for j in theadrows]
```

The first statement finds all the `th` elements we want and creates a Beautiful Soup result set called `theadrows` from the elements it found. The second statement iterates over the `theadrows` Beautiful Soup result set using the `get_text` method to get the text from each element, and stores it in the `labelcols` list.

Step 3 is a little more involved, but makes use of the same Beautiful Soup methods. We find all of the table rows (`tr`) in the target table (`rows = bs.find('table', {'id':'tblDeaths'}).tbody.find_all('tr')`). We then iterate over each of those rows, finding the `th` element and getting the text in that element (`rowlabels = row.find('th').get_text()`). We also find all of the table cells (`td`) for each row (`cells = row.find_all('td', {'class':'data'})` and get the text from all table cells (`cellvalues = [j.get_text() for j in cells]`). Note that this code is dependent on the class of the `td` elements being `data`. Finally, we insert the row labels we get from the `th` elements at the beginning of each list in `datarows`:

```
>>> for i in range(len(datarows)):
...     datarows[i].insert(0, labelrows[i])
```

In *step 4*, we use the `DataFrame` method to load the list we created in *steps 2* and *3* into pandas. We then do some cleaning similar to what we have done in previous recipes in this chapter. We use `string replace` to remove spaces from column names and to remove all non-numeric data, including commas, from what are otherwise valid numeric values. We convert all columns, except for the `rowheadings` column, to numeric.

There's more...

Our scraping code is dependent on several aspects of the web page's structure not changing: the ID of the main table, the presence of `th` tags with column and row labels, and the `td` elements continuing to have their class equal to data. The good news is that if the structure of the web page does change, this will likely only affect the `find` and `find_all` calls. The rest of the code would not need to change.

Persisting JSON data

There are several reasons why we might want to serialize a JSON file:

- We may have retrieved the data with an API, but need to keep a snapshot of the data.

- The data in the JSON file is relatively static and informs our data cleaning and analysis over multiple phases of a project.

- We might decide that the flexibility of a schema-less format such as JSON helps us solve many data cleaning and analysis problems.

It is worth highlighting this last reason to use JSON – that it can solve many data problems. Although tabular data structures clearly have many benefits, particularly for operational data, they are often not the best way to store data for analysis purposes. In preparing data for analysis, a substantial amount of time is spent either merging data from different tables or dealing with data redundancy when working with flat files. Not only are these processes time consuming, but every merge or reshaping leaves the door open to a data error of broad scope. This can also mean that we end up paying too much attention to the mechanics of manipulating data and too little to the conceptual issues at the core of our work.

We return to the Cleveland Museum of Art collections data in this recipe. There are at least three possible units of analysis for this data file – the collection item level, the creator level, and the citation level. JSON allows us to nest citations and creators within collections. (You can examine the structure of the JSON file in the *Getting ready* section of this recipe.) This data cannot be persisted in a tabular structure without flattening the file, which we did in an earlier recipe in this chapter. In this recipe, we will use two different methods to persist JSON data, each with its own advantages and disadvantages.

Getting ready

We will be working with data on the Cleveland Museum of Art's collection of works by African-American artists. The following is the structure of the JSON data returned by the API. It has been abbreviated to save space:

```
{"info": { "total": 778, "parameters": {"african_american_
artists": "" }},
"data": [
{
"id": 165157,
"accession_number": "2007.158",
"title": "Fulton and Nostrand",
"creation_date": "1958",
"citations": [
  {
    "citation": "Annual Exhibition: Sculpture, Paintings...",
    "page_number": "Unpaginated, [8],[12]",
    "url": null
  },
  {
```

```
    "citation": "\"Moscow to See Modern U.S. Art,\"<em> New
York...",
    "page_number": "P. 60",
    "url": null
  }]
"creators": [
    {
    "description": "Jacob Lawrence (American, 1917-2000)",
    "extent": null,
    "qualifier": null,
    "role": "artist",
    "birth_year": "1917",
    "death_year": "2000"
    }
  ]
}
```

How to do it...

We will serialize the JSON data using two different methods:

1. Load the pandas, json, pprint, requests, and msgpack libraries:

    ```
    >>> import pandas as pd
    >>> import json
    >>> import pprint
    >>> import requests
    >>> import msgpack
    ```

2. Load the JSON data from an API. I have abbreviated the JSON output:

    ```
    >>> response = requests.get("https://openaccess-api.
    clevelandart.org/api/artworks/?african_american_artists")
    >>> camcollections = json.loads(response.text)
    >>> print(len(camcollections['data']))
    778
    >>> pprint.pprint(camcollections['data'][0])
    {'accession_number': '2007.158',
    ```

```
 'catalogue_raisonne': None,
 'citations': [{'citation': 'Annual Exhibition:
Sculpture...',
                'page_number': 'Unpaginated, [8],[12]',
                'url': None},
               {'citation': '"Moscow to See Modern
U.S....',
                'page_number': 'P. 60',
                'url': None}]
 'collection': 'American - Painting',
 'creation_date': '1958',
 'creators': [{'biography': 'Jacob Lawrence (born
1917)...',
               'birth_year': '1917',
               'description': 'Jacob Lawrence
(American...',
               'role': 'artist'}],
 'type': 'Painting'}
```

3. Save and reload the JSON file using Python's `json` library.

    Persist the JSON data in human-readable form. Reload it from the saved file and confirm that it worked by retrieving the `creators` data from the first collections item:

```
>>> with open("data/camcollections.json","w") as f:
...     json.dump(camcollections, f)
...
>>> with open("data/camcollections.json","r") as f:
...     camcollections = json.load(f)
...
>>> pprint.pprint(camcollections['data'][0]['creators'])
[{'biography': 'Jacob Lawrence (born 1917) has been a
prominent artist since...'
  'birth_year': '1917',
  'description': 'Jacob Lawrence (American, 1917-2000)',
  'role': 'artist'}]
```

4. Save and reload the JSON file using `msgpack`:

```
>>> with open("data/camcollections.msgpack", "wb") as
outfile:
...        packed = msgpack.packb(camcollections)
...        outfile.write(packed)
...
1586507

>>> with open("data/camcollections.msgpack", "rb") as
data_file:
...        msgbytes = data_file.read()
...
>>> camcollections = msgpack.unpackb(msgbytes)

>>> pprint.pprint(camcollections['data'][0]['creators'])
[{'biography': 'Jacob Lawrence (born 1917) has been a
prominent...',
    'birth_year': '1917',
    'death_year': '2000',
    'description': 'Jacob Lawrence (American, 1917-2000)',
    'role': 'artist'}]
```

How it works...

We use the Cleveland Museum of Art's collections API to retrieve collections items. The `african_american_artists` flag in the query string indicates that we just want collections for those creators. `json.loads` returns a dictionary called `info` and a list of dictionaries called `data`. We check the length of the `data` list. This tells us that there are 778 items in collections. We then display the first item of collections to get a better look at the structure of the data. (I have abbreviated the JSON output.)

We save and then reload the data using Python's JSON library in *step 3*. The advantage of persisting the data in this way is that it keeps the data in human-readable form. Unfortunately, it has two disadvantages: saving takes longer than alternative serialization methods, and it uses more storage space.

In *step 4*, we use `msgpack` to persist our data. This is faster than Python's `json` library, and the saved file uses less space. Of course, the disadvantage is that the resulting JSON is binary rather than text-based.

There's more...

I use both methods for persisting JSON data in my work. When I am working with small amounts of data, and that data is relatively static, I prefer human-readable JSON. A great use case for this is the recipes in the previous chapter where we needed to create value labels.

I use msgpack when I am working with large amounts of data, where that data changes regularly. msgpack files are also great when you want to take regular snapshots of key tables in enterprise databases.

The Cleveland Museum of Art's collections data is similar in at least one important way to the data we work with every day. The unit of analysis frequently changes. Here we are looking at collections, citations, and creators. In our work, we might have to simultaneously look at students and courses, or households and deposits. An enterprise database system for the museum data would likely have separate collections, citations, and creators tables that we would eventually need to merge. The resulting merged file would have data redundancy issues that we would need to account for whenever we changed the unit of analysis.

When we alter our data cleaning process to work directly from JSON or parts of it, we end up eliminating a major source of errors. We do more data cleaning with JSON in the *Classes that handle non-tabular data structures* recipe in *Chapter 10, User-Defined Functions and Classes to Automate Data Cleaning.*

3

Taking the Measure of Your Data

Within a week of receiving a new dataset, at least one person is likely to ask us a familiar question: "so, how does it look?" This is not always asked in a relaxed tone, and others are not usually excited to hear about all of the red flags we have already found. There might be a sense of urgency to declare the data ready for analysis. Of course, if we sign it off too soon, this can create much larger problems; the presentation of invalid results, the misinterpretation of variable relationships, and having to redo major chunks of our analysis. The key is sorting out what we need to know about the data before we explore anything else in the data. The recipes in this chapter offer techniques for determining if the data is in good enough shape to begin the analysis, so that even if we cannot say, "it looks fine," we can at least say, "I'm pretty sure I have identified the main issues, and here they are."

Often our domain knowledge is quite limited, or at least not nearly as good as those who created the data. We have to quickly get a sense of what we are looking at even when we have little substantive understanding of the individuals or events reflected in the data. Many times (for some of us, most of the time) there is not anything like a data dictionary or codebook accompanying the receipt of the data.

Quick. Ask yourself what the first few things you try to find out in this situation are; that is, when you first get data about which you know little. It is probably something like this:

- How are the rows of the dataset uniquely identified? (What is the unit of analysis?)
- How many rows and columns are in the dataset?
- What are the key categorical variables and the frequencies of each value?
- How are important continuous variables distributed?
- How might variables be related to each other – for example, how might the distribution of continuous variables vary according to categories in the data?
- What variable values are out of expected ranges, and how are missing values distributed?

We go over essential tools and strategies for answering the first four questions in this chapter. We look into the last two questions in the following chapter.

I should point out that this first take on our data is important even when the structure of the data is familiar; when, for example, we receive data for a new month or year with the same column names and data types as in previous periods. It is hard to guard against the sense that we can just rerun our old programs; to be as vigilant as we were the first few times we prepared the data for analysis. Most of us have probably been in situations where we receive new data with a familiar structure, but the answers to the preceding questions are meaningfully different: new valid values for key categorical variables; rare values that have always been permissible but that have not been seen for several periods; and unexpected changes in the status of clients/students/customers. It is important to build routines for understanding our data that we follow regardless of our familiarity with it.

Specifically, we will cover the following topics in this chapter:

- Getting a first look at your data
- Selecting and organizing columns
- Selecting rows
- Generating frequencies for categorical variables
- Generating statistics for continuous variables

Technical requirements

The code and notebooks for this chapter are available on GitHub at `https://github.com/PacktPublishing/Python-Data-Cleaning-Cookbook`

Getting a first look at your data

We will work with two datasets in this chapter: The National Longitudinal Survey of Youth for 1997, a survey conducted by the United States government that surveyed the same group of individuals from 1997 through 2017; and the counts of COVID cases and deaths by country from *Our World in Data*.

Getting ready...

We will mainly be using the pandas library for this recipe. We will use pandas tools to take a closer look at the **National Longitudinal Survey (NLS)** and COVID-19 case data.

> **Note**
>
> The NLS of Youth was conducted by the United States Bureau of Labor Statistics. This survey started with a cohort of individuals in 1997 who were born between 1980 and 1985, with annual follow-ups each year through 2017. For this recipe, I pulled 89 variables on grades, employment, income, and attitudes toward government from the hundreds of data items on the survey. Separate files for SPSS, Stata, and SAS can be downloaded from the repository. NLS data can be downloaded from `https://www.nlsinfo.org/ investigator/pages/search`.
>
> *Our World in Data* provides COVID-19 public use data at `https:// ourworldindata.org/coronavirus-source-data`.

How to do it...

We will get an initial look at the NLS and COVID data, including the number of rows and columns, and the data types:

1. Import the libraries and load the DataFrames:

```
>>> import pandas as pd
>>> import numpy as np
>>> nls97 = pd.read_csv("data/nls97.csv")
>>>
>>> covidtotals = pd.read_csv("data/covidtotals.csv",
...     parse_dates=['lastdate'])
```

2.   Set and show the index and the size of the `nls97` data.

Also, check to see whether the index values are unique:

```
>>> nls97.set_index("personid", inplace=True)
>>> nls97.index
Int64Index([100061, 100139, 100284, 100292, 100583,
100833,                        ...
            999543, 999698, 999963],
        dtype='int64', name='personid', length=8984)
>>> nls97.shape
(8984, 88)
>>> nls97.index.nunique()
8984
```

3.   Show the data types and `non-null` value counts:

```
>>> nls97.info()
<class 'pandas.core.frame.DataFrame'>
Int64Index: 8984 entries, 100061 to 999963
Data columns (total 88 columns):
 #    Column               Non-Null Count   Dtype
---   ------               --------------   -----
 0    gender               8984 non-null    object
 1    birthmonth           8984 non-null    int64
 2    birthyear            8984 non-null    int64
 3    highestgradecompleted 6663 non-null   float64
 4    maritalstatus        6672 non-null    object
 5    childathome          4791 non-null    float64
 6    childnotathome       4791 non-null    float64
 7    wageincome           5091 non-null    float64
 8    weeklyhrscomputer    6710 non-null    object
 9    weeklyhrstv          6711 non-null    object
 10   nightlyhrssleep      6706 non-null    float64
 11   satverbal            1406 non-null    float64
 12   satmath              1407 non-null    float64
...

 83   colenroct15          7469 non-null    object
```

```
84   colenrfeb16               7036 non-null    object
85   colenroct16               6733 non-null    object
86   colenrfeb17               6733 non-null    object
87   colenroct17               6734 non-null    object
dtypes: float64(29), int64(2), object(57)
memory usage: 6.1+ MB
```

4. Show the first row of the nls97 data.

    Use transpose to show a little more of the output:

```
>>> nls97.head(2).T
personid                        100061              100139
gender                          Female                Male
birthmonth                           5                   9
birthyear                         1980                1983
highestgradecompleted               13                  12
maritalstatus                  Married             Married
...                                ...                 ...
colenroct15        1. Not enrolled  1. Not enrolled
colenrfeb16        1. Not enrolled  1. Not enrolled
colenroct16        1. Not enrolled  1. Not enrolled
colenrfeb17        1. Not enrolled  1. Not enrolled
colenroct17        1. Not enrolled  1. Not enrolled
```

5. Set and show the index and size for the COVID data.

    Also, check to see whether index values are unqiue:

```
>>> covidtotals.set_index("iso_code", inplace=True)
>>> covidtotals.index
Index(['AFG', 'ALB', 'DZA', 'AND', 'AGO', 'AIA', 'ATG',
'ARG',          ...
        'UZB', 'VAT', 'VEN', 'VNM', 'ESH', 'YEM',
'ZMB','ZWE'],
      dtype='object', name='iso_code', length=210)
>>> covidtotals.shape
(210, 11)
>>> covidtotals.index.nunique()
210
```

6. Show the data types and `non-null` value counts:

```
>>> covidtotals.info()
<class 'pandas.core.frame.DataFrame'>
Index: 210 entries, AFG to ZWE
Data columns (total 11 columns):
 #   Column          Non-Null Count   Dtype
---  ------          --------------   -----
 0   lastdate        210 non-null     datetime64[ns]
 1   location        210 non-null     object
 2   total_cases     210 non-null     int64
 3   total_deaths    210 non-null     int64
 4   total_cases_pm  209 non-null     float64
 5   total_deaths_pm 209 non-null     float64
 6   population      210 non-null     float64
 7   pop_density     198 non-null     float64
 8   median_age      186 non-null     float64
 9   gdp_per_capita  182 non-null     float64
 10  hosp_beds       164 non-null     float64
dtypes: datetime64[ns](1), float64(7), int64(2),
object(1)
memory usage: 19.7+ KB
```

7. Show a sample of a few rows of the COVID case data:

```
>>> covidtotals.sample(2, random_state=1).T
```

iso_code	COG	THA
lastdate	2020-06-01 00:00:00	2020-06-01 00:00:00
location	Congo	Thailand
total_cases	611	3081
total_deaths	20	57
total_cases_pm	110.727	44.14
total_deaths_pm	3.624	0.817
population	5.51809e+06	6.98e+07
pop_density	15.405	135.132
median_age	19	40.1
gdp_per_capita	4881.41	16277.7
hosp_beds	NaN	2.1

This has given us a good foundation for understanding our DataFrames, including their size and column data types.

How it works...

We set and display the index of the nls97 DataFrame, which is called personid, in *step 2*. It is a more meaningful index than the default pandas RangeIndex, which is essentially the row numbers with zero base. Often, there is a unique identifier when working with individuals as the unit of analysis. This is a good candidate for an index. It makes selecting a row by that identifier easier. Rather than using the statement nls97. loc[personid==1000061] to get the row for that person, we can use nls97. loc[1000061]. We try this out in the next recipe.

Pandas makes it easy to view the number of rows and columns, the data type and number of non-missing values for each column, and the values for the columns for a few rows of your data. This can be accomplished by using the shape attribute and calling the info and head, or sample, methods. Using the head(2) method shows the first two rows, but sometimes it is helpful to grab a row from anywhere in the DataFrame, in which case we would use sample (We set the seed when we call sample(random_state=1) to get the same results whenever we run the code). We can chain our call to head or sample with a T to transpose it. This reverses the display of rows and columns. That is helpful when there are more columns than can be shown horizontally and you want to be able to see all of them. By transposing the rows and columns we are able to see all of the columns.

The shape attribute of the nls97 DataFrame tells us that there are 8,984 rows and 88 non-index columns. Since personid is the index, it is not included in the column count. The info method shows us that many of the columns have object data types and that some have a large number of missing values. satverbal and satmath have only about 1,400 valid values.

The shape attribute of the covidtotals DataFrame tells us that there are 210 rows and 11 columns, which does not include the country iso_code column used for the index (iso_code is a unique three-digit identifier for each country). The key variables for most analyses we would do are total_cases, total_deaths, total_cases_pm, and total_deaths_pm. total_cases and total_deaths are present for each country, but total_cases_pm and total_deaths_pm are missing for one country.

There's more...

I find that thinking through the index when working with a data file can remind me of the unit of analysis. That is not actually obvious with the NLS data, as it is actually panel data disguised as person-level data. Panel, or longitudinal, datasets have data for the same individuals over some regular duration. In this case, data was collected for each person over a 21-year span, from 1997 till 2017. The administrators of the survey have flattened it for analysis purposes by creating columns for certain responses over the years, such as college enrollment (`colenroct15` through `colenroct17`). This is a fairly standard practice, but it is likely that we will need to do some reshaping for some analyses.

One thing I pay careful attention to when receiving any panel data is drop-off in responses to key variables over time. Notice the drop off in valid values from `colenroct15` to `colenroct17`. By October of 2017, only 75% of respondents provided a valid response (6,734/8,984). That is definitely worth keeping in mind during subsequent analysis, since the 6,734 remaining respondents may be different in important ways from the overall sample of 8,984.

See also

A recipe in *Chapter 1*, *Anticipating Data Cleaning Issues when Importing Tabular Data into pandas*, shows how to persist pandas DataFrames as feather or pickle files. In later recipes in this chapter, we will look at descriptives and frequencies for these two DataFrames.

We reshape the NLS data in *Chapter 9*, *Tidying and Reshaping Data*, recovering some of its actual structure as panel data. This is necessary for statistical methods such as survival analysis, and is closer to tidy data ideals.

Selecting and organizing columns

We explore several ways to select one or more columns from your DataFrame in this recipe. We can select columns by passing a list of column names to the `[]` bracket operator, or by using the pandas-specific data accessors `loc` and `iloc`.

When cleaning data or doing exploratory or statistical analyses, it is helpful to focus on the variables that are relevant to the issue or analysis at hand. This makes it important to group columns according to their substantive or statistical relationships with each other, or to limit the columns we are investigating at any one time. How many times have we said to ourselves something like, *"Why does variable A have a value of x when variable B has a value of y?"* We can only do that when the amount of data we are viewing at a given moment does not exceed our perceptive abilities at that moment.

Getting ready...

We will continue working with the **NLS** data in this recipe.

How to do it...

We will explore several ways to select columns:

1. Import the pandas library and load the NLS data into pandas.

    Also, convert all columns with object data type in the NLS data to category data type. Do this by selecting object data type columns with select_dtypes and using apply plus a lambda function to change the data type to category:

    ```
    >>> import pandas as pd
    >>> import numpy as np
    >>> nls97 = pd.read_csv("data/nls97.csv")
    >>> nls97.set_index("personid", inplace=True)
    >>> nls97.loc[:, nls97.dtypes == 'object'] = \
    ...    nls97.select_dtypes(['object']). \
    ...    apply(lambda x: x.astype('category'))
    ```

2. Select a column using the pandas [] bracket operator, and the loc and iloc accessors.

    We pass a string matching a column name to the bracket operator to return a pandas series. If we pass a list of one element with that column name (nls97[['gender']]), a DataFrame is returned. We can also use the loc and iloc accessors to select columns:

    ```
    >>> analysisdemo = nls97['gender']
    >>> type(analysisdemo)
    <class 'pandas.core.series.Series'>

    >>> analysisdemo = nls97[['gender']]
    >>> type(analysisdemo)
    <class 'pandas.core.frame.DataFrame'>

    >>> analysisdemo = nls97.loc[:,['gender']]
    >>> type(analysisdemo)
    <class 'pandas.core.frame.DataFrame'>
    ```

```
>>> analysisdemo = nls97.iloc[:,[0]]
>>> type(analysisdemo)
<class 'pandas.core.frame.DataFrame'>
```

3. Select multiple columns from a pandas DataFrame.

Use the bracket operator and `loc` to select a few columns:

```
>>> analysisdemo = nls97[['gender','maritalstatus',
...    'highestgradecompleted']]
>>> analysisdemo.shape
(8984, 3)
>>> analysisdemo.head()
```

personid	gender	maritalstatus	highestgradecompleted
100061	Female	Married	13
100139	Male	Married	12
100284	Male	Never-married	7
100292	Male	NaN	nan
100583	Male	Married	13

```
>>> analysisdemo = nls97.loc[:,['gender','maritalstatus',
...    'highestgradecompleted']]
>>> analysisdemo.shape
(8984, 3)
>>> analysisdemo.head()
```

personid	gender	maritalstatus	highestgradecompleted
100061	Female	Married	13
100139	Male	Married	12
100284	Male	Never-married	7
100292	Male	NaN	nan
100583	Male	Married	13

4. Select multiple columns based on a list of columns.

   If you are selecting more than a few columns, it is helpful to create the list of column names separately. Here, we create a `keyvars` list of key variables for analysis:

```
>>> keyvars = ['gender','maritalstatus',
...   'highestgradecompleted','wageincome',
...   'gpaoverall','weeksworked17','colenroct17']
>>> analysiskeys = nls97[keyvars]
>>> analysiskeys.info()
<class 'pandas.core.frame.DataFrame'>
Int64Index: 8984 entries, 100061 to 999963
Data columns (total 7 columns):
 #   Column                 Non-Null Count   Dtype
---  ------                 --------------   -----
 0   gender                 8984 non-null    category
 1   maritalstatus          6672 non-null    category
 2   highestgradecompleted  6663 non-null    float64
 3   wageincome             5091 non-null    float64
 4   gpaoverall             6004 non-null    float64
 5   weeksworked17          6670 non-null    float64
 6   colenroct17            6734 non-null    category
dtypes: category(3), float64(4)
memory usage: 377.7 KB
```

5. Select one or more columns by filtering on column name.

   Select all of the `weeksworked##` columns using the `filter` operator:

```
>>> analysiswork = nls97.filter(like="weeksworked")
>>> analysiswork.info()
<class 'pandas.core.frame.DataFrame'>
Int64Index: 8984 entries, 100061 to 999963
Data columns (total 18 columns):
 #   Column        Non-Null Count   Dtype
---  ------        --------------   -----
 0   weeksworked00 8603 non-null    float64
 1   weeksworked01 8564 non-null    float64
 2   weeksworked02 8556 non-null    float64
 3   weeksworked03 8490 non-null    float64
```

4	weeksworked04	8458 non-null	float64
5	weeksworked05	8403 non-null	float64
6	weeksworked06	8340 non-null	float64
7	weeksworked07	8272 non-null	float64
8	weeksworked08	8186 non-null	float64
9	weeksworked09	8146 non-null	float64
10	weeksworked10	8054 non-null	float64
11	weeksworked11	7968 non-null	float64
12	weeksworked12	7747 non-null	float64
13	weeksworked13	7680 non-null	float64
14	weeksworked14	7612 non-null	float64
15	weeksworked15	7389 non-null	float64
16	weeksworked16	7068 non-null	float64
17	weeksworked17	6670 non-null	float64

```
dtypes: float64(18)
memory usage: 1.3 MB
```

6. Select all columns with the category data type.

   Use the select_dtypes method to select columns by data type:

```
>>> analysiscats = nls97.select_
dtypes(include=["category"])
>>> analysiscats.info()
<class 'pandas.core.frame.DataFrame'>
Int64Index: 8984 entries, 100061 to 999963
Data columns (total 57 columns):
```

#	Column	Non-Null Count	Dtype
---	------	--------------	-----
0	gender	8984 non-null	category
1	maritalstatus	6672 non-null	category
2	weeklyhrscomputer	6710 non-null	category
3	weeklyhrstv	6711 non-null	category
4	highestdegree	8953 non-null	category
...			
49	colenrfeb14	7624 non-null	category
50	colenroct14	7469 non-null	category
51	colenrfeb15	7469 non-null	category
52	colenroct15	7469 non-null	category

53	colenrfeb16	7036 non-null	category
54	colenroct16	6733 non-null	category
55	colenrfeb17	6733 non-null	category
56	colenroct17	6734 non-null	category

```
dtypes: category(57)
memory usage: 580.0 KB
```

7. Select all columns with numeric data types:

```
>>> analysisnums = nls97.select_dtypes(include=["number"])
>>> analysisnums.info()
<class 'pandas.core.frame.DataFrame'>
Int64Index: 8984 entries, 100061 to 999963
Data columns (total 31 columns):
```

#	Column	Non-Null Count	Dtype
0	birthmonth	8984 non-null	int64
1	birthyear	8984 non-null	int64
2	highestgradecompleted	6663 non-null	float64
...			
23	weeksworked10	8054 non-null	float64
24	weeksworked11	7968 non-null	float64
25	weeksworked12	7747 non-null	float64
26	weeksworked13	7680 non-null	float64
27	weeksworked14	7612 non-null	float64
28	weeksworked15	7389 non-null	float64
29	weeksworked16	7068 non-null	float64
30	weeksworked17	6670 non-null	float64

```
dtypes: float64(29), int64(2)
memory usage: 2.2 MB
```

8. Organize columns using lists of column names.

Use lists to organize the columns in your DataFrame. You can easily change the order of columns or exclude some columns in this way. Here, we move the columns in the demoadult list to the front:

```
>>> demo = ['gender','birthmonth','birthyear']
>>> highschoolrecord =
['satverbal','satmath','gpaoverall',
```

```
...     'gpaenglish','gpamath','gpascience']
>>> govresp = ['govprovidejobs','govpricecontrols',
...     'govhealthcare','govelderliving','govindhelp',
...     'govunemp','govincomediff','govcollegefinance',
...     'govdecenthousing','govprotectenvironment']
>>> demoadult = ['highestgradecompleted','maritalstatus',
...     'childathome','childnotathome','wageincome',
...     'weeklyhrscomputer','weeklyhrstv','nightlyhrssleep',
...     'highestdegree']
>>> weeksworked = ['weeksworked00','weeksworked01',
...     'weeksworked02','weeksworked03','weeksworked04',
...     'weeksworked14','weeksworked15','weeksworked16',
...     'weeksworked17']
>>> colenr = ['colenrfeb97','colenroct97','colenrfeb98',
...     'colenroct98','colenrfeb99','colenroct99',
...         ...
...     'colenrfeb15','colenroct15','colenrfeb16',
...     'colenroct16','colenrfeb17','colenroct17']
```

9. Create the new, reorganized DataFrame:

```
>>> nls97 = nls97[demoadult + demo + highschoolrecord + \
...     govresp + weeksworked + colenr]
>>> nls97.dtypes
highestgradecompleted        float64
maritalstatus                category
childathome                  float64
childnotathome               float64
wageincome                   float64
                                ...
colenroct15                  category
colenrfeb16                  category
colenroct16                  category
colenrfeb17                  category
colenroct17                  category
Length: 88, dtype: object
```

The preceding steps showed how to select columns and change the order of columns in a pandas DataFrame.

How it works...

Both the `[]` bracket operator and the `loc` data accessor are very handy for selecting and organizing columns. Each returns a DataFrame when passed a list of names of columns. The columns will be ordered according to the passed list of column names.

In *step 1*, we use `nls97.select_dtypes(['object'])` to select columns with object data type and chain that with `apply` and a `lambda` function (`apply(lambda x: x.astype('category'))`) to change those columns to `category`. We use the `loc` accessor to only update columns with object data type (`nls97.loc[:, nls97.dtypes == 'object']`). We go into much more detail on `apply` and `lambda` functions in *Chapter 6, Cleaning and Exploring Data with Series Operations*.

We also select columns by data type in *steps 6* and *7*. `select_dtypes` becomes quite useful when passing columns to methods such as `describe` or `value_counts` and you want to limit the analysis to continuous or categorical variables.

In *step 9*, we concatenate six different lists when using the bracket operator. This moves the column names in `demoadult` to the front and organizes all of the columns by those six groups. There are now clear *high school record* and *weeks worked* sections in our DataFrame's columns.

There's more...

We can also use `select_dtypes` to exclude data types. Also, if we are just interested in the `info` results, we can chain the `select_dtypes` call with the `info` method:

```
>>> nls97.select_dtypes(exclude=["category"]).info()
<class 'pandas.core.frame.DataFrame'>
Int64Index: 8984 entries, 100061 to 999963
Data columns (total 31 columns):
 #   Column               Non-Null Count   Dtype
---  ------               --------------   -----
 0   highestgradecompleted 6663 non-null   float64
 1   childathome           4791 non-null   float64
 2   childnotathome        4791 non-null   float64
 3   wageincome            5091 non-null   float64
```

4	nightlyhrssleep	6706 non-null	float64
5	birthmonth	8984 non-null	int64
6	birthyear	8984 non-null	int64
...			
25	weeksworked12	7747 non-null	float64
26	weeksworked13	7680 non-null	float64
27	weeksworked14	7612 non-null	float64
28	weeksworked15	7389 non-null	float64
29	weeksworked16	7068 non-null	float64
30	weeksworked17	6670 non-null	float64

```
dtypes: float64(29), int64(2)
memory usage: 2.2 MB
```

The `filter` operator can also take a regular expression. For example, you can return the columns that have `income` in their names:

```
>>> nls97.filter(regex='income')
>>> nls97.filter(regex='income')
```

	wageincome	govincomediff
personid		
100061	12,500	NaN
100139	120,000	NaN
100284	58,000	NaN
100292	nan	NaN
100583	30,000	NaN
...	...	...
999291	35,000	NaN
999406	116,000	NaN
999543	nan	NaN
999698	nan	NaN
999963	50,000	NaN

See also

Many of these techniques can be used to create pandas series as well as DataFrames. We demonstrate this in *Chapter 6, Cleaning and Exploring Data With Series Operations.*

Selecting rows

When we are taking the measure of our data and otherwise answering the question, *"How does it look?"*, we are constantly zooming in and out. We are looking at aggregated numbers and particular rows. But there are also important data issues that are only obvious at an intermediate zoom level, issues that we only notice when looking at some subset of rows. This recipe demonstrates how to use the pandas tools for detecting data issues in subsets of our data.

Getting ready...

We will continue working with the NLS data in this recipe.

How to do it...

We will go over several techniques for selecting rows in a pandas DataFrame.

1. Import pandas and numpy, and load the nls97 data:

```
>>> import pandas as pd
>>> import numpy as np
>>> nls97 = pd.read_csv("data/nls97.csv")
>>> nls97.set_index("personid", inplace=True)
```

2. Use slicing to start at the 1001st row and go to the 1004th row:

nls97[1000:1004] selects every row starting from the row indicated by the integer to the left of the colon (1000, in this case) to, but not including, the row indicated by the integer to the right of the colon (1004). The row at 1000 is actually the 1001st row because of zero-based indexing. Each row appears as a column in the output since we have transposed the resulting DataFrame:

```
>>> nls97[1000:1004].T
```

personid 195996	195884	195891	195970
gender Female	Male	Male	Female
birthmonth 9	12	9	3
birthyear 1980	1981	1980	1982
highestgradecompleted NaN	NaN	12	17

maritalstatus	NaN	Never-married	Never-married
NaN			
...	...	...	...
...			
colenroct15	NaN	1. Not enrolled	1. Not enrolled
NaN			
colenrfeb16	NaN	1. Not enrolled	1. Not enrolled
NaN			
colenroct16	NaN	1. Not enrolled	1. Not enrolled
NaN			
colenrfeb17	NaN	1. Not enrolled	1. Not enrolled
NaN			
colenroct17	NaN	1. Not enrolled	1. Not enrolled
NaN			

3. Use slicing to start at the 1001st row and go to the 1004th row, skipping every other row.

The integer after the second colon (2 in this case) indicates the size of the step. When the step is excluded it is assumed to be 1. Notice that by setting the value of the step to 2, we are skipping every other row:

```
>>> nls97[1000:1004:2].T
```

personid	195884	195970
gender	Male	Female
birthmonth	12	3
birthyear	1981	1982
highestgradecompleted	NaN	17
maritalstatus	NaN	Never-married
...	...	...
colenroct15	NaN	1. Not enrolled
colenrfeb16	NaN	1. Not enrolled
colenroct16	NaN	1. Not enrolled
colenrfeb17	NaN	1. Not enrolled
colenroct17	NaN	1. Not enrolled

4. Select the first three rows using head and [] operator slicing.

Note that nls97[:3] returns the same DataFrame as nls97.head(3). By not providing a value to the left of the colon in [:3], we are telling the operator to get rows from the start of the DataFrame:

```
>>> nls97.head(3).T
personid             100061          100139
100284
gender               Female            Male
Male
birthmonth                5               9
11
birthyear              1980            1983
1984
...                     ...             ...
...
colenroct15   1. Not enrolled  1. Not enrolled   1. Not
enrolled
colenrfeb16   1. Not enrolled  1. Not enrolled   1. Not
enrolled
colenroct16   1. Not enrolled  1. Not enrolled   1. Not
enrolled
colenrfeb17   1. Not enrolled  1. Not enrolled   1. Not
enrolled
colenroct17   1. Not enrolled  1. Not enrolled   1. Not
enrolled


>>> nls97[:3].T
personid             100061          100139
100284
gender               Female            Male
Male
birthmonth                5               9
11
birthyear              1980            1983
1984
...                     ...             ...
...
colenroct15   1. Not enrolled  1. Not enrolled   1. Not
enrolled
```

colenrfeb16	1. Not enrolled	1. Not enrolled	1. Not enrolled
colenroct16	1. Not enrolled	1. Not enrolled	1. Not enrolled
colenrfeb17	1. Not enrolled	1. Not enrolled	1. Not enrolled
colenroct17	1. Not enrolled	1. Not enrolled	1. Not enrolled

5. Select the last three rows using `tail` and `[]` operator slicing.

   Note that `nls97.tail(3)` returns the same DataFrame as `nls97[-3:]`:

```
>>> nls97.tail(3).T
```

personid	999543	999698	999963
gender	Female	Female	Female
birthmonth	8	5	9
birthyear	1984	1983	1982
...	...	...	...
colenroct15	1. Not enrolled	1. Not enrolled	1. Not enrolled
colenrfeb16	1. Not enrolled	1. Not enrolled	1. Not enrolled
colenroct16	1. Not enrolled	1. Not enrolled	1. Not enrolled
colenrfeb17	1. Not enrolled	1. Not enrolled	1. Not enrolled
colenroct17	1. Not enrolled	1. Not enrolled	1. Not enrolled

```
>>> nls97[-3:].T
```

personid	999543	999698	999963
gender	Female	Female	Female
birthmonth	8	5	9
birthyear	1984	1983	1982

. . .	. . .	. . .	
. . .			
colenroct15	1. Not enrolled	1. Not enrolled	1. Not enrolled
colenrfeb16	1. Not enrolled	1. Not enrolled	1. Not enrolled
colenroct16	1. Not enrolled	1. Not enrolled	1. Not enrolled
colenrfeb17	1. Not enrolled	1. Not enrolled	1. Not enrolled
colenroct17	1. Not enrolled	1. Not enrolled	1. Not enrolled

6. Select a few rows using the `loc` data accessor.

   Use the `loc` accessor to select by `index` label. We can pass a list of index labels
   or we can specify a range of labels. (Recall that we have set `personid` as the
   index.) Note that `nls97.loc[[195884,195891,195970]]` and `nls97.`
   `loc[195884:195970]` return the same DataFrame:

```
>>> nls97.loc[[195884,195891,195970]].T
```

personid	195884	195891
195970		
gender	Male	Male
Female		
birthmonth	12	9
3		
birthyear	1981	1980
1982		
highestgradecompleted	NaN	12
17		
maritalstatus	NaN	Never-married Never-
married		
. . .	. . .	. . .
. . .		
colenroct15	NaN	1. Not enrolled 1. Not enrolled
colenrfeb16	NaN	1. Not enrolled 1. Not enrolled
colenroct16	NaN	1. Not enrolled 1. Not enrolled
colenrfeb17	NaN	1. Not enrolled 1. Not enrolled

| colenroct17 enrolled | NaN | 1. Not enrolled | 1. Not |

```
>>> nls97.loc[195884:195970].T
```

personid 195970	195884	195891
gender Female	Male	Male
birthmonth 3	12	9
birthyear 1982	1981	1980
highestgradecompleted 17	NaN	12
maritalstatus married	NaN	Never-married	Never-
... ...	...	...	
colenroct15 enrolled	NaN	1. Not enrolled	1. Not
colenrfeb16 enrolled	NaN	1. Not enrolled	1. Not
colenroct16 enrolled	NaN	1. Not enrolled	1. Not
colenrfeb17 enrolled	NaN	1. Not enrolled	1. Not
colenroct17 enrolled	NaN	1. Not enrolled	1. Not

7. Select a row from the beginning of the DataFrame with the `iloc` data accessor.

    `iloc` differs from `loc` in that it takes a list of row position integers, rather than index labels. For that reason, it works similarly to bracket operator slicing. In this step, we first pass a one-item list with the value of 0. That returns a DataFrame with the first row:

```
>>> nls97.iloc[[0]].T
```

personid	100061
gender	Female
birthmonth	5
birthyear	1980

highestgradecompleted	13
maritalstatus	Married
...	...
colenroct15	1. Not enrolled
colenrfeb16	1. Not enrolled
colenroct16	1. Not enrolled
colenrfeb17	1. Not enrolled
colenroct17	1. Not enrolled

8. Select a few rows from the beginning of the DataFrame with the `iloc` data accessor.

We pass a three-item list, `[0,1,2]`, to return a DataFrame of the first three rows of `nls97`. We would get the same result if we passed `[0:3]` to the accessor:

```
>>> nls97.iloc[[0,1,2]].T
```

personid	100061	100139	100284
gender	Female	Male	Male
birthmonth	5	9	11
birthyear	1980	1983	1984
...	...	...	...
colenroct15	1. Not enrolled	1. Not enrolled	1. Not enrolled
colenrfeb16	1. Not enrolled	1. Not enrolled	1. Not enrolled
colenroct16	1. Not enrolled	1. Not enrolled	1. Not enrolled
colenrfeb17	1. Not enrolled	1. Not enrolled	1. Not enrolled
colenroct17	1. Not enrolled	1. Not enrolled	1. Not enrolled

```
>>> nls97.iloc[0:3].T
```

personid	100061	100139	100284
gender	Female	Male	Male

birthmonth	5	9
11		
birthyear	1980	1983
1984		
...	...	...
...		
colenroct15	1. Not enrolled	1. Not enrolled	1. Not
enrolled			
colenrfeb16	1. Not enrolled	1. Not enrolled	1. Not
enrolled			
colenroct16	1. Not enrolled	1. Not enrolled	1. Not
enrolled			
colenrfeb17	1. Not enrolled	1. Not enrolled	1. Not
enrolled			
colenroct17	1. Not enrolled	1. Not enrolled	1. Not
enrolled			

9. Select a few rows from the end of the DataFrame with the `iloc` data accessor.

   Use `nls97.iloc[[-3,-2,-1]]`, and `nls97.iloc[-3:]` to retrieve the last three rows of the DataFrame. By not providing a value to the right of the colon in `[-3:]`, we are telling the accessor to get all rows from the third-to-last row to the end of the DataFrame:

```
>>> nls97.iloc[[-3,-2,-1]].T
```

personid	999543	999698
999963		
gender	Female	Female
Female		
birthmonth	8	5
9		
birthyear	1984	1983
1982		
...	...	...
...		
colenroct15	1. Not enrolled	1. Not enrolled	1. Not
enrolled			
colenrfeb16	1. Not enrolled	1. Not enrolled	1. Not
enrolled			
colenroct16	1. Not enrolled	1. Not enrolled	1. Not
enrolled			

colenrfeb17	1. Not enrolled	1. Not enrolled	1. Not enrolled
colenroct17	1. Not enrolled	1. Not enrolled	1. Not enrolled

```
>>> nls97.iloc[-3:].T
```

personid	999543	999698 999963
gender	Female	Female Female
birthmonth	8	5 9
birthyear	1984	1983 1982
...	...	... ...
colenroct15	1. Not enrolled	1. Not enrolled 1. Not enrolled
colenrfeb16	1. Not enrolled	1. Not enrolled 1. Not enrolled
colenroct16	1. Not enrolled	1. Not enrolled 1. Not enrolled
colenrfeb17	1. Not enrolled	1. Not enrolled 1. Not enrolled
colenroct17	1. Not enrolled	1. Not enrolled 1. Not enrolled

10. Select multiple rows conditionally using boolean indexing.

    Create a DataFrame of just individuals receiving very little sleep. About 5% of survey respondents got 4 or fewer hours' sleep per night, of the 6,706 individuals who responded to that question. Test who is getting 4 or fewer hours of sleep with `nls97.nightlyhrssleep<=4`, which generates a pandas series of `True` and `False` values that we assign to `sleepcheckbool`. Pass that series to the `loc` accessor to create a `lowsleep` DataFrame. `lowsleep` has approximately the number of rows we are expecting. We do not need to do the extra step of assigning the boolean series to a variable. This is done here only for explanatory purposes:

```
>>> nls97.nightlyhrssleep.quantile(0.05)
4.0
>>> nls97.nightlyhrssleep.count()
6706
```

```
>>> sleepcheckbool = nls97.nightlyhrssleep<=4
>>> sleepcheckbool
personid
100061      False
100139      False
100284      False
100292      False
100583      False
              ...
999291      False
999406      False
999543      False
999698      False
999963      False
Name: nightlyhrssleep, Length: 8984, dtype: bool
>>> lowsleep = nls97.loc[sleepcheckbool]
>>> lowsleep.shape
(364, 88)
```

11. Select rows based on multiple conditions.

    It may be that folks who are not getting a lot of sleep also have a fair number of children who live with them. Use `describe` to get a sense of the distribution of the number of children for those who have `lowsleep`. About a quarter have three or more children. Create a new DataFrame with individuals who have `nightlyhrssleep` of 4 or less and the number of children at home of 3 or more. The `&` is the logical *and* operator in pandas and indicates that both conditions have to be true for the row to be selected (We would have gotten the same result if we worked from the `lowsleep` DataFrame – `lowsleep3pluschildren = lowsleep.loc[lowsleep.childathome>=3]` – but then we would not have been able to demonstrate testing multiple conditions):

```
>>> lowsleep.childathome.describe()
count     293.00
mean        1.79
std         1.40
min         0.00
25%         1.00
```

```
50%        2.00
75%        3.00
max        9.00
>>> lowsleep3pluschildren = nls97.loc[(nls97.
nightlyhrssleep<=4) & (nls97.childathome>=3)]
>>> lowsleep3pluschildren.shape
(82, 88)
```

12. Select rows and columns based on multiple conditions.

Pass the condition to the `loc` accessor to select rows. Also, pass a list of column names to select:

```
>>> lowsleep3pluschildren = nls97.loc[(nls97.
nightlyhrssleep<=4) & (nls97.childathome>=3),
['nightlyhrssleep','childathome']]
>>> lowsleep3pluschildren
          nightlyhrssleep  childathome
personid
119754                  4            4
141531                  4            5
152706                  4            4
156823                  1            3
158355                  4            4
...                   ...          ...
905774                  4            3
907315                  4            3
955166                  3            3
956100                  4            6
991756                  4            3
```

The preceding steps demonstrated the key techniques for selecting rows in pandas.

How it works...

We used the `[]` bracket operator in *steps 2* through *5* to do standard Python-like slicing to select rows. That operator allows us to easily select rows based on a list or a range of values indicated with slice notation. This notation takes the form of `[start:end:step]`, where a value of `1` for `step` is assumed if no value is provided. When a negative number is used for `start`, it represents the number of rows from the end of the DataFrame.

The `loc` accessor, used in *step 6*, selects rows based on row index labels. Since `personid` is the index for the DataFrame, we can pass a list of one or more `personid` values to the `loc` accessor to get a DataFrame with rows for those index labels. We can also pass a range of index labels to the accessor, which will return a DataFrame with all rows having index labels between the label to the left of the colon and the label to the right (inclusive); so, `nls97.loc[195884:195970]` returns a DataFrame for rows with `personid` between `195884` and `195970`, including those two values.

The `iloc` accessor works very much like the bracket operator. We see this in *steps 7* through *9*. We can pass either a list of integers or a range using slicing notation.

One of the most valuable pandas capabilities is boolean indexing. It makes it easy to select rows conditionally. We see this in *step 10*. A test returns a boolean series. The `loc` accessor selects all rows for which the test is `True`. We actually didn't need to assign the boolean data series to the variable that we then passed to the `loc` operator in. We could have just passed the test to the `loc` accessor with `nls97.loc[nls97.nightlyhrssleep<=4]`.

We should take a closer look at how we used the `loc` accessor to select rows in *step 11*. Each condition in `nls97.loc[(nls97.nightlyhrssleep<=4) & (nls97.childathome>=3)]` is placed in parentheses. An error will be generated if the parentheses are excluded. The `&` operator is the equivalent of `and` in standard Python, meaning that *both* conditions have to be `True` for the row to be selected. We would have used `|` for `or` if we had wanted to select the row if *either* condition was `True`.

Finally, *step 12* demonstrates how to select both rows and columns in one call to the `loc` accessor. The criteria for rows appear before the comma, and the columns to select appear after the comma, as in the following statement:

```
nls97.loc[(nls97.nightlyhrssleep<=4) & (nls97.childathome>=3),
 ['nightlyhrssleep','childathome']]
```

This returns the `nightlyhrssleep` and `childathome` columns for all rows where the individual has `nightlyhrssleep` of less than or equal to 4, and `childathome` greater than or equal to 3.

There's more...

We used three different tools to select rows from a pandas DataFrame in this recipe: the `[]` bracket operator, and two pandas-specific accessors, `loc` and `iloc`. This is a little confusing if you are new to pandas, but it becomes clear which tool to use in which situation after just a few months. If you came to pandas with a fair bit of Python and NumPy experience, you likely find the `[]` operator most familiar. However, the pandas documentation recommends against using the `[]` operator for production code. I have settled on a routine of using that operator only for selecting columns from a DataFrame. I use the `loc` accessor when selecting rows by boolean indexing or by index label, and the `iloc` accessor for selecting rows by row number. Since my workflow has me using a fair bit of boolean indexing, I use `loc` much more than the other methods.

See also

The recipe immediately preceding this one has a more detailed discussion on selecting columns.

Generating frequencies for categorical variables

Many years ago, a very seasoned researcher said to me, *"90% of what we're going to find, we'll see in the frequency distributions."* That message has stayed with me. The more one-way and two-way frequency distributions (crosstabs) I do on a DataFrame, the better I understand it. We will do one-way distributions in this recipe, and crosstabs in subsequent recipes.

Getting ready...

We continue our work with the NLS. We will also be doing a fair bit of column selection using `filter` methods. It is not necessary to review the recipe in this chapter on column selection, but it might be helpful.

How to do it...

We use pandas tools to generate frequencies, particularly the very handy `value_counts`:

1. Load the `pandas` library and the `nls97` file.

   Also, convert the columns with object data type to category data type:

   ```
   >>> import pandas as pd
   >>> nls97 = pd.read_csv("data/nls97.csv")
   >>> nls97.set_index("personid", inplace=True)
   >>> nls97.loc[:, nls97.dtypes == 'object'] = \
   ...    nls97.select_dtypes(['object']). \
   ...    apply(lambda x: x.astype('category'))
   ```

2. Show the names for columns with the category data type and check for the number of missing values.

   Notice that there are no missing values for `gender` and few for `highestdegree`, but many for `maritalstatus` and other columns:

   ```
   >>> catcols = nls97.select_dtypes(include=["category"]).
   columns
   >>> nls97[catcols].isnull().sum()
   gender                  0
   maritalstatus        2312
   weeklyhrscomputer    2274
   weeklyhrstv          2273
   highestdegree          31
                         ...
   colenroct15          1515
   colenrfeb16          1948
   colenroct16          2251
   colenrfeb17          2251
   colenroct17          2250
   Length: 57, dtype: int64
   ```

3. Show the frequencies for marital status:

   ```
   >>> nls97.maritalstatus.value_counts()
   Married             3066
   ```

```
Never-married     2766
Divorced           663
Separated          154
Widowed             23
Name: maritalstatus, dtype: int64
```

4. Turn off sorting by frequency:

```
>>> nls97.maritalstatus.value_counts(sort=False)
Divorced           663
Married           3066
Never-married     2766
Separated          154
Widowed             23
Name: maritalstatus, dtype: int64
```

5. Show percentages instead of counts:

```
>>> nls97.maritalstatus.value_counts(sort=False,
normalize=True)
Divorced          0.10
Married           0.46
Never-married     0.41
Separated         0.02
Widowed           0.00
Name: maritalstatus, dtype: float64
```

6. Show the percentages for all government responsibility columns.

Filter the DataFrame for just the government responsibility columns, then use apply to run value_counts on all columns in that DataFrame:

```
>>> nls97.filter(like="gov").apply(pd.value_counts,
normalize=True)
```

	govprovidejobs	govpricecontrols	...
\			
1. Definitely	0.25	0.54	...
2. Probably	0.34	0.33	...
3. Probably not	0.25	0.09	...

	govprovidejobs	govpricecontrols	
4. Definitely not	0.16	0.04	...

	govdecenthousing	govprotectenvironment
1. Definitely	0.44	0.67
2. Probably	0.43	0.29
3. Probably not	0.10	0.03
4. Definitely not	0.02	0.02

7. Find the percentages for all government responsibility columns of people who are married.

Do what we did in *step 6*, but first select only rows with marital status equal to Married:

```
>>> nls97[nls97.maritalstatus=="Married"].\
... filter(like="gov").\
... apply(pd.value_counts, normalize=True)
```

	govprovidejobs	govpricecontrols	
1. Definitely	0.17	0.46	...
2. Probably	0.33	0.38	...
3. Probably not	0.31	0.11	...
4. Definitely not	0.18	0.05	...

	govdecenthousing	govprotectenvironment
1. Definitely	0.36	0.64
2. Probably	0.49	0.31
3. Probably not	0.12	0.03
4. Definitely not	0.03	0.01

8. Find the frequencies and percentages for all category columns in the DataFrame.

First, open a file to write out the frequencies:

```
>>> freqout = open('views/frequencies.txt', 'w')
>>>
>>> for col in nls97.select_dtypes(include=["category"]):
...     print(col, "---------------------", "frequencies",
...        nls97[col].value_counts(sort=False),"percentages",
...        nls97[col].value_counts(normalize=True,
sort=False),
...        sep="\n\n", end="\n\n\n", file=freqout)
...
>>> freqout.close()
```

This generates a file, the beginning of which looks like this:

```
gender


---------------------


frequencies

Female     4385
Male       4599
Name: gender, dtype: int64


percentages

Female     0.49
Male       0.51
Name: gender, dtype: float64
```

As these steps demonstrate, value_counts is quite useful when we need to generate frequencies for one or more columns of a DataFrame.

How it works...

Most of the columns in the nls97 DataFrame (57 out of 88) have the object data type. If we are working with data that is logically categorical, but does not have a category data type in pandas, there are good reasons to convert it to the category type. Not only does this save memory, it also makes data cleaning a little easier, as we saw in this recipe.

The star of the show for this recipe is the value_counts method. It can generate frequencies for a series, as we do with nls97.maritalstatus.value_counts. It can also be run on a whole DataFrame as we do with nls97.filter(like="gov").apply(pd.value_counts, normalize=True). We first create a DataFrame with just the government responsibility columns and then pass the resulting DataFrame to value_counts with apply.

You probably noticed that in *step 7*, I split the chaining over several lines to make it easier to read. There is no rule about when it makes sense to do that. I generally try to do that whenever the chaining involves three or more operations.

In *step 8*, we iterate over all of the columns with the category data type: for col in nls97.select_dtypes(include=["category"]). For each of those columns, we run value_counts to get frequencies and value_counts again to get percentages. We use a print function so that we can generate the carriage returns necessary to make the output readable. All of this is saved to the frequencies.txt file in the views subfolder. I find it handy to have a bunch of one-way frequencies around just to check before doing any work with categorical variables. *Step 8* accomplishes that.

There's more...

Frequency distributions may be the most important statistical tool for discovering potential data issues with categorical data. The one-way frequencies we generate in this recipe are a good foundation for further insights.

However, we often only detect problems once we examine the relationships between categorical variables and other variables, categorical or continuous. Although we stop short of doing two-way frequencies in this recipe, we do start the process of splitting up the data for investigation in *step 7*. In that step, we look at government responsibility responses for married individuals and see that those responses differ from those for the sample overall.

This raises several questions about our data that we need to explore. Are there important differences in response rates by marital status, and might this matter for the distribution of the government responsibility variables? We also want to be careful about drawing conclusions before considering potential confounding variables. Are married respondents likely to be older or to have more children, and are those more important factors in their government responsibility answers?

I am using the marital status variable as an example of the kind of queries that producing one-way frequencies, like the ones in this recipe, are likely to generate. It is always good to have some bivariate analyses (a correlation matrix, some crosstabs, or a few scatter plots) at the ready should questions like these come up. We will generate those in the next two chapters.

Generating summary statistics for continuous variables

Pandas has a good number of tools we can use to get a sense of the distribution of continuous variables. We will focus on the splendid functionality of `describe` in this recipe and demonstrate the usefulness of histograms for visualizing variable distributions.

Before doing any analysis with a continuous variable it is important to have a good understanding of how it is distributed – its central tendency, its spread, and its skewness. This understanding greatly informs our efforts to identify outliers and unexpected values. But it is also crucial information in and of itself. I do not think it overstates the case to say that we understand a particular variable well if we have a good understanding of how it is distributed, and any interpretation without that understanding will be incomplete or flawed in some way.

Getting ready...

We will work with the COVID totals data in this recipe. You will need **Matplotlib** to run this. If it is not installed on your machine already, you can install it at the terminal by entering `pip install matplotlib`.

How to do it...

We take a look at the distribution of a few key continuous variables:

1. Import `pandas`, `numpy`, and `matplotlib`, and load the COVID case totals data:

```
>>> import pandas as pd
>>> import numpy as np
>>> import matplotlib.pyplot as plt
>>> covidtotals = pd.read_csv("data/covidtotals.csv",
...    parse_dates=['lastdate'])
>>> covidtotals.set_index("iso_code", inplace=True)
```

2. Let's remind ourselves of the structure of the data:

```
>>> covidtotals.shape
(210, 11)
>>> covidtotals.sample(2, random_state=1).T
```

iso_code	COG	THA
lastdate	2020-06-01 00:00:00	2020-06-01 00:00:00
location	Congo	Thailand
total_cases	611	3081
total_deaths	20	57
total_cases_pm	110.73	44.14
total_deaths_pm	3.62	0.82
population	5,518,092.00	69,799,978.00
pop_density	15.40	135.13
median_age	19.00	40.10
gdp_per_capita	4,881.41	16,277.67
hosp_beds	NaN	2.10

```
>>> covidtotals.dtypes
```

lastdate	datetime64[ns]
location	object
total_cases	int64
total_deaths	int64
total_cases_pm	float64
total_deaths_pm	float64
population	float64
pop_density	float64

median_age	float64
gdp_per_capita	float64
hosp_beds	float64
dtype: object	

3. Get the descriptive statistics on the COVID totals and demographic columns:

```
>>> covidtotals.describe()
```

	total_cases	total_deaths	total_cases_pm	...
median_age				
count 186	210	210	209	...
mean 31	29,216	1,771	1,362	...
std 9	136,398	8,706	2,630	...
min 15	0	0	1	...
25% 22	176	4	97	...
50% 30	1,242	26	282	...
75% 39	10,117	241	1,803	...
max 48	1,790,191	104,383	19,771	...

	gdp_per_capita	hosp_beds
count	182	164
mean	19,539	3
std	19,862	2
min	661	0
25%	4,485	1
50%	13,183	2
75%	28,557	4
max	116,936	14

4. Take a closer look at the distribution of values for the cases and deaths columns.

Use NumPy's `arange` method to pass a list of floats from 0 to 1.0 to the `quantile` method of the DataFrame:

```
>>> totvars = ['location','total_cases','total_deaths',
...     'total_cases_pm','total_deaths_pm']
>>> covidtotals[totvars].quantile(np.arange(0.0, 1.1,
0.1))
```

	total_cases	total_deaths	total_cases_pm	total_deaths_pm
0.00	0.00	0.00	0.89	0.00
0.10	22.90	0.00	18.49	0.00
0.20	105.20	2.00	56.74	0.40
0.30	302.00	6.70	118.23	1.73
0.40	762.00	12.00	214.92	3.97
0.50	1,242.50	25.50	282.00	6.21
0.60	2,514.60	54.60	546.05	12.56
0.70	6,959.80	137.20	1,074.03	26.06
0.80	16,847.20	323.20	2,208.74	50.29
0.90	46,513.10	1,616.90	3,772.00	139.53
1.00	1,790,191.00	104,383.00	19,771.35	1,237.55

5. View the distribution of total cases:

```
>>> plt.hist(covidtotals['total_cases']/1000, bins=12)
>>> plt.title("Total Covid Cases")
>>> plt.xlabel('Cases')
>>> plt.ylabel("Number of Countries")
>>> plt.show()
```

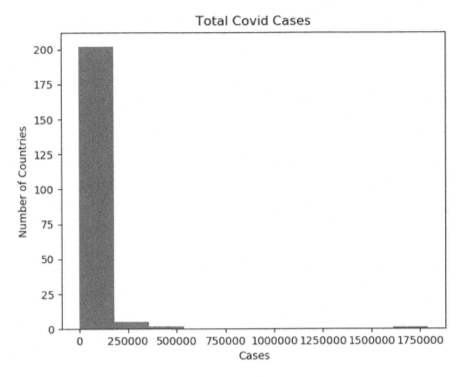

Figure 3.1 – Total COVID Cases

The preceding steps demonstrated the use of `describe` and Matplotlib's `hist` method, which are essential tools when working with continuous variables.

How it works...

We use the `describe` method in *step 3* to examine some summary statistics and the distribution of the key variables. It is often a red flag when the mean and median (50%) have dramatically different values. Cases and deaths are heavily skewed to the right (reflected in the mean being much higher than the median). This alerts us to the presence of outliers at the upper end. This is true even with the adjustment for population size, as both `total_cases_pm` and `total_deaths_pm` show this same skew. We do more analysis of outliers in the next chapter.

The more detailed percentile data in *step 4* further supports this sense of skewness. For instance, the gap between the 90th-percentile and 100th-percentile values for cases and deaths is substantial. These are good first indicators that we are not dealing with normally distributed data here. Even if this is not due to errors, this matters for the statistical testing we will do down the road. On the list of things we want to note when asked, *"How does the data look?"* this is one of the first things we want to say.

We should also note the large number of zero values for total deaths, over 10%. This will also matter for statistical testing when we get to that point.

The histogram of total cases confirms that much of the distribution is between 0 and 150,000, with a few outliers and 1S extreme outlier. Visually, the distribution looks much more log-normal than normal. Log-normal distributions have fatter tails and do not have negative values.

See also

We take a closer look at outliers and unexpected values in the next chapter. We do much more with visualizations in *Chapter 5, Using Visualizations for the Identification of Unexpected Values.*

4
Identifying Missing Values and Outliers in Subsets of Data

Outliers and unexpected values may not be errors. They often are not. Individuals and events are complicated and surprise the analyst. Some people really are 7'4" tall and some really have $50 million salaries. Sometimes, data is messy because people and situations are messy; however, extreme values can have an outsized impact on our analysis, particularly when we are using parametric techniques that assume a normal distribution.

These issues may become even more apparent when working with subsets of data. That is not just because extreme or unexpected values have more weight in smaller samples. It is also because they may make less sense when bivariate and multivariate relationships are considered. When the 7'4" person, or the person making $50 million, is 10 years old, the red flag gets even redder. We take these complications into account in this chapter when considering strategies for detecting outliers, unexpected values, and missing values.

Specifically, the recipes in this chapter examine the following:

- Finding missing values
- Identifying outliers with one variable

- Identifying outliers and unexpected values in bivariate relationships
- Using subsetting to examine logical inconsistencies in variable relationships
- Using linear regression to identify data points with significant influence
- Using k-nearest neighbor to find outliers
- Using Isolation Forest to find anomalies

Technical requirements

The code and notebooks for this chapter are available on GitHub at `https://github.com/PacktPublishing/Python-Data-Cleaning-Cookbook`

Finding missing values

Before starting any analysis, we need to have a good sense of the number of missing values for each variable, and why those values are missing. We also want to know which rows in our data frame are missing values for several key variables. We can get this information with just a couple of statements in pandas.

We also need good strategies for dealing with missing values before we begin statistical modeling, since those models do not typically handle missing values flexibly. We introduce imputation strategies in this recipe and go into more detail in subsequent recipes in this chapter.

Getting ready

We will work with cumulative data on coronavirus cases and deaths by country. The DataFrame has other relevant information, including population density, age, and GDP.

> **Note**
>
> Our World in Data provides COVID-19 public use data at `https://ourworldindata.org/coronavirus-source-data`. The data used in this recipe was downloaded on June 1, 2020. The Covid case and death data were missing for Hong Kong as of this date, but this problem was rectified in files after that.

We will also be doing some routine plotting with Matplotlib in this recipe to help us visualize the distributions of Covid cases and deaths. You can install Matplotlib using `pip install matplotlib`.

How to do it...

We make good use of the `isnull` and `sum` functions to count the number of missing values for selected columns and the number of rows that have missing values for several key variables. We then use the very handy data frame `fillna` method to impute missing values:

1. Load the `pandas`, `numpy`, and `matplotlib` libraries, along with the Covid case data file.

    Also, set up the Covid case and demographic columns:

    ```
    >>> import pandas as pd
    >>> import numpy as np
    >>> import matplotlib.pyplot as plt
    >>> covidtotals = pd.read_csv("data/
    covidtotalswithmissings.csv")
    >>> totvars = ['location','total_cases','total_
    deaths','total_cases_pm',
    ...    'total_deaths_pm']
    >>>
    >>> demovars = ['population','pop_density','median_
    age','gdp_per_capita',
    ...    'hosp_beds']
    ```

2. Check the demographic columns for missing data.

    Set the axis to 0 (the default) to check for the count of countries that are missing values for each of the demographic variables (missing values down columns). Notice that 46 out of 210 countries, more than 20 percent of countries, are missing `hosp_beds`. Set the axis to 1 to check for the number of demographic variables that are missing for each country (missing values across rows). Next, get `value_counts` on the resulting `demovarsmisscnt` series to see whether some countries have missing values for much of the demographic data. Notice that 10 countries are missing values for 3 out of the 5 demographic variables, while 8 countries are missing values for 4 out of 5 demographic variables:

    ```
    >>> covidtotals[demovars].isnull().sum(axis=0)
    population       0
    pop_density     12
    median_age      24
    ```

```
gdp_per_capita       28
hosp_beds            46
dtype: int64
```

```
>>> demovarsmisscnt = covidtotals[demovars].isnull().
sum(axis=1)
```

```
>>> demovarsmisscnt.value_counts()
0      156
1       24
2       12
3       10
4        8
dtype: int64
```

3.   List the countries with three or more missing values for the demographic data.

Index alignment and Boolean indexing allow us to use the count of missing values (demovarsmisscnt) to select rows. Append the location to the demovars list to see the country. (We only show the first five of these countries here.):

```
>>> covidtotals.loc[demovarsmisscnt>=3, ['location'] +
demovars].head(5).T
```

iso_code BES \	AND	AIA	
location ...	Andorra	Anguilla	Bonaire Sint
population 26,221	77,265	15,002	
pop_density NaN	164	NaN	
median_age NaN	NaN	NaN	
gdp_per_capita NaN	NaN	NaN	
hosp_beds NaN	NaN	NaN	
iso_code		VGB	FRO

location	British Virgin Islands	Faeroe Islands
population	30,237	48,865
pop_density	208	35
median_age	NaN	NaN
gdp_per_capita	NaN	NaN
hosp_beds	NaN	NaN

```
>>> type(demovarsmisscnt)
<class 'pandas.core.series.Series'>
```

4. Check the Covid case data for missing values.

   Notice that only one country has missing values for any of this data:

```
>>> covidtotals[totvars].isnull().sum(axis=0)
location            0
total_cases         0
total_deaths        0
total_cases_pm      1
total_deaths_pm     1
dtype: int64
>>> totvarsmisscnt = covidtotals[totvars].isnull().
sum(axis=1)
>>> totvarsmisscnt.value_counts()
0     209
2       1
dtype: int64
>>> covidtotals.loc[totvarsmisscnt>0].T
iso_code                           HKG
lastdate           2020-05-26 00:00:00
location                     Hong Kong
total_cases                          0
total_deaths                         0
total_cases_pm                     NaN
total_deaths_pm                    NaN
population                   7,496,988
pop_density                      7,040
```

median_age	45
gdp_per_capita	56,055
hosp_beds	NaN

5. Use the `fillna` method to fix the missing cases data for the one country affected (Hong Kong).

    We could just set the values to `0`, since the numerator is `0` in both cases. However, it is helpful in terms of code reuse to use the correct logic:

```
>>> covidtotals.total_cases_pm.fillna(covidtotals.total_
cases/
...    (covidtotals.population/1000000), inplace=True)

>>> covidtotals.total_deaths_pm.fillna(covidtotals.total_
deaths/
...    (covidtotals.population/1000000), inplace=True)

>>> covidtotals[totvars].isnull().sum(axis=0)
location            0
total_cases         0
total_deaths        0
total_cases_pm      0
total_deaths_pm     0
dtype: int64
```

These steps give us a good sense of the number of missing values that we have for each column, and which countries have many missing values.

How it works...

Step 2 shows that there is a fair bit of missing data for the demographic variables, particularly for the number of hospital beds. 18 countries have at least 3 of the 5 demographic variables missing. We will either have to exclude those variables from any multivariate analyses we will do in the future or impute values for those variables. We make no attempt to fix those values here. We look more at fixing missing values, including by imputing values, in subsequent chapters.

The key Covid case data is relatively free of missing values. We have one country with missing cases or death data, which we resolve in *step 5*. We use `fillna` to fix the missing value. We could have also used `fillna` to set the missing value to `0`.

We should not gloss over the little bit of pandas magic in *steps 2 and 3*. We create a series, `demovarsmisscnt`, which has the count of demographic columns that have missing values for each country. We are able to use that series, along with the three or more test series (`demovarsmisscnt>=3`), because of pandas index alignment and Boolean indexing. That's magic I say!

See also

We examine other pandas techniques for fixing missing values in *Chapter 6, Cleaning and Exploring Data with Series Operations.*

Identifying outliers with one variable

The concept of an outlier is somewhat subjective but is closely tied to the properties of a particular distribution; to its central tendency, spread, and shape. We make assumptions about whether a value is expected or unexpected based on how likely we are to get that value given the variable's distribution. We are more inclined to view a value as an outlier if it is multiple standard deviations away from the mean and it is from a distribution that is approximately normal; one that is symmetrical (has low skew) and has relatively skinny tails (low kurtosis).

This becomes clear if we imagine trying to identify outliers from a uniform distribution. There is no central tendency and there are no tails. Each value is equally likely. If, for example, Covid cases per country were uniformly distributed, with a minimum of 1 and a maximum of 10,000,000, neither 1 nor 10,000,000 would be considered an outlier.

We need to understand how a variable is distributed, then, before we can identify outliers. Several Python libraries provide tools to help us understand how variables of interest are distributed. We use a couple of them in this recipe to identify when a value is sufficiently out of range to be of concern.

Getting ready

You will need the `matplotlib`, `statsmodels`, and `scipy` libraries, in addition to `pandas` and `numpy`, to run the code in this recipe. You can install `matplotlib`, `statsmodels`, and `scipy` by entering `pip install matplotlib`, `pip install statsmodels`, and `pip install scipy` in a terminal client or PowerShell (in Windows).

We continue to work with the Covid case data.

How to do it...

We take a good look at the distribution of some of the key continuous variables in the Covid data. We examine the central tendency and shape of the distribution, generating measures and visualizations of normality:

1. Load the `pandas`, `numpy`, `matplotlib`, `statsmodels`, and `scipy` libraries, and the Covid case data file.

   Also, set up the Covid case and demographic columns:

   ```
   >>> import pandas as pd
   >>> import numpy as np
   >>> import matplotlib.pyplot as plt
   >>> import statsmodels.api as sm
   >>> import scipy.stats as scistat


   >>> covidtotals = pd.read_csv("data/covidtotals.csv")
   >>> covidtotals.set_index("iso_code", inplace=True)
   >>> totvars = ['location','total_cases','total_
   deaths','total_cases_pm',
   ...    'total_deaths_pm']
   >>> demovars = ['population','pop_density','median_
   age','gdp_per_capita',
   ...    'hosp_beds']
   ```

2. Get descriptive statistics for the Covid case data.

   Create a data frame with just the key case data:

   ```
   >>> covidtotalsonly = covidtotals.loc[:, totvars]
   >>> covidtotalsonly.describe()
          total_cases  total_deaths  total_cases_pm  total_
   deaths_pm
   count          210           210             210
   210
   mean        29,216         1,771           1,355
   56
   std        136,398         8,706           2,625
   145
   min              0             0               0
   0
   ```

25% 1	176	4	93
50% 6	1,242	26	281
75% 32	10,117	241	1,801
max 1,238	1,790,191	104,383	19,771

3. Show more detailed percentile data.

Also show skewness and kurtosis. Skewness and kurtosis describe how symmetrical the distribution is and how fat the tails of the distribution are, respectively. Both measures are significantly higher than we would expect if our variables were distributed normally:

```
>>> covidtotalsonly.quantile(np.arange(0.0, 1.1, 0.1))
```

	total_cases	total_deaths	total_cases_pm	total_ deaths_pm
0.00 0.00	0.00	0.00	0.00	
0.10 0.00	22.90	0.00	18.00	
0.20 0.38	105.20	2.00	56.29	
0.30 1.72	302.00	6.70	115.43	
0.40 3.96	762.00	12.00	213.97	
0.50 6.15	1,242.50	25.50	280.93	
0.60 12.25	2,514.60	54.60	543.96	
0.70 25.95	6,959.80	137.20	1,071.24	
0.80 49.97	16,847.20	323.20	2,206.30	
0.90 138.90	46,513.10	1,616.90	3,765.14	

```
1.00 1,790,191.00      104,383.00         19,771.35
1,237.55


>>> covidtotalsonly.skew()
total_cases          10.80
total_deaths          8.93
total_cases_pm        4.40
total_deaths_pm       4.67
dtype: float64
>>> covidtotalsonly.kurtosis()
total_cases         134.98
total_deaths         95.74
total_cases_pm       25.24
total_deaths_pm      27.24
dtype: float64
```

4. Test the Covid data for normality.

Use the Shapiro-Wilk test from the `scipy` library. Print out the p-value from the test. (The `null` hypothesis of a normal distribution can be rejected at the 95% level at any p-value below 0.05.):

```
>>> def testnorm(var, df):
...     stat, p = scistat.shapiro(df[var])
...     return p
...
>>> testnorm("total_cases", covidtotalsonly)
3.753789128593843e-29
>>> testnorm("total_deaths", covidtotalsonly)
4.3427896631016077e-29
>>> testnorm("total_cases_pm", covidtotalsonly)
1.3972683006509067e-23
>>> testnorm("total_deaths_pm", covidtotalsonly)
1.361060423265974e-25
```

5. Show normal quantile-quantile plots (qqplots) of total cases and total cases per million.

    The straight lines show what the distributions would look like if they were normal:

```
>>> sm.qqplot(covidtotalsonly[['total_cases']]. \
...     sort_values(['total_cases']), line='s')
>>> plt.title("QQ Plot of Total Cases")
>>> sm.qqplot(covidtotals[['total_cases_pm']]. \
...     sort_values(['total_cases_pm']), line='s')
>>> plt.title("QQ Plot of Total Cases Per Million")
>>> plt.show()
```

This results in the following scatter plots:

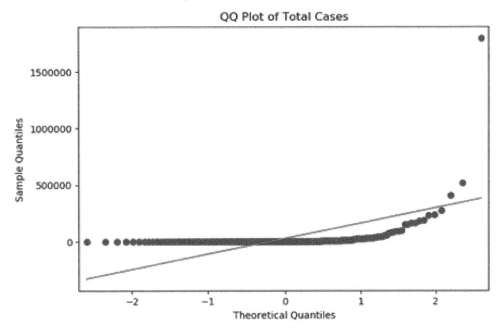

Figure 4.1 – Distribution of Covid cases compared with a normal distribution

Even when adjusted by population with the total cases per million column, the distribution is substantially different from normal:

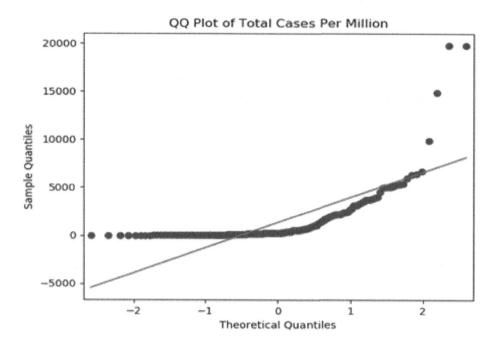

Figure 4.2 – Distribution of Covid cases per million compared with a normal distribution

6. Show the outlier range for total cases.

One way to define an outlier for a continuous variable is by distance above the third quartile or below the first quartile. If that distance is more than 1.5 times the interquartile range (the distance between the first and third quartiles), that value is considered an outlier. In this case, since only 0 or positive values are possible, any total cases value above 25,028 is considered an outlier:

```
>>> thirdq, firstq = covidtotalsonly.total_cases.
quantile(0.75), covidtotalsonly.total_cases.
quantile(0.25)
>>> interquartilerange = 1.5*(thirdq-firstq)
>>> outlierhigh, outlierlow = interquartilerange+thirdq,
firstq-interquartilerange
>>> print(outlierlow, outlierhigh, sep=" <--> ")
-14736.125 <--> 25028.875
```

7. Generate a data frame of outliers and write it to Excel.

Iterate over the four Covid case columns. Calculate the outlier thresholds for each column as we did in the previous step. Select from the data frame those rows above the high threshold or below the low threshold. Add columns that indicate the variable examined (`varname`) for outliers and the threshold levels:

```
>>> def getoutliers():
...     dfout = pd.DataFrame(columns=covidtotals.columns,
data=None)
...     for col in covidtotalsonly.columns[1:]:
...         thirdq, firstq = covidtotalsonly[col].
quantile(0.75),\
...             covidtotalsonly[col].quantile(0.25)
...         interquartilerange = 1.5*(thirdq-firstq)
...         outlierhigh, outlierlow =
            interquartilerange+thirdq,\
...             firstq-interquartilerange
...         df = covidtotals.
loc[(covidtotals[col]>outlierhigh) | \
...             (covidtotals[col]<outlierlow)]
...         df = df.assign(varname = col,
            threshlow = outlierlow,\
...             threshhigh = outlierhigh)
...         dfout = pd.concat([dfout, df])
...     return dfout
...
>>> outliers = getoutliers()
>>> outliers.varname.value_counts()
total_deaths      36
total_cases       33
total_deaths_pm   28
total_cases_pm    17
Name: varname, dtype: int64
>>> outliers.to_excel("views/outlierscases.xlsx")
```

8. Look a little more closely at outliers for cases per million.

Use the varname column we created in the previous step to select the outliers for total_cases_pm. Also show columns (pop_density and gdp_per_capita) that might help to explain the extreme values and the interquartile range for those columns:

```
>>> outliers.loc[outliers.varname=="total_cases_pm",\
...     ['location','total_cases_pm','pop_density','gdp_
per_capita']].\
...       sort_values(['total_cases_pm'], ascending=False)
            location  total_cases_pm  pop_density  gdp_per_
capita
SMR       San Marino     19,771.35       556.67
56,861.47
QAT            Qatar     19,753.15       227.32
116,935.60
VAT          Vatican     14,833.13          nan
nan
AND          Andorra      9,888.05       163.75
nan
BHR          Bahrain      6,698.47     1,935.91
43,290.71
LUX       Luxembourg      6,418.78       231.45
94,277.96
KWT           Kuwait      6,332.42       232.13
65,530.54
SGP        Singapore      5,962.73     7,915.73
85,535.38
USA    United States      5,408.39        35.61
54,225.45
ISL          Iceland      5,292.31         3.40
46,482.96
CHL            Chile      5,214.84        24.28
22,767.04
ESP            Spain      5,120.95        93.11
34,272.36
IRL          Ireland      5,060.96        69.87
67,335.29
BEL          Belgium      5,037.35       375.56
42,658.58
```

GIB nan	Gibraltar	5,016.18	3,457.10
PER 12,236.71	Peru	4,988.38	25.13
BLR 17,167.97	Belarus	4,503.60	46.86

```
>>> covidtotals[['pop_density','gdp_per_capita']].
quantile([0.25,0.5,0.75])
```

	pop_density	gdp_per_capita
0.25	37.42	4,485.33
0.50	87.25	13,183.08
0.75	214.12	28,556.53

9. Show a histogram of total cases:

```
>>> plt.hist(covidtotalsonly['total_cases']/1000, bins=7)
>>> plt.title("Total Covid Cases (thousands)")
>>> plt.xlabel('Cases')
>>> plt.ylabel("Number of Countries")
>>> plt.show()
```

This code produces the following plot:

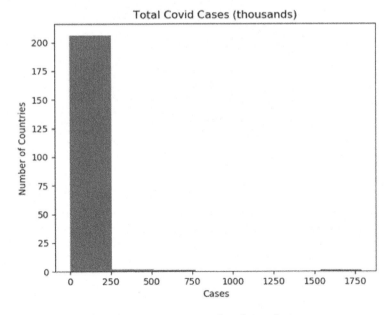

Figure 4.3 – Histogram of total Covid cases

10. Perform a log transformation of the Covid data. Show a histogram of the log transformation of total cases:

```
>>> covidlogs = covidtotalsonly.copy()
>>> for col in covidtotalsonly.columns[1:]:
...     covidlogs[col] = np.log1p(covidlogs[col])
>>> plt.hist(covidlogs['total_cases'], bins=7)
>>> plt.title("Total Covid Cases (log)")
>>> plt.xlabel('Cases')
>>> plt.ylabel("Number of Countries")
>>> plt.show()
```

This code produces the following:

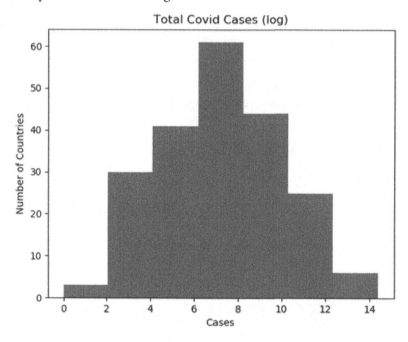

Figure 4.4 – Histogram of total Covid cases with log transformation

The tools we used in the preceding steps tell us a fair bit about how Covid cases and deaths are distributed, and about where outliers are located.

How it works...

The percentile data shown in *step 3* reflects the skewness of the cases and deaths data. If, for example, we look at the range of values between the 20th and 30th percentiles, and compare it with the range from the 70th to the 80th percentiles, we see that the range is much greater in the higher percentiles for each variable. This is confirmed by the very high values for skewness and kurtosis, compared with normal distribution values of 0 and 3, respectively. We run formal tests of normality in *step 4*, which indicate that the distributions of the Covid variables are not normal at high levels of significance.

This is consistent with the `qqplots` we run in *step 5*. The distributions of both total cases and total cases per million differ significantly from normal, as represented by the straight line. Many cases hover around zero, and there is a dramatic increase in slope at the right tail.

We identify outliers in *steps 6 and 7*. Using 1.5 times the interquartile range to determine outliers is a reasonable rule of thumb. I like to output those values to an Excel file, along with associated data, to see what patterns I can detect in the data. This often leads to more questions, of course. We will try to answer some of them in the next recipe, but one question we can consider now is what accounts for the countries with high cases per million, displayed in *step 8*. Some of the countries with extreme values are very small, in terms of land mass, so perhaps population density matters. But half of the countries on this list are near or below the 75th percentile in population density. On the other hand, most countries on this list are above the 75th percentile in GDP per capita. It is worth exploring these bivariate relationships further, which we do in subsequent recipes.

Our identification of outliers in *step 7* assumes a normal distribution, an assumption that we have shown to be unwarranted. Looking again at the distribution in *step 9*, it seems much more like a log-normal distribution, with values clustered around 0 and a right skew. We transform the data in *step 10* and plot the results of the transformation.

There's more...

We could have also used standard deviation, rather than interquartile ranges, to identify outliers in *steps 6 and 7*.

I should add here that outliers are not necessarily data collection or measurement errors, and we may or may not need to make adjustments to the data. However, extreme values can have a meaningful and persistent impact on our analysis, particularly with small datasets like this one.

The overall impression we should have of the Covid case data is that it is relatively clean; that is, there are not many invalid values, narrowly defined. Looking at each variable independently of how it moves with other variables does not identify much that screams out as a clear data error. However, the distribution of the variables is quite problematic statistically. Building statistical models dependent on these variables will be complicated, as we might have to rule out parametric tests.

It is also worth remembering that our sense of what constitutes an outlier is shaped by our assumption of a normal distribution. If, instead, we allow our expectations to be guided by the actual distribution of the data, we have a different understanding of extreme values. If our data reflects a social, or biological, or physical process that is inherently not normally distributed (uniform, logarithmic, exponential, Weibull, Poisson, and so on), our sense of what constitutes an outlier should adjust accordingly.

See also

Box plots might have also been illuminating here. We do a few box plots on this data in *Chapter 5, Using Visualizations for the Identification of Unexpected Values*.

We explore bivariate relationships in this same dataset in the next recipe for any insights they might provide about outliers and unexpected values. In subsequent chapters, we consider strategies for imputing values for missing data and for making adjustments to extreme values.

Identifying outliers and unexpected values in bivariate relationships

A value might be unexpected, even if it is not an extreme value, when it does not deviate significantly from the distribution mean. Some values for a variable are unexpected when a second variable has certain values. This is easy to illustrate when one variable is categorical and the other is continuous.

The following diagram illustrates the number of bird sightings per day over a several year period, but shows different distributions for each of the two sites. One site has a mean sightings per day of 33, and the other 52. (This is fictional data.) The overall mean (not shown) is 42. What should we make of a value of 58 for daily sightings? Is that an outlier? That clearly depends on which of the two sites was being observed. If there were 58 sightings on a day at site A, 58 would be an unusually high number. Not so for site B, where 58 sightings would not be very different from the mean for that site:

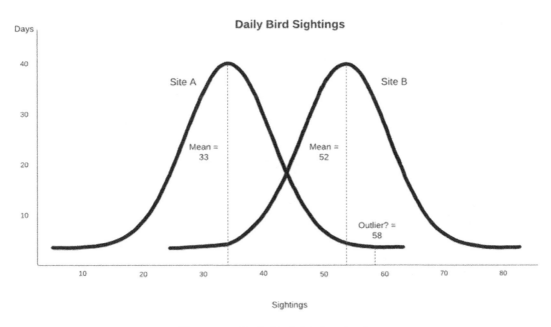

Figure 4.5 – Daily bird sightings by site

This hints at useful rule of thumb: whenever a variable of interest is significantly correlated with another variable, we should take that relationship into account when trying to identify outliers (or any statistical analysis with that variable actually). It is helpful to state this a little more precisely, and extend it to cases where both variables are continuous. If we assume a linear relationship between variable x and variable y, we can describe that relationship with the familiar $y = mx + b$ equation, where m is the slope and b is the y-intercept. We can then expect for y to increase by m for every 1 unit increase in x. Unexpected values are those that deviate substantially from this relationship, where the value of y is much higher or lower than what would be predicted given the value of x. This can be extended to multiple x, or predictor, variables.

In this recipe, we demonstrate how to identify outliers and unexpected values by examining the relationship of a variable to one other variable. In subsequent recipes in this chapter, we use multivariate techniques to make additional improvements in our outlier detection.

Getting ready

We use the matplotlib and seaborn libraries in this recipe. You can install them with pip by entering pip install matplotlib and pip install seaborn with a terminal client or powershell (in Windows).

How to do it...

We examine the relationship between total cases and total deaths. We take a closer look at those countries where deaths are higher or lower than expected given the number of cases:

1. Load pandas, numpy, matplotlib, seaborn, and the Covid cumulative data:

```
>>> import pandas as pd
>>> import numpy as np
>>> import matplotlib.pyplot as plt
>>> import seaborn as sns
>>> covidtotals = pd.read_csv("data/covidtotals.csv")
>>> covidtotals.set_index("iso_code", inplace=True)
>>> totvars = ['location','total_cases','total_
deaths','total_cases_pm',
...     'total_deaths_pm']
>>> demovars = ['population','pop_density','median_
age','gdp_per_capita',
...     'hosp_beds']
```

2. Generate a correlation matrix for the cumulative and demographic columns.

Unsurprisingly, there is a very high correlation (0.93) between total cases and total deaths, and a smaller (0.59) but still substantial one between total cases per million and total deaths per million. There is a strong (0.65) relationship between GDP per capita and cases per million:

```
>>> covidtotals.corr(method="pearson")
```

	total_cases	total_deaths	total_cases_pm
total_deaths_pm			
total_cases 0.25	1.00	0.93	0.18
total_deaths 0.39	0.93	1.00	0.18
total_cases_pm 0.59	0.18	0.18	1.00
total_deaths_pm 1.00	0.25	0.39	0.59
population -0.01	0.27	0.21	-0.06
pop_density 0.03	-0.03	-0.03	0.11

median_age	0.16	0.21	0.31	0.39
gdp_per_capita	0.19	0.20	0.65	0.38
hosp_beds	0.03	0.02	0.08	0.12

	population	pop_density	median_age	gdp_per_capita	hosp_beds
total_cases	0.27	-0.03	0.16	0.19	0.03
total_deaths	0.21	-0.03	0.21	0.20	0.02
total_cases_pm	-0.06	0.11	0.31	0.65	0.08
total_deaths_pm	-0.01	0.03	0.39	0.38	0.12
population	1.00	-0.02	0.02	-0.06	-0.04
pop_density	-0.02	1.00	0.18	0.32	0.31
median_age	0.02	0.18	1.00	0.65	0.66
gdp_per_capita	-0.06	0.32	0.65	1.00	0.30
hosp_beds	-0.04	0.31	0.66	0.30	1.00

3. Check to see whether some countries have unexpectedly high or low total deaths, given total cases.

First create a data frame with only the cases and deaths columns. Use qcut to create a column that breaks the data into quantiles. Show a crosstab of total cases quantiles by total deaths quantiles:

```
>>> covidtotalsonly = covidtotals.loc[:, totvars]
>>> covidtotalsonly['total_cases_q'] = pd.\
...    qcut(covidtotalsonly['total_cases'],
...    labels=['very low','low','medium',
...    'high','very high'], q=5, precision=0)

>>> covidtotalsonly['total_deaths_q'] = pd.\
```

```
...     qcut(covidtotalsonly['total_deaths'],
...     labels=['very low','low','medium',
...     'high','very high'], q=5, precision=0)

>>> pd.crosstab(covidtotalsonly.total_cases_q,
...     covidtotalsonly.total_deaths_q)
```

total_deaths_q	very low	low	medium	high	very high
total_cases_q					
very low	34	7	1	0	0
low	12	19	10	1	0
medium	1	13	15	13	0
high	0	0	12	24	6
very high	0	0	2	4	36

4. Take a look at countries that do not fit along the diagonal.

These are countries with very high total cases but medium total deaths. (There are no countries with high total cases and low or very low deaths.) Also, look at countries with low cases but high deaths. (Since the covidtotals and covidtotalsonly data frames have the same index, we can use Boolean series created from the latter to return selected rows from the former.):

```
>>> covidtotals.loc[(covidtotalsonly.total_cases_q=="very
high") & (covidtotalsonly.total_deaths_q=="medium")].T
```

iso_code	QAT	SGP
lastdate	2020-06-01 00:00:00	2020-06-01 00:00:00
location	Qatar	Singapore
total_cases	56910	34884
total_deaths	38	23
total_cases_pm	19,753.15	5,962.73
total_deaths_pm	13.19	3.93
population	2,881,060.00	5,850,343.00
pop_density	227.32	7,915.73
median_age	31.90	42.40
gdp_per_capita	116,935.60	85,535.38
hosp_beds	1.20	2.40

```
>>> covidtotals.loc[(covidtotalsonly.total_cases_
q=="low") & (covidtotalsonly.total_deaths_q=="high")].T
```

iso_code	YEM
lastdate	2020-06-01 00:00:00

location	Yemen
total_cases	323
total_deaths	80
total_cases_pm	10.83
total_deaths_pm	2.68
population	29,825,968.00
pop_density	53.51
median_age	20.30
gdp_per_capita	1,479.15
hosp_beds	0.70
>>> covidtotals.hosp_beds.mean()	
3.012670731707318	

5. Do a scatter plot of total cases by total deaths.

Use Seaborn's `regplot` method to generate a linear regression line in addition to the scatter plot:

```
>>> ax = sns.regplot(x="total_cases", y="total_deaths",
data=covidtotals)
>>> ax.set(xlabel="Cases", ylabel="Deaths", title="Total
Covid Cases and Deaths by Country")
>>> plt.show()
```

This produces the following scatter plot:

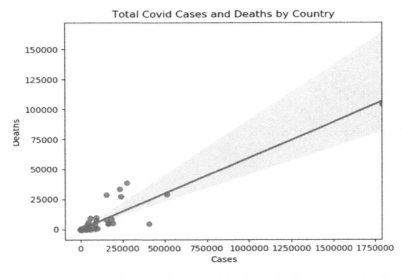

Figure 4.6 – Scatter plot of total cases and deaths with a linear regression line

6. Examine unexpected values above the regression line.

It is good to take a closer look at countries with cases and deaths coordinates that are noticeably above or below the regression line through the data. There are four countries with fewer than 300,000 cases and more than 20,000 deaths:

```
>>> covidtotals.loc[(covidtotals.total_cases<300000) &
(covidtotals.total_deaths>20000)].T
```

iso_code	FRA	ITA
lastdate	2020-06-01 00:00:00	2020-06-01 00:00:00
location	France	Italy
total_cases	151753	233019
total_deaths	28802	33415
total_cases_pm	2,324.88	3,853.99
total_deaths_pm	441.25	552.66
population	65,273,512.00	60,461,828.00
pop_density	122.58	205.86
median_age	42.00	47.90
gdp_per_capita	38,605.67	35,220.08
hosp_beds	5.98	3.18

iso_code	ESP	GBR
lastdate	2020-05-31 00:00:00	2020-06-01 00:00:00
location	Spain	United Kingdom
total_cases	239429	274762
total_deaths	27127	38489
total_cases_pm	5,120.95	4,047.40
total_deaths_pm	580.20	566.97
population	46,754,783.00	67,886,004.00
pop_density	93.11	272.90
median_age	45.50	40.80
gdp_per_capita	34,272.36	39,753.24
hosp_beds	2.97	2.54

7. Examine unexpected values below the regression line.

There is one country with more than 300,000 cases but fewer than 10,000 deaths:

```
>>> covidtotals.loc[(covidtotals.total_cases>300000) &
(covidtotals.total_deaths<10000)].T
```

iso_code	RUS
lastdate	2020-06-01 00:00:00
location	Russia
total_cases	405843
total_deaths	4693
total_cases_pm	2,780.99
total_deaths_pm	32.16
population	145,934,460.00
pop_density	8.82
median_age	39.60
gdp_per_capita	24,765.95
hosp_beds	8.05

8. Do a scatter plot of total cases per million by total deaths per million:

```
>>> ax = sns.regplot(x="total_cases_pm", y="total_deaths_
pm", data=covidtotals)
```

```
>>> ax.set(xlabel="Cases Per Million", ylabel="Deaths Per
Million", title="Total Covid Cases per Million and Deaths
per Million by Country")
```

```
>>> plt.show()
```

This produces the following scatter plot:

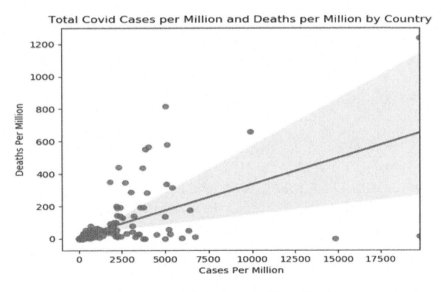

Figure 4.7 – Scatter plot of cases and deaths per million with a linear regression line

9. Examine deaths per million above and below the regression line:

```
>>> covidtotals.loc[(covidtotals.total_cases_pm<7500) \
...    & (covidtotals.total_deaths_pm>250),\
...    ['location','total_cases_pm','total_deaths_pm']]
                             location  total_cases_pm
total_deaths_pm
iso_code
BEL                            Belgium           5,037
817
FRA                             France           2,325
441
IRL                            Ireland           5,061
335
IMN                        Isle of Man           3,951
282
ITA                              Italy           3,854
553
JEY                             Jersey           3,047
287
NLD                        Netherlands           2,710
348
SXM         Sint Maarten (Dutch part)           1,796
350
ESP                              Spain           5,121
580
SWE                             Sweden           3,717
435
GBR                     United Kingdom           4,047
567
USA                      United States           5,408
315


>>> covidtotals.loc[(covidtotals.total_cases_pm>5000) \
...    & (covidtotals.total_deaths_pm<=50), \
...    ['location','total_cases_pm','total_deaths_pm']]
           location  total_cases_pm  total_deaths_pm
iso_code
BHR         Bahrain           6,698               11
```

GIB	Gibraltar	5,016	0
ISL	Iceland	5,292	29
KWT	Kuwait	6,332	50
QAT	Qatar	19,753	13
SGP	Singapore	5,963	4
VAT	Vatican	14,833	0

The preceding steps examined the relationship between variables in order to identify outliers.

How it works...

A number of questions are raised by looking at the bivariate relationships that did not surface in our univariate exploration in the previous recipe. There is confirmation of anticipated relationships, such as with total cases and total deaths, but this makes deviations from this all the more curious. There are possible substantive explanations for unusually high death rates, given a certain number of cases, but measurement error or poor reporting of cases cannot be ruled out either.

Step 2 shows a high correlation (0.93) between total cases and total deaths, but there is variation even there. We divide the cases and deaths into quantiles in *step 3* and then do a crosstab of the quantile values. Most countries are along the diagonal or close to it. However, two countries have a very high number of cases but medium deaths, Qatar and Singapore. This is also a reminder that both countries have very high total cases per million, well into the 90th percentile. It is reasonable to wonder if there are potential reporting issues.

One country, Yemen, had a low number of cases but a high number of deaths. This could perhaps be seen as consistent with the very low number of hospital beds per 100,000 people in Yemen. But it could also mean that coronavirus cases have been under-reported.

We do a scatter plot in *step 5* of total cases and deaths. The strong upward sloping relationship between the two is confirmed, but there are a number of countries whose deaths are above the regression line. We can see that four countries (France, Italy, Spain, and Great Britain) have higher deaths than would be predicted by the number of cases. One country (Russia) has a much lower number of deaths. It is at least worth wondering about whether this is a reporting problem, or reflects differences in how countries define a Covid death.

Not surprisingly, there is even more scatter around the regression line in the scatter plot of cases per million and deaths per million. Countries such as Belgium, France, Ireland, Italy, and the Netherlands have much higher deaths per million than the number of cases per million would suggest. Countries such as Bahrain, Iceland, Kuwait, Qatar, and Singapore have significantly lower rates.

There's more...

We are beginning to get a good sense of what our data looks like, but the data in this form does not enable us to examine how the univariate distributions and bivariate relationships might change over time. For example, one reason why countries might have more deaths per million than the number of cases per million would indicate could be that more time has passed since the first confirmed cases. We are not able to explore that in the cumulative data. We need the daily data for that, which we look at in subsequent chapters.

This recipe, and the previous one, show how much data cleaning can bleed into exploratory data analysis, even when you are first starting to get a sense of your data. I would definitely draw a distinction between data exploration and what we are doing here. We are trying to get a sense of how the data hangs together, why certain variables take on certain values in certain situations and not others. We want to get to the point where there are not huge surprises when we begin to do the analysis.

I find it helpful to do small things to formalize this process. I use different naming conventions for files that are not quite ready for analysis. If nothing else, this helps remind me that any numbers produced at this point are far from ready for distribution.

See also

We still have not done much to examine possible data issues that only become apparent when examining subsets of data; for example, positive wage income values for people who say they are not working (both variables are on the National Longitudinal Survey). We do that in the next recipe.

We do much more with Matplotlib and Seaborn in *Chapter 5, Using Visualizations for the Identification of Unexpected Values.*

Using subsetting to examine logical inconsistencies in variable relationships

At a certain point, data issues come down to deductive logic problems, such as variable x has to be greater than some quantity a when variable y is less than some quantity b. Once we are through some initial data cleaning, it is important to check for logical inconsistencies. pandas makes this kind of error checking relatively straightforward with subsetting tools such as loc and Boolean indexing. This can be combined with summary methods on series and data frames to allow us to easily compare values for a particular row to values for the whole dataset or some subset of rows. We can also easily aggregate over columns. Just about any question we might have about the logical relationships between variables can be answered with these tools. We work through some examples in this recipe.

Getting ready

We will work with the **National Longitudinal Survey of Youth (NLS)**, mainly with data on employment and education. We use `apply` and `lambda` functions several times in this recipe, but go into more detail on their use in *Chapter 7, Fixing Messy Data when Aggregating*. It is not necessary to review *Chapter 7* to follow along, however, even if you have no experience with those tools.

> **Data note**
>
> The NLS, administered by the United States Bureau of Labor Statistics, is a longitudinal survey of individuals who were in high school in 1997 when the survey started. Participants were surveyed each year through 2017.

How to do it...

We run a number of logical checks on the NLS data, such as individuals with post-graduate enrollment but no undergraduate enrollment, or having wage income but no weeks worked. We also check for large changes in key values for a given individual from one period to the next:

1. Import `pandas` and `numpy`, and then load the NLS data:

    ```
    >>> import pandas as pd
    >>> import numpy as np
    >>> nls97 = pd.read_csv("data/nls97.csv")
    >>> nls97.set_index("personid", inplace=True)
    ```

2. Look at some of the employment and education data.

    The dataset has weeks worked each year from 2000 through 2017, and college enrollment status each month from February 1997 through October 2017. We use the ability of the `loc` accessor to choose all columns from the column indicated on the left of the colon through the column indicated on the right; for example, `nls97.loc[:, "colenroct09":"colenrfeb14"]`:

    ```
    >>> nls97[['wageincome','highestgradecompleted',
    'highestdegree']].head(3).T
    personid                    100061      100139
    100284
    wageincome                  12,500      120,000
    58,000
    ```

highestgradecompleted 7		13		12	
highestdegree None		2. High School	2. High School		0.

```
>>> nls97.loc[:, "weeksworked12":"weeksworked17"].
head(3).T
```

personid	100061	100139	100284
weeksworked12	40	52	0
weeksworked13	52	52	nan
weeksworked14	52	52	11
weeksworked15	52	52	52
weeksworked16	48	53	47
weeksworked17	48	52	0

```
>>> nls97.loc[:, "colenroct09":"colenrfeb14"].head(3).T
```

	100061	100139	100284
colenroct09	1. Not enrolled	1. Not enrolled	1. Not enrolled
colenrfeb10	1. Not enrolled	1. Not enrolled	1. Not enrolled
colenroct10	1. Not enrolled	1. Not enrolled	1. Not enrolled
colenrfeb11	1. Not enrolled	1. Not enrolled	1. Not enrolled
colenroct11	3. 4-year college	1. Not enrolled	1. Not enrolled
colenrfeb12	3. 4-year college	1. Not enrolled	1. Not enrolled
colenroct12	3. 4-year college	1. Not enrolled	1. Not enrolled
colenrfeb13	1. Not enrolled	1. Not enrolled	1. Not enrolled
colenroct13	1. Not enrolled	1. Not enrolled	1. Not enrolled
colenrfeb14	1. Not enrolled	1. Not enrolled	1. Not enrolled

3. Show individuals with wage income but no weeks worked.

    The wage income variable reflects wage income for 2016:

    ```
    >>> nls97.loc[(nls97.weeksworked16==0) & nls97.
    wageincome>0, ['weeksworked16','wageincome']]
                 weeksworked16   wageincome
    personid
    102625                   0        1,200
    109403                   0        5,000
    118704                   0       25,000
    130701                   0       12,000
    131151                   0       65,000
    . . .                 . . .        . . .
    957344                   0       90,000
    966697                   0       65,000
    969334                   0        5,000
    991756                   0        9,000
    992369                   0       35,000

    [145 rows x 2 columns]
    ```

4. Check for whether an individual was ever enrolled in a 4-year college course.

    Chain several methods. First, create a data frame with columns that start with
    `colenr` (`nls97.filter(like="colenr")`). These are the college enrollment
    columns for October and February of each year. Then, use `apply` to run a
    `lambda` function that examines the first character of each `colenr` column
    (`apply(lambda x: x.str[0:1]=='3')`). This returns a value of `True` or
    `False` for all of the college enrollment columns; `True` if the first value of the
    string is 3, meaning enrollment at a 4-year college. Finally, use the `any` function
    to test whether any of the values returned from the previous step has a value of
    `True` (`any(axis=1)`). This will identify whether the individual was enrolled in a
    4-year college course between February 1997 and October 2017. The first statement
    here shows the results of the first two steps for explanatory purposes only. Only the
    second statement needs to be run to get the desired results: whether the individual
    was enrolled at a 4-year college course at some point:

    ```
    >>> nls97.filter(like="colenr").apply(lambda x:
    x.str[0:1]=='3').head(2).T
    personid       100061   100139
    . . .
    ```

```
colenroct09     False     False
colenrfeb10     False     False
colenroct10     False     False
colenrfeb11     False     False
colenroct11      True     False
colenrfeb12      True     False
colenroct12      True     False
colenrfeb13     False     False
colenroct13     False     False
colenrfeb14     False     False
...
>>> nls97.filter(like="colenr").apply(lambda x:
x.str[0:1]=='3').\
...     any(axis=1).head(2)
personid
100061      True
100139      False
dtype: bool
```

5. Show individuals with post-graduate enrollment but no bachelor's enrollment.

We can use what we tested in *step 4* to do some checking. We want individuals who have a 4 (graduate enrollment) as the first character for `colenr` any month, but who never had a 3 (bachelor enrollment). Note the "~" before the second half of the test, for negation. There are 22 individuals who fall into this category:

```
>>> nobach = nls97.loc[nls97.filter(like="colenr").\
...     apply(lambda x: x.str[0:1]=='4').\
...     any(axis=1) & ~nls97.filter(like="colenr").\
...     apply(lambda x: x.str[0:1]=='3').\
...     any(axis=1), "colenrfeb97":"colenroct17"]

>>> len(nobach)
22
>>> nobach.head(3).T
personid                        153051              154535
184721

...
colenroct08     1. Not enrolled     1. Not enrolled
1. Not enrolled
```

```
colenrfeb09    1. Not enrolled       1. Not enrolled
1. Not enrolled
colenroct09    1. Not enrolled       1. Not enrolled
1. Not enrolled
colenrfeb10    1. Not enrolled       1. Not enrolled
1. Not enrolled
colenroct10    1. Not enrolled  4. Graduate program  4.
Graduate program
colenrfeb11    1. Not enrolled  4. Graduate program
NaN
colenroct11    1. Not enrolled  4. Graduate program
NaN
colenrfeb12    1. Not enrolled  4. Graduate program
NaN
colenroct12    1. Not enrolled  4. Graduate program
NaN
colenrfeb13 4. Graduate program 4. Graduate program
NaN
colenroct13    1. Not enrolled  4. Graduate program
NaN
colenrfeb14 4. Graduate program 4. Graduate program
NaN
```

6. Show individuals with bachelor's degrees or more, but no 4-year college enrollment.

   Use `isin` to compare the first character in `highestdegree` with all of the values in a list (`nls97.highestdegree.str[0:1].isin(['4','5','6','7'])`):

```
>>> nls97.highestdegree.value_counts(sort=False)
0. None           953
1. GED           1146
2. High School   3667
3. Associates     737
4. Bachelors     1673
5. Masters        603
6. PhD             54
7. Professional   120
Name: highestdegree, dtype: int64
>>> no4yearenrollment = nls97.loc[nls97.highestdegree.str[0:1].\
```

```
...     isin(['4','5','6','7']) & ~nls97.
filter(like="colenr").\
...     apply(lambda x: x.str[0:1]=='3').\
...     any(axis=1), "colenrfeb97":"colenroct17"]
>>> len(no4yearenrollment)
39
>>> no4yearenrollment.head(3).T
personid                    113486                  118749
124616

colenroct01  2. 2-year college      1. Not enrolled
1. Not enrolled
colenrfeb02  2. 2-year college      1. Not enrolled  2.
2-year college
colenroct02  2. 2-year college      1. Not enrolled  2.
2-year college
colenrfeb03  2. 2-year college      1. Not enrolled  2.
2-year college
colenroct03  2. 2-year college      1. Not enrolled  2.
2-year college
colenrfeb04  2. 2-year college      1. Not enrolled  2.
2-year college
colenroct04     1. Not enrolled     1. Not enrolled  2.
2-year college
colenrfeb05     1. Not enrolled     1. Not enrolled  2.
2-year college
colenroct05     1. Not enrolled     1. Not enrolled
1. Not enrolled
colenrfeb06     1. Not enrolled     1. Not enrolled
1. Not enrolled
colenroct06     1. Not enrolled     1. Not enrolled
1. Not enrolled
colenrfeb07     1. Not enrolled  2. 2-year college
1. Not enrolled
colenroct07     1. Not enrolled  2. 2-year college
1. Not enrolled
colenrfeb08     1. Not enrolled     1. Not enrolled
1. Not enrolled
...
```

7. Show individuals with a high wage income.

Define high wages as 3 standard deviations above the mean. It looks as though wage income values have been truncated at $235,884:

```
>>> highwages = nls97.loc[nls97.wageincome >
nls97.wageincome.mean()+(nls97.wageincome.
std()*3),['wageincome']]
```

```
>>> highwages
```

personid	wageincome
131858	235,884
133619	235,884
151863	235,884
164058	235,884
164897	235,884
...	...
964406	235,884
966024	235,884
976141	235,884
983819	235,884
989896	235,884

```
[121 rows x 1 columns]
```

8. Show individuals with large changes in weeks worked for the most recent year.

Calculate the average value for weeks worked between 2012 and 2016 for each person (nls97.loc[:, "weeksworked12":"weeksworked16"].mean(axis=1)). We indicate axis=1 to calculate the mean across columns for each individual, rather than over individuals. We then check to see whether the mean is either less than 50% of the weeks worked in 2017 value or more than twice as much. We also indicate that we are not interested in rows that satisfy those criteria by being null for weeks worked in 2017. There are 1,160 individuals with sharp changes in weeks worked in 2017:

```
>>> workchanges = nls97.loc[~nls97.loc[:,
...     "weeksworked12":"weeksworked16"].mean(axis=1).\
...     between(nls97.weeksworked17*0.5,nls97.
weeksworked17*2) \
...     & ~nls97.weeksworked17.isnull(),
```

```
...       "weeksworked12":"weeksworked17"]
>>> len(workchanges)
1160
>>> workchanges.head(7).T
personid          100284   101526   101718   101724   102228
102454   102625
weeksworked12          0        0       52       52       52
52        14
weeksworked13        nan        0        9       52       52
52         3
weeksworked14         11        0        0       52       17
7        52
weeksworked15         52        0       32       17        0
0        44
weeksworked16         47        0        0        0        0
0         0
weeksworked17          0       45        0       17        0
0         0
```

9. Show inconsistencies in the highest grade completed and the highest degree.

   Use the `crosstab` function to show `highestgradecompleted` by `highestdegree` for people with `highestgradecompleted` less than 12. A good number of these individuals indicate that they have completed high school, which is unusual in the United States if the highest grade completed is less than 12:

```
>>> ltgrade12 = nls97.loc[nls97.highestgradecompleted<12,
['highestgradecompleted','highestdegree']]
>>> pd.crosstab(ltgrade12.highestgradecompleted,
ltgrade12.highestdegree)
```

highestdegree	0. None	1. GED	2. High School
highestgradecompleted			
5	0	0	1
6	11	5	0
7	24	6	1
8	113	78	7
9	112	169	8
10	111	204	13
11	120	200	41

These steps reveal a number of logical inconsistences in the NLS data.

How it works...

The syntax required to do the kind of subsetting that we have done in this recipe may seem a little complicated if you are seeing it for the first time. You do get used to it, however, and it allows for quickly running any query against the data that you might imagine.

Some of the inconsistencies or unexpected values suggest either respondent or entry error, so warrant further investigation. It is hard to explain positive values for wage income when weeks worked is 0. Other unexpected values might not be data problems at all, but suggest that we should be careful about how we use that data. For example, we might not want to use the weeks worked in 2017 by itself. Instead, we might consider using three-year averages in many analyses.

See also

The *Selecting and organizing columns* and *Selecting rows* recipes in *Chapter 3*, *Taking the Measure of Your Data*, demonstrate some of the techniques for subsetting the data used here. We examine `apply` functions in more detail in *Chapter 7*, *Fixing Messy Data when Aggregating*.

Using linear regression to identify data points with significant influence

The remaining recipes in this chapter use statistical modeling to identify outliers. The advantage of these techniques is that they are less dependent on the distribution of the variable of concern, and take more into account than can be revealed in either univariate or bivariate analyses. This allows us to identify outliers that are not otherwise apparent. On the other hand, by taking more factors into account, multivariate techniques may provide evidence that a previously suspect value is actually within an expected range, and provides meaningful information.

In this recipe, we use linear regression to identify observations (rows) that have an outsized influence on models of a target or dependent variable. This can indicate that one or more values for a few observations are so extreme that they compromise model fit for all of the other observations.

Getting ready

The code in this recipe requires the `matplotlib` and `statsmodels` libraries. You can install Matplotlib and Statsmodels by entering `pip install matplotlib` and `pip install statsmodels` in a terminal window or `powershell` (in Windows).

We will be working with data on total COVID-19 cases and deaths per country.

How to do it...

We will use the statsmodels `OLS` method to fit a linear regression model of total cases per million of the population. We then identify those countries that have the greatest influence on that model:

1. Import `pandas`, `matplotlib`, and `statsmodels`, and load the COVID case data:

    ```
    >>> import pandas as pd
    >>> import matplotlib.pyplot as plt
    >>> import statsmodels.api as sm
    >>> covidtotals = pd.read_csv("data/covidtotals.csv")
    >>> covidtotals.set_index("iso_code", inplace=True)
    ```

2. Create an analysis file and generate descriptive statistics.

    Get just the columns required for analysis. Drop any row with missing data for the analysis columns:

    ```
    >>> xvars = ['pop_density','median_age','gdp_per_capita']
    >>> covidanalysis = covidtotals.loc[:,['total_cases_pm']
    + xvars].dropna()
    >>> covidanalysis.describe()
    ```

	total_cases_pm	pop_density	median_age	gdp_per_capita
count	175	175	175	175
mean	1,134	247	31	19,008
std	2,101	822	9	19,673
min	0	2	15	661
25%	67	36	22	4,458
50%	263	82	30	12,952
75%	1,358	208	39	27,467
max	19,753	7,916	48	116,936

3. Fit a linear regression model.

There are good conceptual reasons to believe that population density, median age, and GDP per capita may be predictors of total cases per million. We use all three variables in our model:

```
>>> def getlm(df):
...     Y = df.total_cases_pm
...     X = df[['pop_density','median_age','gdp_per_
capita']]
...     X = sm.add_constant(X)
...     return sm.OLS(Y, X).fit()
...
>>> lm = getlm(covidanalysis)
>>> lm.summary()
```

	coef	std err	t	P>|t| [0.025	0.975]
const	944.47 102.17	426.71 1786.77	2.21	0.028	
pop_density	-0.21 -0.49	0.14 0.075	-1.45	0.150	
median_age	-49.44 -81.05	16.01 -17.832	-3.09	0.002	
gdp_per_capita	0.09 0.077	0.01 0.107	12.02	0.000	

4. Identify those countries with an outsized influence on the model.

Cook's distance values of greater than 0.5 should be scrutinized closely:

```
>>> influence = lm.get_influence().summary_frame()
>>> influence.loc[influence.cooks_d>0.5, ['cooks_d']]
        cooks_d
iso_code
HKG        0.78
QAT        5.08
>>> covidanalysis.loc[influence.cooks_d>0.5]
```

	total_cases_pm	pop_density	median_age	gdp_per_capita
iso_code				
HKG	0.00	7,039.71	44.80	56,054.92
QAT	19,753.15	227.32	31.90	116,935.60

5. Do an influence plot.

Countries with higher Cook's Distance values have larger circles:

```
>>> fig, ax = plt.subplots(figsize=(10,6))
```
```
>>> sm.graphics.influence_plot(lm, ax = ax,
criterion="cooks")
```
```
>>> plt.show()
```

This produces the following plot:

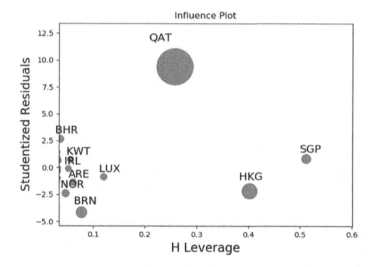

Figure 4.8 – Influence plot, including countries with the highest Cook's Distance

6. Run the model without the two outliers.

Removing these outliers, particularly Qatar, has a dramatic effect on the model. The estimates for median_age and for the constant are no longer significant:

```
>>> covidanalysisminusoutliers = covidanalysis.
loc[influence.cooks_d<0.5]
```
```
>>> lm = getlm(covidanalysisminusoutliers)
```

```
>>> lm.summary()
```

	coef	std err	t	P>|t|
[0.025	0.975]			
--				
----------------				
const	44.09	349.92	0.13	0.900
-646.70	734.87			
pop_density	0.24	0.15	1.67	0.098
-0.05	0.53			
median_age	-2.52	13.53	-0.19	0.853
-29.22	24.18			
gdp_per_capita	0.06	0.01	7.88	0.000
0.04	0.07			

This gives us a sense of the countries that are most unlike the others in terms of the relationship between demographic variables and total cases per million in population.

How it works...

Cook's Distance is a measure of how much each observation influences the model. The large impact of the two outliers is confirmed in *step 6* when we rerun the model without them. The question for the analyst is whether outliers such as these add important information or distort the model and limit its applicability. The coefficient of -49 for median age in the first regression results indicates that every one-year increase in median age is associated with a 49 point reduction in cases per million people. But this seems largely due to the model trying to fit a quite extreme total cases per million value for Qatar. Without Qatar, the coefficient on age is no longer significant.

The P>|t| value in the regression output tells us whether the coefficient is significantly different from 0. In the first regression, the coefficients for median_age and gdp_per_capita are significant at the 99% level; that is, the P>|t| value is less than 0.01. Only gdp_per_capita is significant when the model is run without the two outliers.

There's more...

We run a linear regression model in this recipe, not so much because we are interested in the parameter estimates of the model, but because we want to determine whether there are observations with potential outsized influence on any multivariate analysis we might conduct. That definitely seems to be true in this case.

Often, it makes sense to remove the outliers, as we have done here, but that is not always true. When we have independent variables that do a good job of capturing what makes outliers different, then the parameter estimates for the other independent variables are less vulnerable to distortion. We also might consider transformations, such as the log transformation we did in a previous recipe, and the scaling we will do in the next two recipes. An appropriate transformation, given your data, can reduce the influence of outliers by limiting the size of residuals at the extremes.

Using k-nearest neighbor to find outliers

Unsupervised machine learning tools can help us identify observations that are unlike others when we have unlabeled data; that is, when there is no target or dependent variable. (In the previous recipe, we used total cases per million as the dependent variable.) Even when selecting targets and factors is relatively straightforward, it might be helpful to identify outliers without making any assumptions about relationships between variables. We can use *k*-nearest neighbor to find observations that are most unlike others, those where there is the greatest difference between their values and their nearest neighbors' values.

Getting ready

You will need PyOD (Python outlier detection) and scikit-learn to run the code in this recipe. You can install both by entering `pip install pyod` and `pip install sklearn` in the terminal or `powershell` (in Windows).

How to do it...

We will use k-nearest neighbor to identify countries whose attributes indicate that they are most anomalous:

1. Load `pandas`, `pyod`, and `scikit-learn`, along with the Covid case data:

```
>>> import pandas as pd
>>> from pyod.models.knn import KNN
>>> from sklearn.preprocessing import StandardScaler
>>> covidtotals = pd.read_csv("data/covidtotals.csv")
>>> covidtotals.set_index("iso_code", inplace=True)
```

2. Create a standardized data frame of the analysis columns:

```
>>> standardizer = StandardScaler()
>>> analysisvars = ['location','total_cases_pm','total_
deaths_pm',\
...     'pop_density','median_age','gdp_per_capita']
>>> covidanalysis = covidtotals.loc[:, analysisvars].
dropna()
>>> covidanalysisstand = standardizer.fit_
transform(covidanalysis.iloc[:, 1:])
```

3. Run the KNN model and generate anomaly scores.

    We create an arbitrary number of outliers by setting the contamination parameter to 0.1:

```
>>> clf_name = 'KNN'
>>> clf = KNN(contamination=0.1)
>>> clf.fit(covidanalysisstand)
KNN(algorithm='auto', contamination=0.1, leaf_size=30,
method='largest',
   metric='minkowski', metric_params=None, n_jobs=1, n_
neighbors=5, p=2,
   radius=1.0)
>>> y_pred = clf.labels_
>>> y_scores = clf.decision_scores_
```

4. Show the predictions from the model.

    Create a data frame from the y_pred and y_scores NumPy arrays. Set the index to the covidanalysis data frame index so that we can easily combine it with that data frame later. Notice that the decision scores for outliers are all higher than those for the inliers (outlier = 0):

```
>>> pred = pd.DataFrame(zip(y_pred, y_scores),
...     columns=['outlier','scores'],
...     index=covidanalysis.index)
>>>
>>> pred.sample(10, random_state=1)
          outlier  scores
iso_code
```

LBY	0	0.37
NLD	1	1.56
BTN	0	0.19
HTI	0	0.43
EST	0	0.46
LCA	0	0.43
PER	0	1.41
BRB	0	0.77
MDA	0	0.91
NAM	0	0.31

```
>>> pred.outlier.value_counts()
0    157
1     18
Name: outlier, dtype: int64
>>> pred.groupby(['outlier'])[['scores']].
agg(['min','median','max'])
```

	scores		
	min	median	max
outlier			
0	0.08	0.36	1.52
1	1.55	2.10	9.48

5. Show the COVID data for the outliers.

First, merge the `covidanalysis` and `pred` data frames:

```
>>> covidanalysis.join(pred).loc[pred.outlier==1,\
...    ['location','total_cases_pm','total_deaths_
pm','scores']].\
...    sort_values(['scores'], ascending=False)
```

	location	total_cases_pm	total_deaths_pm	scores
iso_code				
SGP	Singapore	5,962.73	3.93	9.48
QAT	Qatar	19,753.15	13.19	8.00
HKG	Hong Kong	0.00	0.00	7.77

BEL		Belgium	5,037.35
816.85	3.54		
BHR		Bahrain	6,698.47
11.17	2.84		
LUX		Luxembourg	6,418.78
175.73	2.44		
ESP		Spain	5,120.95
580.20	2.18		
KWT		Kuwait	6,332.42
49.64	2.13		
GBR		United Kingdom	4,047.40
566.97	2.10		
ITA		Italy	3,853.99
552.66	2.09		
IRL		Ireland	5,060.96
334.56	2.07		
BRN		Brunei	322.30
4.57	1.92		
USA		United States	5,408.39
315.35	1.89		
FRA		France	2,324.88
441.25	1.86		
MDV		Maldives	3,280.04
9.25	1.82		
ISL		Iceland	5,292.31
29.30	1.58		
NLD		Netherlands	2,710.38
347.60	1.56		
ARE		United Arab Emirates	3,493.99
26.69	1.55		

These steps show how we can use *k*-nearest neighbor to identify outliers based on multivariate relationships.

How it works...

PyOD is a package of Python outlier detection tools. We use it here as a wrapper around scikit-learn's KNN package. This simplifies some tasks.

Our focus in this recipe is not on building a model, but on getting a quick sense of which observations (countries) are significant outliers once we take all the data we have into account. This analysis supports our developing sense that Singapore, Qatar, and Hong Kong are very different observations than the others in our dataset. They have very high decision scores. (The table in *step 5* is sorted in descending order of score.)

Countries such as Belgium, Bahrain, and Luxembourg might also be considered outliers, though that is less clear cut. The previous recipe did not indicate that they had an overwhelming influence on a regression model. But that model did not take both cases per million and deaths per million into account at the same time. That could also explain why Singapore is even more of an outlier than Qatar here. It has both high cases per million and below-average deaths per million.

Scikit-learn makes scaling very easy. We use the standard scaler in *step 2*, which returns the *z*-score for each value in the data frame. The *z*-score subtracts the variable mean from each variable value and divides it by the standard deviation for the variable. Many machine learning tools require standardized data to run well.

There's more...

K-nearest neighbor is a very popular machine learning algorithm. It is easy to run and interpret. Its main limitation is that it will run slowly on large datasets.

We have skipped steps we might usually take when building machine learning models. We did not create separate training and test datasets, for example. PyOD allows this to be done easily, but this is not necessary for our purposes here.

See also

The PyOD toolkit has a large number of supervised and unsupervised learning techniques for detecting anomalies in data. You can get the documentation for this at `https://pyod.readthedocs.io/en/latest/`.

Using Isolation Forest to find anomalies

Isolation Forest is a relatively new machine learning technique for identifying anomalies. It has quickly become popular, partly because its algorithm is optimized to find anomalies, rather than normal values. It finds outliers by successive partitioning of the data until a data point has been isolated. Points that require fewer partitions to be isolated receive higher anomaly scores. This process turns out to be fairly easy on system resources. In this recipe, we demonstrate how to use it to detect outlier COVID-19 cases and deaths.

Getting ready

You will need scikit-learn and Matplotlib to run the code in this recipe. You can install them by entering `pip install sklearn` and `pip install matplotlib` in the terminal or `powershell` (in Windows).

How to do it...

We will use Isolation Forest to find the countries whose attributes indicate that they are most anomalous:

1. Load `pandas`, `matplotlib`, and the `StandardScaler` and `IsolationForest` modules from scikit-learn:

```
>>> import pandas as pd
>>> import matplotlib.pyplot as plt
>>> from sklearn.preprocessing import StandardScaler
>>> from sklearn.ensemble import IsolationForest
>>> from mpl_toolkits.mplot3d import Axes3D
>>> covidtotals = pd.read_csv("data/covidtotals.csv")
>>> covidtotals.set_index("iso_code", inplace=True)
```

2. Create a standardized analysis data frame.

First, remove all rows with missing data:

```
>>> analysisvars = ['location','total_cases_pm','total_
deaths_pm',
...     'pop_density','median_age','gdp_per_capita']
>>> standardizer = StandardScaler()
>>> covidtotals.isnull().sum()
lastdate          0
location          0
total_cases       0
total_deaths      0
total_cases_pm    0
total_deaths_pm   0
population        0
pop_density       12
median_age        24
gdp_per_capita    28
```

```
hosp_beds              46
dtype: int64
>>> covidanalysis = covidtotals.loc[:, analysisvars].
dropna()
>>> covidanalysisstand = standardizer.fit_
transform(covidanalysis.iloc[:, 1:])
```

3. Run an Isolation Forest model to detect outliers.

    Pass the standardized data to the `fit` method. 18 countries are identified as outliers. (These countries have anomaly values of -1.) This is determined by the contamination number of `0.1`:

```
>>> clf=IsolationForest(n_estimators=100, max_
samples='auto',
...    contamination=.1, max_features=1.0)
>>> clf.fit(covidanalysisstand)
IsolationForest(behaviour='deprecated', bootstrap=False,
contamination=0.1,
                max_features=1.0, max_samples='auto',
                n_estimators=100,
                n_jobs=None, random_state=None,
verbose=0, warm_start=False)


>>> covidanalysis['anomaly'] = clf.
predict(covidanalysisstand)
>>> covidanalysis['scores'] = clf.decision_
function(covidanalysisstand)
>>> covidanalysis.anomaly.value_counts()
 1     157
-1      18
Name: anomaly, dtype: int64
```

4. Create outlier and inlier data frames.

    List the top 10 outliers according to anomaly score:

```
>>> inlier, outlier = covidanalysis.loc[covidanalysis.
anomaly==1],\
...    covidanalysis.loc[covidanalysis.anomaly==-1]
```

```
>>> outlier[['location','total_cases_pm','total_deaths_
pm',\
...     'median_age','gdp_per_capita','scores']].\
...     sort_values(['scores']).\
...     head(10)
```

	location	total_cases_pm	total_deaths_pm	median_age
iso_code				
SGP	Singapore	5,962.73	3.93	42.40
QAT	Qatar	19,753.15	13.19	31.90
HKG	Hong Kong	0.00	0.00	44.80
BEL	Belgium	5,037.35	816.85	41.80
BHR	Bahrain	6,698.47	11.17	32.40
LUX	Luxembourg	6,418.78	175.73	39.70
ITA	Italy	3,853.99	552.66	47.90
ESP	Spain	5,120.95	580.20	45.50
NLD	Netherlands	2,710.38	347.60	43.20
MDV	Maldives	3,280.04	9.25	30.60

	gdp_per_capita	scores
iso_code		
SGP	85,535.38	-0.23
QAT	116,935.60	-0.21
HKG	56,054.92	-0.18
BEL	42,658.58	-0.14
BHR	43,290.71	-0.09
LUX	94,277.96	-0.09

ITA	35,220.08	-0.08
ESP	34,272.36	-0.06
NLD	48,472.54	-0.03
MDV	15,183.62	-0.03

5. Plot the outliers and inliers:

```
>>> ax = plt.axes(projection='3d')
>>> ax.set_title('Isolation Forest Anomaly Detection')
>>> ax.set_zlabel("Cases Per Million")
>>> ax.set_xlabel("GDP Per Capita")
>>> ax.set_ylabel("Median Age")
>>> ax.scatter3D(inlier.gdp_per_capita, inlier.median_
age, inlier.total_cases_pm, label="inliers", c="blue")
>>> ax.scatter3D(outlier.gdp_per_capita, outlier.median_
age, outlier.total_cases_pm, label="outliers", c="red")
>>> ax.legend()
>>> plt.tight_layout()
>>> plt.show()
```

This produces the following plot:

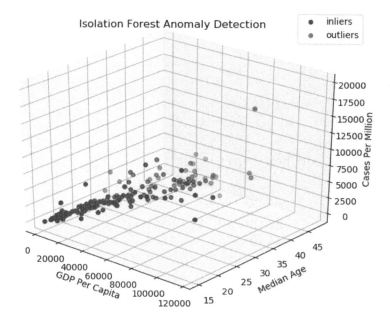

Figure 4.9 – Inlier and outlier countries by GDP, median age, and cases per million

The preceding steps demonstrate the use of Isolation Forest as an alternative to k-nearest neighbor for anomaly detection.

How it works...

We use Isolation Forest in this recipe much like we used k-nearest neighbor in the previous recipe. In *step 3*, we pass a standardized dataset to the Isolation Forest `fit` method, and then use its `predict` and `decision_function` methods to get the anomaly flag and score, respectively. We use the anomaly flag in *step 4* to separate the data into inliers and outliers.

We plot the inliers and outliers in *step 5*. Since there are only three dimensions in the plot, it does not quite capture all of the features in our Isolation Forest model, but the outliers (the red dots) clearly have higher GDP per capita and median age; these are typically to the right of, and behind, the inliers.

The results from Isolation Forest are quite similar to the k-nearest neighbor results. Qatar, Singapore, and Hong Kong have the highest (most negative) anomaly scores. Belgium is not far behind, just as with the KNN model. This is most likely due to an exceptionally high total of deaths per million for Belgium, the highest in the dataset. We should consider removing these four observations from any multivariate analyses we conduct.

There's more...

Isolation Forest is a good alternative to k-nearest neighbor, particularly when working with large datasets. The efficiency of its algorithm allows it to handle large samples and a high number of features (variables).

The anomaly detection techniques we have used in the last three recipes were designed to improve multivariate analyses and the training of machine learning models. However, we might want to exclude the outliers they help us identify much earlier in the analysis process. For example, if it makes sense to exclude Qatar from our modeling, it might also make sense to exclude Qatar from some descriptive statistics.

See also

In addition to being useful for anomaly detection, the Isolation Forest algorithm is quite satisfying intuitively. (I think the same could be said about k-nearest neighbor.) You can read more about Isolation Forest here: `https://cs.nju.edu.cn/zhouzh/zhouzh.files/publication/icdm08b.pdf`.

5

Using Visualizations for the Identification of Unexpected Values

We dipped our toes in the water with visualizations in several recipes in the previous chapter. We used histograms and QQ plots to examine the distribution of a single variable, and scatter plots to view how two variables are related. But we were just scratching the surface of the rich visualization tools available in the Matplotlib and Seaborn libraries. Getting comfortable with these tools, and their seemingly inexhaustible capabilities, can help us uncover patterns and oddities that are not obvious when we run the standard battery of descriptives.

Boxplots, for example, are a great tool for visualizing values outside of a certain range. These can be extended with grouped boxplots or violin plots that allow us to compare distributions across subsets of data. We can also do much more with scatter plots than we did in the last chapter, including getting some sense of multivariate relationships. Histograms, too, can sometimes offer additional insight if we display several histograms on one plot or create a stacked histogram. We explore all of these capabilities in this chapter.

Specifically, the recipes in this chapter demonstrate the following topics:

- Using histograms to examine the distribution of continuous variables
- Using boxplots to identify outliers for continuous variables
- Using grouped boxplots to uncover unexpected values in a particular group
- Examining both the distribution shape and outliers with violin plots
- Using scatter plots to view bivariate relationships
- Using line plots to examine trends in continuous variables
- Generating a heat map based on a correlation matrix

Technical requirements

The code and notebooks for this chapter are available on GitHub at `https://github.com/PacktPublishing/Python-Data-Cleaning-Cookbook`

Using histograms to examine the distribution of continuous variables

The go-to visualization tool for statisticians trying to understand how single variables are distributed is the histogram. Histograms plot a continuous variable on the x axis, in bins determined by the researcher, and the frequency of occurrence on the y axis.

Histograms provide a clear and meaningful illustration of the shape of a distribution, including central tendency, skewness (symmetry), excess kurtosis (relatively fat tails), and spread. This matters for statistical testing, as many tests make assumptions about a variable's distribution. Moreover, our expectation of what data values to expect should be guided by our understanding of the distribution's shape. For example, a value at the 90th percentile has very different implications when it comes from a normal distribution rather than from a uniform distribution.

One of the first tasks I ask introductory statistics students to do is construct a histogram manually from a small sample. We do boxplots in the following class. Together, histograms and boxplots provide a solid foundation for subsequent analysis. In my data science work, I try to remember to construct histograms and boxplots on all continuous variables of interest shortly after the initial importing and cleaning of data. We create histograms in this recipe, and boxplots in the following two recipes.

Getting ready

We will use the Matplotlib library to generate histograms. Some tasks can be done quickly and straightforwardly in Matplotlib. Histograms are one of those tasks. We will switch between Matplotlib and Seaborn (which is built on Matplotlib) in this chapter, based on which tool gets us to the required graphic more easily.

We will also use the statsmodels library. You can install Matplotlib and statsmodels with pip using `pip install matplotlib` and `pip install statsmodels`.

We will work with data on land temperature and on coronavirus cases in this recipe. The land temperature DataFrame has one row per weather station. The coronavirus data frame has one row per country and reflects totals as of July 18, 2020.

> **Data note**
>
> The land temperature DataFrame has the average temperature reading (in °C) in 2019 from over 12,000 stations across the world, though a majority of the stations are in the United States. The raw data was retrieved from the *Global Historical Climatology Network* integrated database. It is made available for public use by the United States National Oceanic and Atmospheric Administration at `https://www.ncdc.noaa.gov/data-access/land-based-station-data/land-based-datasets/global-historical-climatology-network-monthly-version-4`.
>
> *Our World in Data* provides Covid-19 public use data at `https://ourworldindata.org/coronavirus-source-data`. The data used in this recipe was downloaded on June 1, 2020. Some of the data was missing for Hong Kong as of this date, but this problem was fixed in files after that.

How to do it...

We take a close look at the distribution of land temperatures by weather station in 2019 and total coronavirus cases per million of the population for each country. We start with a few descriptive statistics before doing a QQ plot, histograms, and stacked histograms.

1. Import the `pandas`, `matplotlib`, and `statsmodels` libraries.

   Also, load the data on land temperatures and COVID cases:

   ```
   >>> import pandas as pd
   >>> import matplotlib.pyplot as plt
   >>> import statsmodels.api as sm
   >>> landtemps = pd.read_csv("data/landtemps2019avgs.csv")
   ```

```
>>> covidtotals = pd.read_csv("data/covidtotals.csv",
parse_dates=["lastdate"])
>>> covidtotals.set_index("iso_code", inplace=True)
```

2. Show some of the station temperature rows.

The `latabs` column is the value of latitude without the North or South indicators; so, Cairo, Egypt at approximately 30 degrees north, and Porto Alegre, Brazil at about 30 degrees south have the same value:

```
>>> landtemps[['station','country','latabs','elevation',
'avgtemp']].\
...      sample(10, random_state=1)
                      station          country  latabs
elevation   avgtemp
10526            NEW_FORK_LAKE  United States       43
2,542           2
1416                 NEIR_AGDM         Canada       51
1,145           2
2230                    CURICO          Chile       35
225          16
6002       LIFTON_PUMPING_STN  United States       42
1,809           4
2106                   HUAILAI          China       40
538          11
2090                MUDANJIANG          China       45
242           6
7781     CHEYENNE_6SW_MESONET  United States       36
694          15
10502               SHARKSTOOTH  United States       38
3,268           4
11049               CHALLIS_AP  United States       45
1,534           7
2820                   METHONI         Greece       37
52           18
```

3. Show some descriptive statistics.

Also, look at the skew and the kurtosis:

```
>>> landtemps.describe()
          latabs   elevation   avgtemp
count     12,095      12,095    12,095
mean          40         589        11
std           13         762         9
```

min	0	-350	-61
25%	35	78	5
50%	41	271	10
75%	47	818	17
max	90	9,999	34

```
>>> landtemps.avgtemp.skew()
-0.2678382583481769
>>> landtemps.avgtemp.kurtosis()
2.1698313707061074
```

4. Do a histogram of average temperatures.

    Also, draw a line at the overall mean:

```
>>> plt.hist(landtemps.avgtemp)
>>> plt.axvline(landtemps.avgtemp.mean(), color='red',
linestyle='dashed', linewidth=1)
>>> plt.title("Histogram of Average Temperatures
(Celsius)")
>>> plt.xlabel("Average Temperature")
>>> plt.ylabel("Frequency")
>>> plt.show()
```

This results in the following histogram:

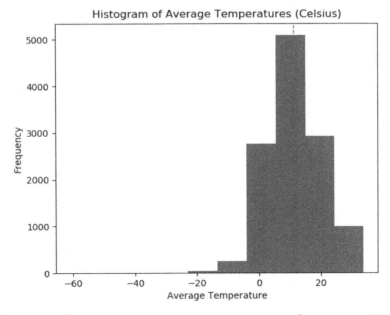

Figure 5.1 – Histogram of average temperatures across weather stations in 2019

5. Run a QQ plot to examine where the distribution deviates from a normal distribution.

    Notice that much of the distribution of temperatures falls along the red line (all dots would fall on the red line if the distribution were perfectly normal, but the tails fall off dramatically from the normal):

    ```
    >>> sm.qqplot(landtemps[['avgtemp']].sort_
    values(['avgtemp']), line='s')
    ```
    ```
    >>> plt.title("QQ Plot of Average Temperatures")
    ```
    ```
    >>> plt.show()
    ```

    This results in the following QQ plot:

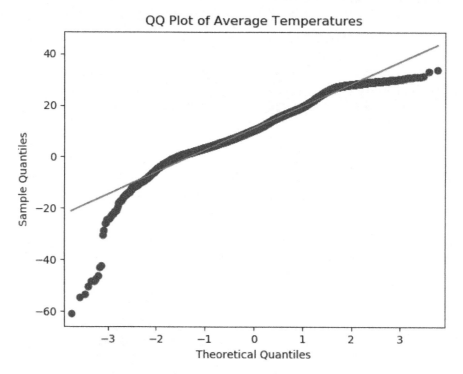

Figure 5.2 – Plot of average temperature by station compared with the normal distribution

6. Show the skewness and kurtosis for total Covid cases per million.

    This is from the COVID-19 data frame, which has one row for each country:

```
>>> covidtotals.total_cases_pm.skew()
4.284484653881833
>>> covidtotals.total_cases_pm.kurtosis()
26.137524276840452
```

7. Do a stacked histogram of the Covid case data.

    Select data from four of the regions. (Stacked histograms can get messy with any more categories than that.) Define a getcases function that returns a series for total_cases_pm for the countries of a region. Pass those series to the hist method ([getcases(k) for k in showregions]) to create the stacked histogram. Notice that much of the distribution—almost 40 countries out of the 65 countries in these regions—has cases per million below 2,000:

```
>>> showregions = ['Oceania / Aus','East Asia','Southern
Africa', 'Western Europe']
>>>
>>> def getcases(regiondesc):
...     return covidtotals.loc[covidtotals.
region==regiondesc,
...         'total_cases_pm']
...
>>> plt.hist([getcases(k) for k in showregions],\
...     color=['blue','mediumslateblue','plum',
'mediumvioletred'],\
...     label=showregions,\
...     stacked=True)
>>>
>>> plt.title("Stacked Histogram of Cases Per Million for
Selected Regions")
>>> plt.xlabel("Cases Per Million")
>>> plt.ylabel("Frequency")
>>> plt.xticks(np.arange(0, 22500, step=2500))
>>> plt.legend()
>>> plt.show()
```

This results in the following stacked histogram:

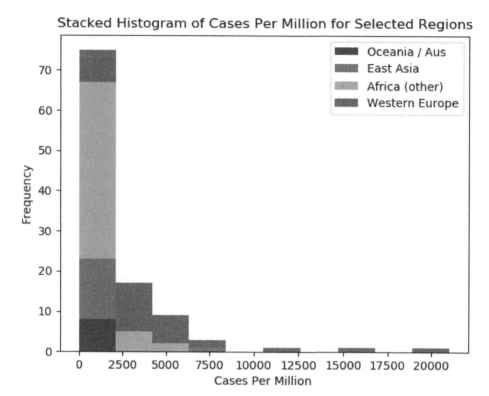

Figure 5.3 – Stacked histogram of number of countries per region at different cases per million levels

8.   Show multiple histograms on one figure.

This allows different *x* and *y* axis values. We need to loop through each axis and select a different region from `showregions` for each subplot:

```
>>> fig, axes = plt.subplots(2, 2)
>>> fig.subtitle("Histograms of Covid Cases Per Million
by Selected Regions")
>>> axes = axes.ravel()
>>> for j, ax in enumerate(axes):
...     ax.hist(covidtotals.loc[covidtotals.
region==showregions[j]].\
...        total_cases_pm, bins=5)
...     ax.set_title(showregions[j], fontsize=10)
...     for tick in ax.get_xticklabels():
```

```
...          tick.set_rotation(45)
...
>>> plt.tight_layout()
>>> fig.subplots_adjust(top=0.88)
>>> plt.show()
```

This results in the following histograms:

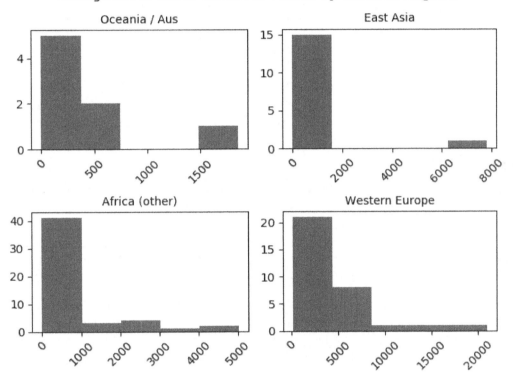

Figure 5.4 – Histograms by region with numbers of countries at different cases per million levels

The preceding steps demonstrated how to visualize the distribution of a continuous variable using histograms and QQ plots.

How it works...

Step 4 shows how easy it is to display a histogram. This can be done by passing a series to the `hist` method of Matplotlib's `pyplot` module. (We use an alias of `plt` for matplotlib.) We could have also passed any `ndarray`, or even a list of data series.

We also get great access to the attributes of the figure and its axes. We can set the labels for each axis, as well as the tick marks and tick labels. We can also specify the content and look and feel of the legend. We will be taking advantage of this functionality often in this chapter.

We pass multiple series to the `hist` method in *Step 7* to produce the stacked histogram. Each series is the `total_cases_pm` (cases per million of population) value for the countries in a region. To get the series for each region, we call the `getcases` function for each item in `showregions`. We choose colors for each series rather than allowing that to happen automatically. We also use the `showregions` list to select labels for the legend.

In *Step 8*, we start by indicating that we want four subplots, in two rows and two columns. That is what we get with `plt.subplots(2, 2)`, which returns both a figure and the four axes. We loop through the axes with `for j, ax in enumerate(axes)`. Within each loop, we select a different region for the histogram from `showregions`. Within each axis, we loop through the tick labels and change the rotation. We also adjust the start of the subplots to make enough room for the figure title. Note that we need to use `suptitle` to add a title in this case. Using `title` would add the title to a subplot.

There's more...

The land temperature data is not quite normally distributed, as the histograms and the skew and kurtosis measures show. It is skewed to the left (skew of `-0.26`) and actually has somewhat skinnier tails than normal (kurtosis of 2.17, compared with 3). Although there are some extreme values, there are not that many of them relative to the overall size of the dataset. While it is not perfectly bell-shaped, the land temperature data frame is a fair bit easier to deal with than the Covid case data.

The skew and kurtosis of the Covid `cases per million` variable show that it is some distance from normal. The skew of 4 and kurtosis of 26 indicates a high positive skew and much fatter tails than with a normal distribution. This is also reflected in the histograms, even when we look at the numbers by region. There are a number of countries at very low levels of cases per million in most regions, and just a few countries with high levels of cases. The *Using grouped boxplots to uncover unexpected values in a particular group* recipe in this chapter shows that there are outliers in almost every region.

If you work through all of the recipes in this chapter, and you are relatively new to Matplotlib and Seaborn, you will find those libraries either usefully flexible or confusingly flexible. It is difficult to even pick one strategy and stick with it because you might need to set up your figure and axes in a particular way to get the visualization you want. It is helpful to keep two things in mind when working through these recipes: first, you will generally need to create a figure and one or more subplots; and second, the main plotting functions work similarly regardless, so `plt.hist` and `ax.hist` will both often work.

Using boxplots to identify outliers for continuous variables

Boxplots are essentially a graphical representation of our work in the *Identifying outliers with one variable* recipe in *Chapter 4, Identifying Missing Values and Outliers in Subsets of Data*. There, we used the concept of **interquartile range (IQR)**—the distance between the value at the first quartile and the value at the third quartile—to determine outliers. Any value greater than $(1.5 * IQR)$ + the third quartile value, or less than the first quartile value – $(1.5 * IQR)$, was considered an outlier. That is precisely what is revealed in a boxplot.

Getting ready

We will work with cumulative data on coronavirus cases and deaths by country, and the **National Longitudinal Surveys (NLS)** data. You will need the Matplotlib library to run the code on your computer.

How to do it...

We use boxplots to show the shape and spread of **Scholastic Assessment Test (SAT)** scores, weeks worked, and Covid cases and deaths:

1. Load the `pandas` and `matplotlib` libraries.

   Also, load the NLS and Covid data:

   ```
   >>> import pandas as pd
   >>> import matplotlib.pyplot as plt
   >>> nls97 = pd.read_csv("data/nls97.csv")
   >>> nls97.set_index("personid", inplace=True)
   >>> covidtotals = pd.read_csv("data/covidtotals.csv",
   parse_dates=["lastdate"])
   >>> covidtotals.set_index("iso_code", inplace=True)
   ```

2. Do a boxplot of SAT verbal scores.

   Produce some descriptives first. The `boxplot` method produces a rectangle that represents the IQR, the values between the first and third quartile. The whiskers go from that rectangle to 1.5 times the IQR. Any values above or below the whiskers (what we have labeled the outlier threshold) are considered outliers (we use `annotate` to point to the first and third quartile points, the median, and to the outlier thresholds):

   ```
   >>> nls97.satverbal.describe()
   count    1,406
   ```

mean	500
std	112
min	14
25%	430
50%	500
75%	570
max	800

Name: satverbal, dtype: float64

```
>>> plt.boxplot(nls97.satverbal.dropna(), labels=['SAT
Verbal'])
```

```
>>> plt.annotate('outlier threshold',
xy=(1.05,780), xytext=(1.15,780), size=7,
arrowprops=dict(facecolor='black', headwidth=2,
width=0.5, shrink=0.02))
```

```
>>> plt.annotate('3rd quartile',
xy=(1.08,570), xytext=(1.15,570), size=7,
arrowprops=dict(facecolor='black', headwidth=2,
width=0.5, shrink=0.02))
```

```
>>> plt.annotate('median', xy=(1.08,500),
xytext=(1.15,500), size=7,
arrowprops=dict(facecolor='black', headwidth=2,
width=0.5, shrink=0.02))
```

```
>>> plt.annotate('1st quartile',
xy=(1.08,430), xytext=(1.15,430), size=7,
arrowprops=dict(facecolor='black', headwidth=2,
width=0.5, shrink=0.02))
```

```
>>> plt.annotate('outlier threshold',
xy=(1.05,220), xytext=(1.15,220), size=7,
arrowprops=dict(facecolor='black', headwidth=2,
width=0.5, shrink=0.02))
```

```
>>> #plt.annotate('outlier threshold',
xy=(1.95,15), xytext=(1.55,15), size=7,
arrowprops=dict(facecolor='black', headwidth=2,
width=0.5, shrink=0.02))
```

```
>>> plt.show()
```

This results in the following boxplot:

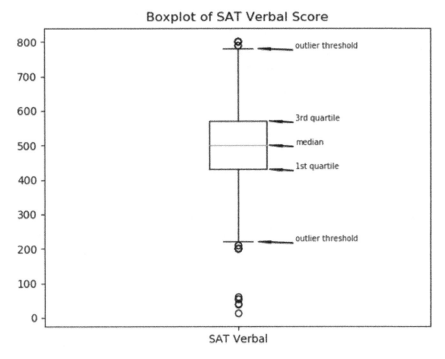

Figure 5.5 – Boxplot of SAT verbal scores with labels for quartile range and outliers

3.   Show some descriptives on weeks worked:

```
>>> weeksworked = nls97.loc[:,
['highestdegree','weeksworked16', 'weeksworked17']]
>>>
>>> weeksworked.describe()
       weeksworked16  weeksworked17
count          7,068          6,670
mean              39             39
std               21             19
min                0              0
25%               23             37
50%               53             49
75%               53             52
max               53             52
```

4. Do boxplots of weeks worked:

```
>>> plt.boxplot([weeksworked.weeksworked16.dropna(),
...     weeksworked.weeksworked17.dropna()],
...     labels=['Weeks Worked 2016','Weeks Worked 2017'])
>>> plt.title("Boxplots of Weeks Worked")
>>> plt.tight_layout()
>>> plt.show()
```

This results in the following boxplots:

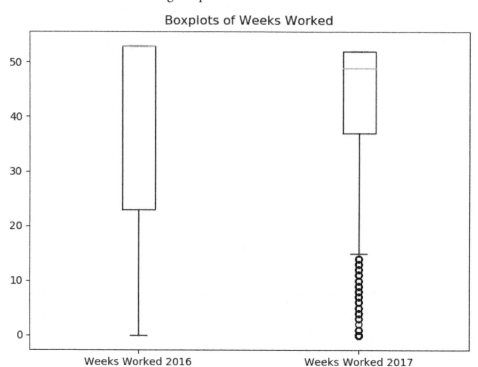

Figure 5.6 – Boxplots of two variables side by side

5. Show some descriptives for the Covid data.

Create a list of labels (`totvarslabels`) for columns to use in a later step:

```
>>> totvars = ['total_cases','total_deaths','total_cases_
pm', 'total_deaths_pm']
>>> totvarslabels = ['cases','deaths','cases per
million','deaths per million']
>>> covidtotalsonly = covidtotals[totvars]
>>> covidtotalsonly.describe()
```

	total_cases	total_deaths	total_cases_pm	total_deaths_pm
count	209	209	209	209
mean	60,757	2,703	2,297	74
std	272,440	11,895	4,040	156
min	3	0	1	0
25%	342	9	203	3
50%	2,820	53	869	15
75%	25,611	386	2,785	58
max	3,247,684	134,814	35,795	1,238

6. Do boxplots of cases and deaths per million:

```
>>> fig, ax = plt.subplots()
>>> plt.title("Boxplots of Covid Cases and Deaths Per
Million")
>>> ax.boxplot([covidtotalsonly.total_cases_
pm,covidtotalsonly.total_deaths_pm],\
...    labels=['cases per million','deaths per million'])
>>> plt.tight_layout()
>>> plt.show()
```

This results in the following boxplots:

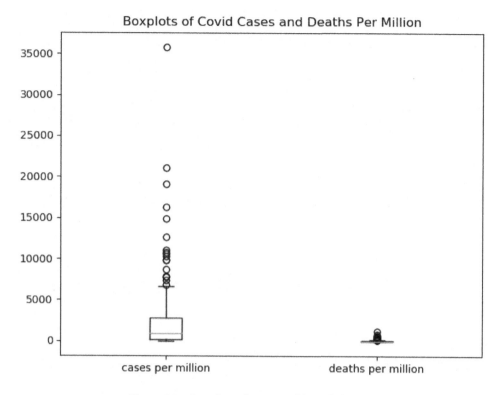

Figure 5.7 – Boxplots of two variables side by side

7.   Show the boxplots as separate subplots on one figure.

It is hard to view multiple boxplots on one figure when the variable values are very different, as is true for Covid cases and deaths. Fortunately, `matplotlib` allows us to create multiple subplots on each figure, each of which can use different x and y axes:

```
>>> fig, axes = plt.subplots(2, 2)
>>> fig.suptitle("Boxplots of Covid Cases and Deaths")
>>> axes = axes.ravel()
>>> for j, ax in enumerate(axes):
...    ax.boxplot(covidtotalsonly.iloc[:, j],
labels=[totvarslabels[j]])
...
>>> plt.tight_layout()
>>> fig.subplots_adjust(top=0.94)
>>> plt.show()
```

This results in the following boxplots:

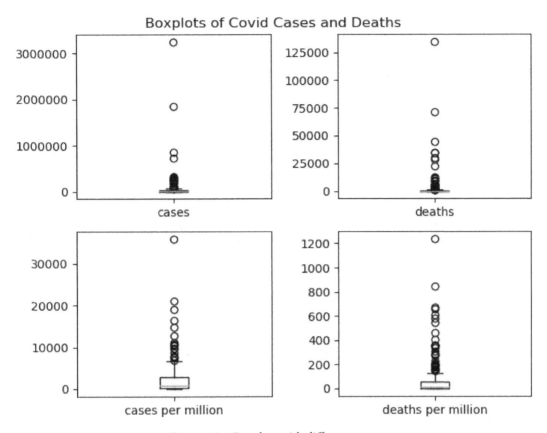

Figure 5.8 – Boxplots with different y axes

Boxplots are a relatively straightforward but exceedingly useful way to view how variables are distributed. They make it easy to visualize spread, central tendency, and outliers, all in one graphic.

How it works...

It is fairly easy to create a boxplot with matplotlib, as *Step 2* shows. Passing a series to pyplot is all that is required (we use the plt alias). We call the show method of pyplot to show the figure. This step also demonstrates how to use annotations to add text and symbols to your figure. We show multiple boxplots in *Step 4* by passing multiple series to pyplot.

It can be difficult to show multiple boxplots in a single figure when the scales are very different, as is the case with the Covid outcome data (cases, deaths, cases per million, and deaths per million). *Step 7* shows one way to deal with that. We can create several subplots on one plot. We start by indicating that we want four subplots, in two columns and two rows. That is what we get with `plt.subplots(2, 2)`, which returns both a figure and the four axes. We can then loop through the axes, calling `boxplot` on each one. Nifty!

However, it is still hard to see the IQR for cases and deaths because of some of the extreme values. In the next recipe, we remove some of the extreme values to give us a better visualization of the remaining data.

There's more...

The boxplot of SAT verbal scores in *Step 2* suggests a relatively normal distribution. The median is close to the center of the IQR. This is not surprising given that the descriptives we ran show that mean and median have the same value. There is, however, substantially more room for outliers at the lower end than at the upper end. (Indeed, the very low SAT verbal scores seem implausible and should be checked.)

The boxplots of weeks worked in 2016 and 2017 in *Step 4* show variables that are distributed much differently than SAT scores. The medians are near the top of the IQR and are much greater than the means. This suggests a negative skew. Also, notice that there are no whiskers or outliers at the upper end of the distribution as the median value is at, or near, the maximum.

See also

Some of these boxplots suggest that the data we are examining is not normally distributed. The *Identifying outliers with one variable* recipe in *Chapter 4, Identifying Missing Values and Outliers in Subsets of Data*, covers some normal distribution tests. It also shows how to take a closer look at the values outside of the outlier thresholds: the circles in the boxplots.

Using grouped boxplots to uncover unexpected values in a particular group

We saw in the previous recipe that boxplots are a great tool for examining the distribution of continuous variables. They can also be useful when we want to see if those variables are distributed differently for parts of our dataset: salaries for different age groups; number of children by marital status; litter size for different mammal species. Grouped boxplots are a handy and intuitive way to view differences in variable distribution by categories in our data.

Getting ready

We will work with the NLS and the Covid case data. You will need Matplotlib and Seaborn installed on your computer to run the code in this recipe.

How to do it...

We generate descriptive statistics of weeks worked by highest degree earned. We then use grouped boxplots to visualize the spread of the weeks worked distribution by degree, and of Covid cases by region:

1. Import the pandas, matplotlib, and seaborn libraries:

```
>>> import pandas as pd
>>> import matplotlib.pyplot as plt
>>> import seaborn as sns
>>> nls97 = pd.read_csv("data/nls97.csv")
>>> nls97.set_index("personid", inplace=True)
>>> covidtotals = pd.read_csv("data/covidtotals.csv",
parse_dates=["lastdate"])
>>> covidtotals.set_index("iso_code", inplace=True)
```

2. View the median, and first and third quartile values for weeks worked for each degree attainment level.

   First, define a function that returns those values as a series, then use apply to call it for each group:

```
>>> def gettots(x):
...     out = {}
...     out['min'] = x.min()
...     out['qr1'] = x.quantile(0.25)
...     out['med'] = x.median()
...     out['qr3'] = x.quantile(0.75)
...     out['max'] = x.max()
...     out['count'] = x.count()
...     return pd.Series(out)
...
>>> nls97.groupby(['highestdegree'])['weeksworked17'].\
...     apply(gettots).unstack()
```

	min	qr1	med	qr3	max	count
highestdegree						
0. None	0	0	40	52	52	510
1. GED	0	8	47	52	52	848
2. High School	0	31	49	52	52	2,665
3. Associates	0	42	49	52	52	593
4. Bachelors	0	45	50	52	52	1,342
5. Masters	0	46	50	52	52	538
6. PhD	0	46	50	52	52	51
7. Professional	0	47	50	52	52	97

3. Do a boxplot of weeks worked by highest degree earned.

Use Seaborn for these boxplots. First, create a subplot and name it `myplt`. This makes it easier to access subplot attributes later. Use the `order` parameter of `boxplot` to order by highest degree earned. Notice that there are no outliers or whiskers at the lower end for individuals with no degree ever received. This is because the IQR for those individuals covers the whole range of values; that is, the value at the 25th percentile is 0 and the value at the 75th percentile is 52:

```
>>> myplt = sns.boxplot('highestdegree','weeksworked17',
data=nls97,
...    order=sorted(nls97.highestdegree.dropna().
unique()))
>>> myplt.set_title("Boxplots of Weeks Worked by Highest
Degree")
>>> myplt.set_xlabel('Highest Degree Attained')
>>> myplt.set_ylabel('Weeks Worked 2017')
>>> myplt.set_xticklabels(myplt.get_xticklabels(),
rotation=60, horizontalalignment='right')
>>> plt.tight_layout()
>>> plt.show()
```

This results in the following boxplots:

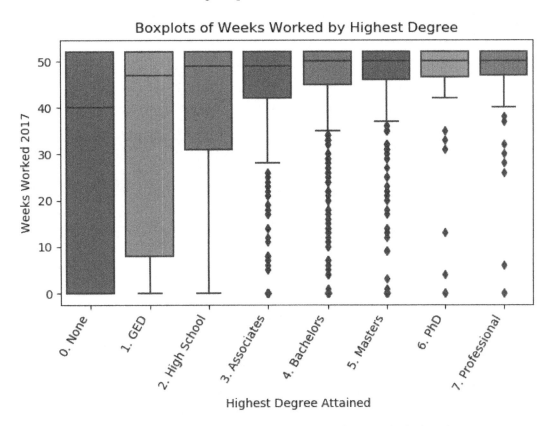

Figure 5.9 – Boxplots of weeks worked with IQR and outliers by highest degree

4. View the minimum, maximum, median, and first and third quartile values for total cases per million by region.

Use the gettots function defined in *Step 2*:

```
>>> covidtotals.groupby(['region'])['total_cases_pm'].\
...     apply(gettots).unstack()
```

	min	qr1	med	qr3	max	count
region						
Caribbean	95	252	339	1,726	4,435	22
Central Africa	15	71	368	1,538	3,317	11
Central America	93	925	1,448	2,191	10,274	7

Central Asia	374	919	1,974	2,907	10,594	6
East Africa	9	65	190	269	5,015	13
East Asia	3	16	65	269	7,826	16
Eastern Europe	347	883	1,190	2,317	6,854	22
North Africa	105	202	421	427	793	5
North America	2,290	2,567	2,844	6,328	9,812	3
Oceania / Aus	1	61	234	424	1,849	8
South America	284	395	2,857	4,044	16,323	13
South Asia	106	574	885	1,127	19,082	9
Southern Africa	36	86	118	263	4,454	9
West Africa	26	114	203	780	2,862	17
West Asia	23	273	2,191	5,777	35,795	16
Western Europe	200	2,193	3,769	5,357	21,038	32

5. Do boxplots of cases per million by region.

Flip the axes since there are a large number of regions. Also, do a swarm plot to give some sense of the number of countries by region. The swarm plot displays a dot for each country in each region. Some of the IQRs are hard to see because of the extreme values:

```
>>> sns.boxplot('total_cases_pm', 'region',
data=covidtotals)
```

```
>>> sns.swarmplot(y="region", x="total_cases_pm",
data=covidtotals, size=2, color=".3", linewidth=0)
```

```
>>> plt.title("Boxplots of Total Cases Per Million by
Region")
```

```
>>> plt.xlabel("Cases Per Million")
```

```
>>> plt.ylabel("Region")
```

```
>>> plt.tight_layout()
```

```
>>> plt.show()
```

This results in the following boxplots:

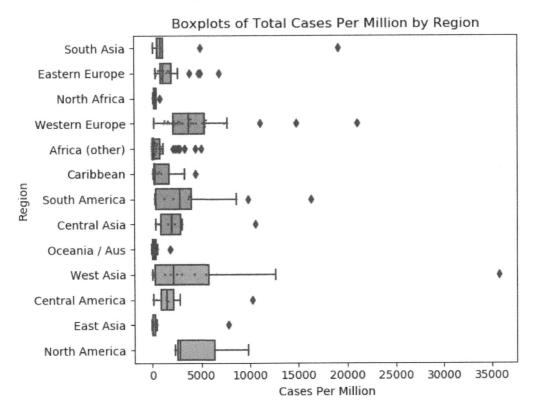

Figure 5.10 – Boxplots and swarm plots of cases per million by region, with IQR and outliers

6. Show the most extreme values for cases per million:

```
>>> covidtotals.loc[covidtotals.total_cases_pm>=14000,\
...     ['location','total_cases_pm']]
             location   total_cases_pm
iso_code
BHR           Bahrain           19,082
CHL             Chile           16,323
QAT             Qatar           35,795
SMR        San Marino           21,038
VAT           Vatican           14,833
```

7.   Redo the boxplots without the extreme values:

```
>>> sns.boxplot('total_cases_pm', 'region',
data=covidtotals.loc[covidtotals.total_cases_pm<14000])
>>> sns.swarmplot(y="region", x="total_cases_pm",
data=covidtotals.loc[covidtotals.total_cases_pm<14000],
size=3, color=".3", linewidth=0)
>>> plt.title("Total Cases Without Extreme Values")
>>> plt.xlabel("Cases Per Million")
>>> plt.ylabel("Region")
>>> plt.tight_layout()
>>> plt.show()
```

This results in the following boxplots:

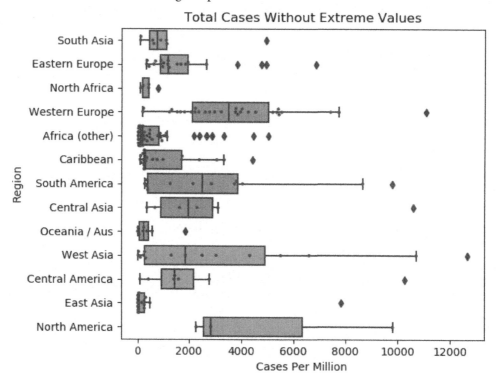

Figure 5.11 – Boxplots of cases per million by region without the extreme values

These grouped boxplots reveal how much the distribution of cases, adjusted by population, varies by region.

How it works...

We use Seaborn for the figures we create in this recipe. We could have also used Matplotlib. Seaborn is actually built on top of Matplotlib, extending it in some areas, and making some things easier. It sometimes produces more aesthetically pleasing figures with the default settings than Matplotlib does.

It is a good idea to have some descriptives in front of us before creating figures with multiple boxplots. In *Step 2*, we get the first and third quartile values, and the median, for each degree attainment level. We do this by first creating a function called gettots, which returns a series with those values. We apply gettots to each group in the data frame with the following statement:

```
nls97.groupby(['highestdegree'])['weeksworked17'].
apply(gettots).unstack()
```

The groupby method creates a data frame with grouping information, which is passed to the apply function. gettots then calculates summary values for each group. unstack reshapes the returned rows, from multiple rows per group (one for each summary statistic) to one row per group, with columns for each summary statistic.

In *Step 3*, we generate a boxplot for each degree attainment level. We do not normally need to name the subplot object we create when we use Seaborn's boxplot method. We do so in this step, naming it myplt, so that we can easily change attributes—such as tick labels—later. We rotate the labels on the *x* axis using set_xticklabels so that the labels do not run into each other.

We flip the axes for the boxplots in *Step 5* since there are more group levels (regions) than there are ticks for the continuous variable, cases per million. We do that by making total_cases_pm the value for the first argument, rather than the second. We also do a swarm plot to give some sense of the number of observations (countries) in each region.

Extreme values can sometimes make it difficult to view a boxplot. Boxplots show both the outliers and the IQR, but the IQR rectangle will be so small that it is not viewable when outliers are several times the third or first quartile value. In *Step 5*, we remove all values of total_cases_pm greater than or equal to 14,000. This improves the presentation of each IQR.

There's more...

The boxplots of weeks worked by educational attainment in *Step 3* reveal high variation in weeks worked, something that is not obvious in univariate analysis. The lower the educational attainment level, the greater the spread in weeks worked. There is substantial variability in weeks worked in 2017 for individuals with less than a high school degree, and very little variability for individuals with college degrees.

This is quite relevant, of course, to our understanding of what is an outlier in terms of weeks worked. For example, someone with a college degree who worked 20 weeks is an outlier, but they would not be an outlier if they had less than a high school diploma.

The `Cases Per Million` boxplots also invite us to think more flexibly about what an outlier is. For example, none of the outliers for cases per million in East Africa would have been identified as an outlier in the dataset as a whole. In addition, those values are all lower than the third quartile value for North America. But they definitely are outliers for East Africa.

One of the first things I notice when looking at a boxplot is where the median is in the IQR. When the median is not at all close to the center, I know I am not dealing with a normally distributed variable. It also gives me a good sense of the direction of the skew. If it is near the bottom of the IQR, meaning that the median is much closer to the first quartile than the third, then there is positive skew. Compare the boxplot for the Caribbean to that of Western Europe. A large number of low values and a few high values brings the median close to the first quartile value for the Caribbean.

See also

We work much more with `groupby` in *Chapter 7, Fixing Messy Data when Aggregating*. We work more with `stack` and `unstack` in *Chapter 9, Tidying and Reshaping Data*.

Examining both the distribution shape and outliers with violin plots

Violin plots combine histograms and boxplots in one plot. They show the IQR, median, and whiskers, as well as the frequency of observations at all ranges of values. It is hard to visualize how that is possible without seeing an actual violin plot. We generate a few violin plots on the same data we used for boxplots in the previous recipe, to make it easier to grasp how they work.

Getting ready

We will work with the NLS and the Covid case data. You need Matplotlib and Seaborn installed on your computer to run the code in this recipe.

How to do it...

We do violin plots to view both the spread and shape of the distribution on the same graphic. We then do violin plots by groups:

1. Load pandas, matplotlib, and seaborn, and the Covid case and NLS data:

```
>>> import pandas as pd
>>> import numpy as np
>>> import matplotlib.pyplot as plt
>>> import seaborn as sns
>>> nls97 = pd.read_csv("data/nls97.csv")
>>> nls97.set_index("personid", inplace=True)
>>> covidtotals = pd.read_csv("data/covidtotals.csv",
parse_dates=["lastdate"])
>>> covidtotals.set_index("iso_code", inplace=True)
```

2. Do a violin plot of the SAT verbal score:

```
>>> sns.violinplot(nls97.satverbal, color="wheat",
orient="v")
>>> plt.title("Violin Plot of SAT Verbal Score")
>>> plt.ylabel("SAT Verbal")
>>> plt.text(0.08, 780, "outlier threshold",
horizontalalignment='center', size='x-small')
>>> plt.text(0.065, nls97.satverbal.quantile(0.75), "3rd
quartile", horizontalalignment='center', size='x-small')
>>> plt.text(0.05, nls97.satverbal.median(), "Median",
horizontalalignment='center', size='x-small')
>>> plt.text(0.065, nls97.satverbal.quantile(0.25), "1st
quartile", horizontalalignment='center', size='x-small')
>>> plt.text(0.08, 210, "outlier threshold",
horizontalalignment='center', size='x-small')
>>> plt.text(-0.4, 500, "frequency",
horizontalalignment='center', size='x-small')
>>> plt.show()
```

This results in the following violin plot:

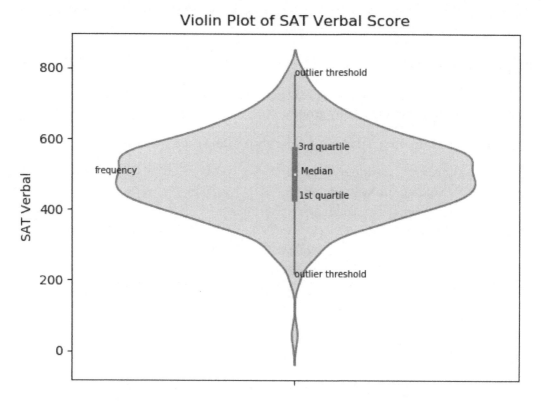

Figure 5.12 – Violin plot of SAT verbal score with labels for the IQR and outlier threshold

3. Get some descriptives for weeks worked:

```
>>> nls97.loc[:, ['weeksworked16','weeksworked17']].
describe()
```

	weeksworked16	weeksworked17
count	7,068	6,670
mean	39	39
std	21	19
min	0	0
25%	23	37
50%	53	49
75%	53	52
max	53	52

4. Show weeks worked for 2016 and 2017.

Use a more object-oriented approach to make it easier to access some axes' attributes. Notice that the weeksworked distributions are bimodal, with bulges near the top and the bottom of the distribution. Also, note the very different IQR for 2016 and 2017:

```
>>> myplt = sns.violinplot(data=nls97.loc[:, ['weeksworke
d16','weeksworked17']])
>>> myplt.set_title("Violin Plots of Weeks Worked")
>>> myplt.set_xticklabels(["Weeks Worked 2016","Weeks
Worked 2017"])
>>> plt.show()
```

This results in the following violin plots:

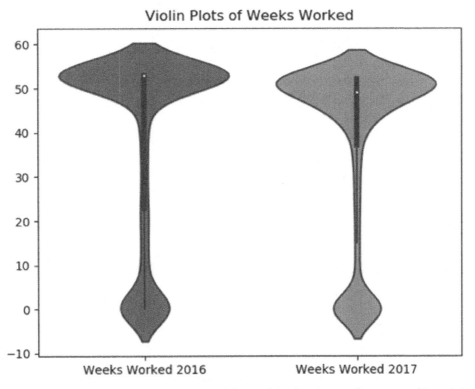

Figure 5.13 – Violin plots showing the spread and shape of the distribution for two variables side by side

5.   Do a violin plot of wage income by gender and marital status.

First, create a collapsed marital status column. Specify gender for the *x* axis, salary for the *y* axis, and a new collapsed marital status column for hue. The hue parameter is used for grouping, which will be added to any grouping already used for the *x* axis. We also indicate `scale="count"` to generate violin plots sized according to the number of observations in each category:

```
>>> nls97["maritalstatuscollapsed"] = nls97.
maritalstatus.\
...    replace(['Married','Never-married','Divorced','Sepa
rated','Widowed'],\
...    ['Married','Never Married','Not Married','Not
Married','Not Married'])
>>> sns.violinplot(nls97.gender, nls97.wageincome,
hue=nls97.maritalstatuscollapsed, scale="count")
>>> plt.title("Violin Plots of Wage Income by Gender and
Marital Status")
>>> plt.xlabel('Gender')
>>> plt.ylabel('Wage Income 2017')
>>> plt.legend(title="", loc="upper center",
framealpha=0, fontsize=8)
>>> plt.tight_layout()
>>> plt.show()
```

This results in the following violin plots:

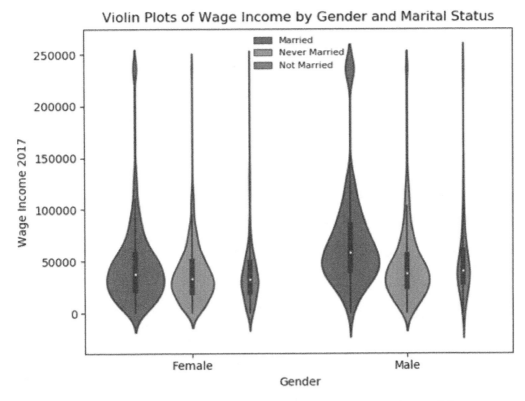

Figure 5.14 – Violin plots showing the spread and shape of the distribution by two different groups

6.   Do violin plots of weeks worked by highest degree attained:

```
>>> myplt = sns.
violinplot('highestdegree','weeksworked17', data=nls97,
rotation=40)
```

```
>>> myplt.set_xticklabels(myplt.get_xticklabels(),
rotation=60, horizontalalignment='right')
```

```
>>> myplt.set_title("Violin Plots of Weeks Worked by
Highest Degree")
```

```
>>> myplt.set_xlabel('Highest Degree Attained')
```

```
>>> myplt.set_ylabel('Weeks Worked 2017')
```

```
>>> plt.tight_layout()
```

```
>>> plt.show()
```

This results in the following violin plots:

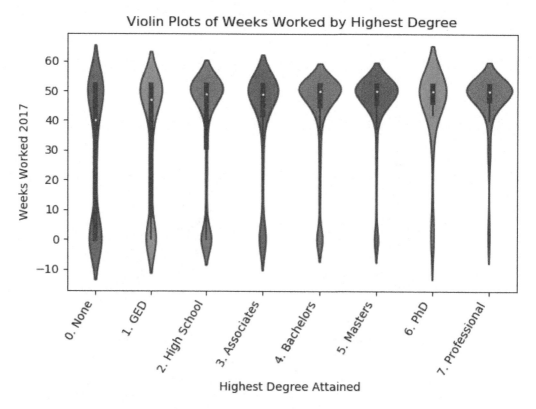

Figure 5.15 – Violin plots showing the spread and shape of the distribution by group

These steps show just how much violin plots can tell us about how continuous variables in our data frame are distributed, and how that might vary by group.

How it works...

Similar to boxplots, violin plots show the median, first and third quartiles, and the whiskers. They also show the relative frequency of variable values. (When the violin plot is displayed vertically, the relative frequency is the width at a given point.) The violin plot produced in *Step 2*, and the associated annotations, provide a good illustration. We can tell from the violin plot that the distribution of SAT verbal scores is not dramatically different from the normal, other than the extreme values at the lower end. The greatest bulge (greatest width) is at the median, declining fairly symmetrically from there. The median is relatively equidistant from the first and third quartiles.

We can create a violin plot in Seaborn by passing one or more data series to the `violinplot` method. We can also pass a whole data frame of one or more columns. We do that in *Step 4* because we want to plot more than one continuous variable.

We sometimes need to experiment with the legend a bit to get it to be both informative and unobtrusive. In *Step 5*, we used the following command to remove the legend title (since it is clear from the values), locate it in the best place in the figure, and make the box transparent (`framealpha=0`):

```
plt.legend(title="", loc="upper center", framealpha=0,
fontsize=8)
```

We can pass data series to `violinplot` in a variety of ways. If you do not indicate an axis with `"x="` or `"y="`, or grouping with `"hue="`, Seaborn will figure that out based on order. For example, in *Step 5*, we did the following:

```
sns.violinplot(nls97.gender, nls97.wageincome, hue=nls97.
maritalstatuscollapsed, scale="count")
```

We would have got the same results if we had done the following:

```
sns.violinplot(x=nls97.gender, y=nls97.wageincome, hue=nls97.
maritalstatuscollapsed, scale="count")
```

We could have also done this to obtain the same result:

```
sns.violinplot(y=nls97.wageincome, x=nls97.gender,  hue=nls97.
maritalstatuscollapsed, scale="count")
```

Although I have highlighted this flexibility in this recipe, these techniques for sending data to Matplotlib and Seaborn apply to all of the plotting methods discussed in this chapter (though not all of them have a `hue` parameter).

There's more...

Once you get the hang of violin plots, you will appreciate the enormous amount of information they make available on one figure. We get a sense of the shape of the distribution, its central tendency, and its spread. We can also easily show that information for different subsets of our data.

The distribution of weeks worked in 2016 is different enough from weeks worked in 2017 to give the careful analyst pause. The IQR is quite different—30 for 2016 (23 to 53), and 15 for 2017 (37 to 52).

An unusual fact about the distribution of wage income is revealed when examining the violin plots produced in *Step 5*. There is a bunching-up of incomes at the top of the distribution for married males, and somewhat for married females. That is quite unusual for a wage income distribution. As it turns out, it looks like there is a ceiling on wage income of $235,884. This is something that we definitely want to take into account in future analyses that include wage income.

The income distributions have a similar shape across gender and marital status, with bulges slightly below the median and extended positive tails. The IQRs have relatively similar lengths. However, the distribution for married males is noticeably higher (or to the right, depending on chosen orientation) than that for the other groups.

The violin plots of weeks worked by degree attained show very different distributions by group, as we also discovered in the boxplots of the same data in the previous recipe. What is more clear here, though, is the bimodal nature of the distribution at lower levels of education. There is a bunching at low levels of weeks worked for individuals without college degrees. Individuals without high school diplomas or a **GED** (a **Graduate Equivalency Diploma**) were nearly as likely to work 5 or fewer weeks in 2017 as they were to work 50 or more weeks.

We used Seaborn exclusively to produce violin plots in this recipe. Violin plots can also be produced with Matplotlib. However, the default graphics in Matplotlib for violin plots look very different from those for Seaborn.

See also

It might be helpful to compare the violin plots in this recipe to the histograms, boxplots, and grouped boxplots in the previous recipes in this chapter.

Using scatter plots to view bivariate relationships

My sense is that there are few plots that data analysts rely more on than scatter plots, with the possible exception of histograms. We are all very used to looking at relationships that can be illustrated in two dimensions. Scatter plots capture important real-world phenomena (the relationship between variables) and are quite intuitive for most people. This makes them a valuable addition to our visualization toolkit.

Getting ready

You will need Matplotlib and Seaborn for this recipe. We will be working with the landtemps dataset, which provides the average temperature in 2019 for 12,095 weather stations across the world.

How to do it...

We level up our scatter plot skills from the previous chapter and visualize more complicated relationships. We display the relationship between average temperature, latitude, and elevation by showing multiple scatter plots on one chart, creating 3D scatter plots, and showing multiple regression lines:

1. Load pandas, numpy, matplotlib, the Axes3D module, and seaborn:

```
>>> import pandas as pd
>>> import numpy as np
>>> import matplotlib.pyplot as plt
>>> from mpl_toolkits.mplot3d import Axes3D
>>> import seaborn as sns
>>> landtemps = pd.read_csv("data/landtemps2019avgs.csv")
```

2. Run a scatter plot of latitude (latabs) by average temperature:

```
>>> plt.scatter(x="latabs", y="avgtemp", data=landtemps)
>>> plt.xlabel("Latitude (N or S)")
>>> plt.ylabel("Average Temperature (Celsius)")
>>> plt.yticks(np.arange(-60, 40, step=20))
>>> plt.title("Latitude and Average Temperature in 2019")
>>> plt.show()
```

This results in the following scatter plot:

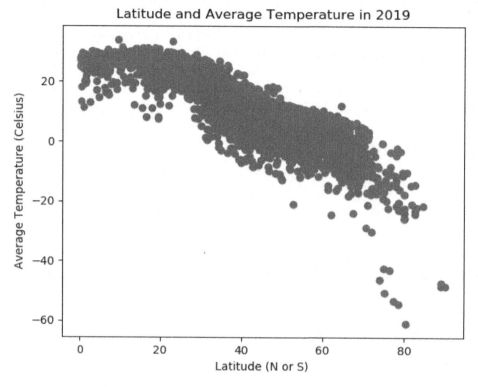

Figure 5.16 – Scatter plot of latitude by average temperature

3.　Show the high elevation points in red.

Create low and high elevation data frames. Notice that the high elevation points are generally lower (that is, cooler) on the figure at each latitude:

```
>>> low, high = landtemps.loc[landtemps.elevation<=1000],
landtemps.loc[landtemps.elevation>1000]
```

```
>>> plt.scatter(x="latabs", y="avgtemp", c="blue",
data=low)
```

```
>>> plt.scatter(x="latabs", y="avgtemp", c="red",
data=high)
```

```
>>> plt.legend(('low elevation', 'high elevation'))
```

```
>>> plt.xlabel("Latitude (N or S)")
```

```
>>> plt.ylabel("Average Temperature (Celsius)")
```

```
>>> plt.title("Latitude and Average Temperature in 2019")
```

```
>>> plt.show()
```

This results in the following scatter plot:

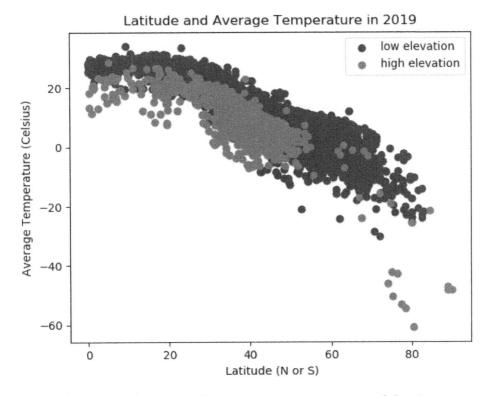

Figure 5.17 – Scatter plot of latitude by average temperature and elevation

4. View a three-dimensional plot of temperature, latitude, and elevation.

It looks like there is a somewhat steeper decline in temperature, with increases in latitude for high elevation stations:

```
>>> fig = plt.figure()
>>> plt.suptitle("Latitude, Temperature, and Elevation in
2019")
>>> ax.set_title('Three D')
>>> ax = plt.axes(projection='3d')
>>> ax.set_xlabel("Elevation")
>>> ax.set_ylabel("Latitude")
>>> ax.set_zlabel("Avg Temp")
>>> ax.scatter3D(low.elevation, low.latabs, low.avgtemp,
label="low elevation", c="blue")
```

```
>>> ax.scatter3D(high.elevation, high.latabs, high.
avgtemp, label="high elevation", c="red")
```

```
>>> ax.legend()
```

```
>>> plt.show()
```

This results in the following scatter plot:

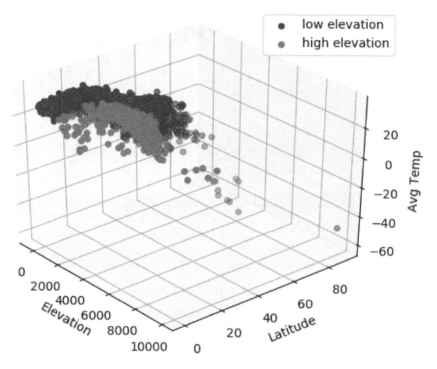

Figure 5.18 – 3D scatter plot of latitude and elevation by average temperature

5. Show a regression line of latitude on the temperature data.

Use regplot to get a regression line:

```
>>> sns.regplot(x="latabs", y="avgtemp", color="blue",
data=landtemps)
```

```
>>> plt.title("Latitude and Average Temperature in 2019")
```

```
>>> plt.xlabel("Latitude (N or S)")
```

```
>>> plt.ylabel("Average Temperature")
```

```
>>> plt.show()
```

This results in the following scatter plot:

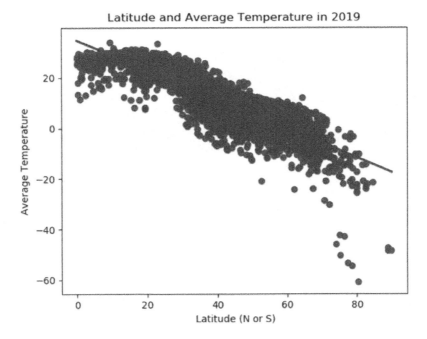

Figure 5.19 – Scatter plot of latitude by average temperature with regression line

6. Show separate regression lines for low and high elevation stations.

We use `lmplot` this time instead of `regplot`. The two methods have similar functionality. Unsurprisingly, high elevation stations appear to have both lower intercepts (where the line crosses the *y* axis) and steeper negative slopes:

```
>>> landtemps['elevation_group'] = np.where(landtemps.
elevation<=1000,'low','high')
```
```
>>> sns.lmplot(x="latabs", y="avgtemp", hue="elevation_
group", palette=dict(low="blue", high="red"), legend_
out=False, data=landtemps)
```
```
>>> plt.xlabel("Latitude (N or S)")
```
```
>>> plt.ylabel("Average Temperature")
```
```
>>> plt.legend(('low elevation', 'high elevation'),
loc='lower left')
```
```
>>> plt.yticks(np.arange(-60, 40, step=20))
```
```
>>> plt.title("Latitude and Average Temperature in 2019")
```
```
>>> plt.tight_layout()
```
```
>>> plt.show()
```

This results in the following scatter plot:

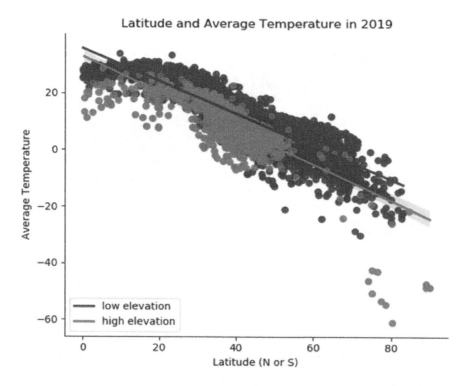

Figure 5.20 – Scatter plot of latitude by temperature with separate regression lines for elevation

7.   Show some stations above the low and high elevation regression lines:

```
>>> high.loc[(high.latabs>38) & (high.avgtemp>=18),\
...
['station','country','latabs','elevation','avgtemp']]
            station       country  latabs   elevation
avgtemp
3985       LAJES_AB       Portugal      39       1,016
18
5870    WILD_HORSE_6N  United States     39       1,439
23
>>> low.loc[(low.latabs>47) & (low.avgtemp>=14),
...
['station','country','latabs','elevation','avgtemp']]
                station         country   latabs
elevation   avgtemp
```

1062 61	SAANICHTON_CDA 18	Canada	49
1160 50	CLOVERDALE_EAST 15	Canada	49
6917 401	WINNIBIGOSHISH_DAM 18	United States	47
7220 988	WINIFRED 16	United States	48

8. Show some stations below the low and high elevation regression lines:

```
>>> high.loc[(high.latabs<5) & (high.avgtemp<18),\
...
['station','country','latabs','elevation','avgtemp']]
              station   country   latabs   elevation
avgtemp
2273   BOGOTA_ELDORADO   Colombia        5       2,548
15
2296           SAN_LUIS   Colombia        1       2,976
11
2327           IZOBAMBA    Ecuador        0       3,058
13
2331              CANAR    Ecuador        3       3,083
13
2332   LOJA_LA_ARGELIA    Ecuador        4       2,160
17
>>> low.loc[(low.latabs<50) & (low.avgtemp<-9),
...
['station','country','latabs','elevation','avgtemp']]
                  station        country   latabs
elevation   avgtemp
1204   FT_STEELE_DANDY_CRK           Canada       50
856        -12
1563               BALDUR           Canada       49
450        -11
1852        POINTE_CLAVEAU           Canada       48
4          -11
1881      CHUTE_DES_PASSES           Canada       50
398        -13
6627          PRESQUE_ISLE   United States       47
183        -10
```

Scatter plots are a great way to view the relationship between two variables. These steps also show how we can display that relationship for different subsets of our data.

How it works...

We can run a scatter plot by just providing column names for x and y and a data frame. Nothing more is required. We get the same access to the attributes of the figure and its axes that we get when we run histograms and boxplots—titles, axis labels, tick marks and labels, and so on. Note that to access attributes such as labels on an axis (rather than on the figure), we use set_xlabels or set_ylabels, not xlabels or ylabels.

3D plots are a little more complicated. First, we need to have imported the Axes3D module. Then, we set the projection of our axes to 3d—plt.axes(projection='3d'), as we do in *Step 4*. We can then use the scatter3D method for each subplot.

Since scatter plots are designed to illustrate the relationship between a regressor (the x variable) and a dependent variable, it is quite helpful to see a least-squares regression line on the scatter plot. Seaborn provides two methods for doing that: regplot and lmplot. I use regplot typically, since it is less resource-intensive. But sometimes, I need the features of lmplot. We use lmplot and its hue attribute in *Step 6* to generate separate regression lines for each elevation level.

In *Steps 7* and *8*, we view some of the outliers: those stations with temperatures much higher or lower than the regression line for their group. We would want to investigate the data for the LAJES_AB station in Portugal and the WILD_HORSE_6N station in the United States ((high.latabs>38) & (high.avgtemp>=18)). The average temperatures are higher than would be predicted at the latitude and elevation level. Similarly, there are four stations in Canada and one in the United States that are at low elevation and have lower average temperatures than would be expected (low.latabs<50) & (low.avgtemp<-9)).

There's more...

We see the expected relationship between latitude and average temperatures. Temperatures fall as latitude increases. But elevation is another important factor. Being able to visualize all three variables at once helps us identify outliers more easily. Of course, there are additional factors that matter for temperatures, such as warm ocean currents. That data is not in this dataset, unfortunately.

Scatter plots are great for visualizing the relationship between two continuous variables. With some tweaking, Matplotlib's and Seaborn's scatter plot tools can also provide some sense of relationships between three variables—by adding a third dimension, creative use of colors (when the third dimension is categorical), or changing the size of the dots (the *Using linear regression to identify data points with high influence* recipe in *Chapter 4, Identifying Missing Values and Outliers in Subsets of Data*, provides an example of that).

See also

This is a chapter on visualization, and identifying unexpected values through visualizations. But these figures also scream out for the kind of multivariate analyses we did in *Chapter 4, Identifying Missing Values and Outliers in Subsets of Data*. In particular, linear regression analysis, and a close look at the residuals, would be useful for identifying outliers.

Using line plots to examine trends in continuous variables

A typical way to visualize values for a continuous variable over regular intervals of time is through a line plot, though sometimes bar charts are used for small numbers of intervals. We will use line plots in this recipe to display variable trends, and examine sudden deviations in trends and differences in values over time by groups.

Getting ready

We will work with daily Covid case data in this recipe. In previous recipes, we have used totals by country. The daily data provides us with the number of new cases and new deaths each day by country, in addition to the same demographic variables we used in other recipes. You will need Matplotlib installed to run the code in this recipe.

How to do it...

We use line plots to visualize trends in daily coronavirus cases and deaths. We create line plots by region, and stacked plots to get a better sense of how much one country can drive the number of cases for a whole region:

1. Import pandas, matplotlib, and the matplotlib dates and date formatting utilities:

```
>>> import pandas as pd
>>> import numpy as np
>>> import matplotlib.pyplot as plt
```

```
>>> import matplotlib.dates as mdates
>>> from matplotlib.dates import DateFormatter
>>> coviddaily = pd.read_csv("data/coviddaily720.csv",
parse_dates=["casedate"])
```

2. View a couple of rows of the Covid daily data:

```
>>> coviddaily.sample(2, random_state=1).T
                       2478              9526
iso_code                BRB               FRA
casedate         2020-06-11        2020-02-16
location           Barbados            France
continent     North America            Europe
new_cases                 4                 0
new_deaths                0                 0
population          287,371        65,273,512
pop_density             664               123
median_age               40                42
gdp_per_capita       16,978            38,606
hosp_beds                 6                 6
region            Caribbean   Western Europe
```

3. Calculate new cases and deaths by day.

   Select dates between 2020-02-01 and 2020-07-12, and then use groupby to
   summarize cases and deaths across all countries for each day:

```
>>> coviddailytotals = coviddaily.loc[coviddaily.
casedate.between('2020-02-01','2020-07-12')].\
...     groupby(['casedate'])[['new_cases','new_deaths']].\
...     sum().\
...     reset_index()
>>>
>>> coviddailytotals.sample(7, random_state=1)
        casedate  new_cases  new_deaths
44    2020-03-16     12,386         757
47    2020-03-19     20,130         961
94    2020-05-05     77,474       3,998
78    2020-04-19     80,127       6,005
160   2020-07-10    228,608       5,441
11    2020-02-12      2,033          97
117   2020-05-28    102,619       5,168
```

4. Show line plots for new cases and new deaths by day.

Show cases and deaths on different subplots:

```
>>> fig = plt.figure()
>>> plt.suptitle("New Covid Cases and Deaths By Day
Worldwide in 2020")
>>> ax1 = plt.subplot(2,1,1)
>>> ax1.plot(coviddailytotals.casedate, coviddailytotals.
new_cases)
>>> ax1.xaxis.set_major_formatter(DateFormatter("%b"))
>>> ax1.set_xlabel("New Cases")
>>> ax2 = plt.subplot(2,1,2)
>>> ax2.plot(coviddailytotals.casedate, coviddailytotals.
new_deaths)
>>> ax2.xaxis.set_major_formatter(DateFormatter("%b"))
>>> ax2.set_xlabel("New Deaths")
>>> plt.tight_layout()
>>> fig.subplots_adjust(top=0.88)
>>> plt.show()
```

This results in the following line plots:

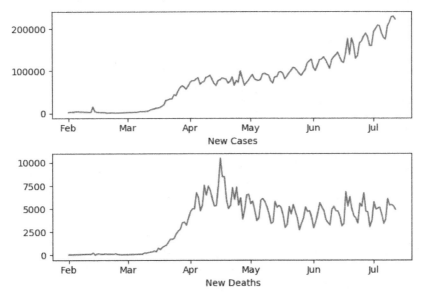

Figure 5.21 – Daily trend lines of worldwide Covid cases and deaths

5. Calculate new cases and deaths by day and region:

```
>>> regiontotals = coviddaily.loc[coviddaily.casedate.
between('2020-02-01','2020-07-12')].\
...    groupby(['casedate','region'])[['new_cases','new_
deaths']].\
...    sum().\
...    reset_index()
>>>
>>> regiontotals.sample(7, random_state=1)
        casedate           region  new_cases  new_deaths
1518  2020-05-16     North Africa        634          28
2410  2020-07-11     Central Asia      3,873          26
870   2020-04-05   Western Europe     30,090       4,079
1894  2020-06-08   Western Europe      3,712         180
790   2020-03-31   Western Europe     30,180       2,970
2270  2020-07-02     North Africa      2,006          89
306   2020-02-26   Oceania / Aus          0           0
```

6. Show line plots of new cases by selected regions.

    Loop through the regions in showregions. Do a line plot of the total new_cases
    by day for each region. Use the gca method to get the *x* axis and set the date format:

```
>>> showregions = ['East Asia','Southern Africa','North
America',
...    'Western Europe']
>>>
>>> for j in range(len(showregions)):
...    rt = regiontotals.loc[regiontotals.
region==showregions[j],
...        ['casedate','new_cases']]
...    plt.plot(rt.casedate, rt.new_cases,
label=showregions[j])
...
>>> plt.title("New Covid Cases By Day and Region in
2020")
>>> plt.gca().get_xaxis().set_major_
formatter(DateFormatter("%b"))
>>> plt.ylabel("New Cases")
>>> plt.legend()
>>> plt.show()
```

This results in the following line plots:

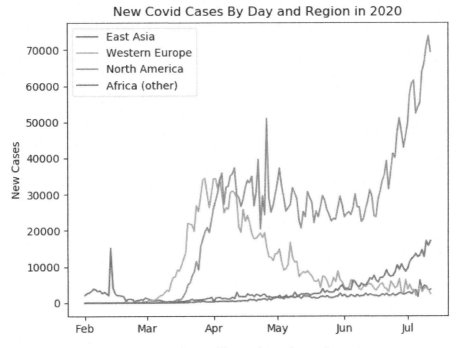

Figure 5.22 – Daily trend lines of Covid cases by region

7. Use a stacked plot to examine the uptick in Southern Africa more closely.

See whether one country (South Africa) in Southern Africa is driving the trend line. Create a data frame (af) for new_cases by day for Southern Africa (the region). Add a series for new_cases in South Africa (the country) to the af data frame. Then, create a new series in the af data frame for Southern Africa cases minus South African cases (afcasesnosa). Select only data from April or later, since that is when we start to see an increase in new cases:

```
>>> af = regiontotals.loc[regiontotals.region=='Southern
Africa',
...     ['casedate','new_cases']].rename(columns={'new_
cases':'afcases'})
>>> sa = coviddaily.loc[coviddaily.location=='South
Africa',
...     ['casedate','new_cases']].rename(columns={'new_
cases':'sacases'})
>>> af = pd.merge(af, sa, left_on=['casedate'], right_
on=['casedate'], how="left")
```

```
>>> af.sacases.fillna(0, inplace=True)
>>> af['afcasesnosa'] = af.afcases-af.sacases
>>> afabb = af.loc[af.casedate.between('2020-04-
01','2020-07-12')]
>>> fig = plt.figure()
>>> ax = plt.subplot()
>>> ax.stackplot(afabb.casedate, afabb.sacases, afabb.
afcasesnosa, labels=['South Africa','Other Southern
Africa'])
>>> ax.xaxis.set_major_formatter(DateFormatter("%m-%d"))
>>> plt.title("New Covid Cases in Southern Africa")
>>> plt.tight_layout()
>>> plt.legend(loc="upper left")
>>> plt.show()
```

This results in the following stacked plot:

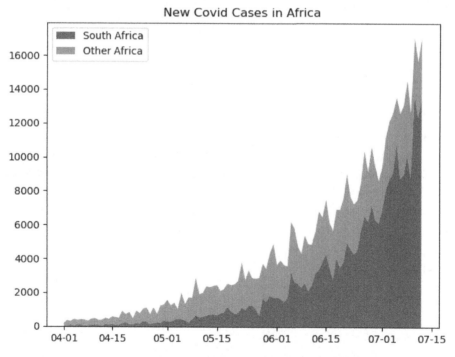

Figure 5.23 – Stacked daily trends of cases in South Africa and the rest of that region (Southern Africa)

These steps show how to use line plots to examine trends in a variable over time, and how to display trends for different groups on one figure.

How it works...

We need to do some manipulation of the daily Covid data before we do the line charts. We use `groupby` in *Step 3* to summarize new cases and deaths over all countries for each day. We use `groupby` in *Step 5* to summarize cases and deaths for each region and day.

In *Step 4*, we set up our first subplot with `plt.subplot(2,1,1)`. That will give us a figure with two rows and one column. The `1` for the third argument indicates that this subplot will be the first, or top, subplot. We can pass a data series for date and for the values for the *y* axis. So far, this is pretty much what we have done with the `hist`, `scatterplot`, `boxplot`, and `violinplot` methods. But since we are working with dates here, we take advantage of Matplotlib's utilities for date formatting and indicate that we want only the month to show, with `xaxis.set_major_formatter(DateFormatter("%b"))`. Since we are working with subplots, we use `set_xlabel` rather than `xlabel` to indicate the label we want for the *x* axis.

We show line plots for four selected regions in *Step 6*. We do this by calling `plot` for each region that we want plotted. We could have done it for all of the regions, but it would have been too difficult to view.

We have to do some additional manipulation in *Step 7* to pull the South African (the country) cases out of the cases for Southern Africa (the region). Once we do that, we can do a stacked plot with the Southern Africa cases (minus South Africa) and South Africa. This figure suggests that the increase in cases in Southern Africa is almost completely driven by increases in South Africa.

There's more...

The figure produced in *Step 6* reveals a couple of potential data issues. There are unusual spikes in mid-February in East Asia and in late April in North America. It is important to examine these anomalies to see if there is a data collection error.

It is difficult to miss how much the trends differ by region. There are substantive reasons for this, of course. The different lines reflect what we know to be reality about different rates of spread by country and region. However, it is worth exploring any significant change in the direction or slope of trend lines to make sure that we can confirm that the data is accurate. We want to be able to explain what happened in Western Europe in early April and in North America and Southern Africa in early June. One question is whether the trends reflect changes in the whole region (such as with the decline in Western Europe in early April) or for one or two large countries in the region (the United States in North America and South Africa in Southern Africa).

See also

We cover `groupby` in more detail in *Chapter 7, Fixing Messy Data When Aggregating*. We go over merging data, as we did in *Step 7*, in *Chapter 8, Addressing Data Issues when Combining DataFrames*.

Generating a heat map based on a correlation matrix

The correlation between two variables is a measure of how much they move together. A correlation of 1 means that the two variables are perfectly positively correlated. As one variable increases in size, so does the other. A value of -1 means that they are perfectly negatively correlated. As one variable increases in size, the other decreases. Correlations of 1 or -1 only rarely happen, but correlations above 0.5 or below -0.5 might still be meaningful. There are several tests that can tell us whether the relationship is statistically significant (such as Pearson, Spearman, and Kendall). Since this is a chapter on visualizations, we will focus on viewing important correlations.

Getting ready

You will need Matplotlib and Seaborn installed to run the code in this recipe. Both can be installed by using `pip`, with the `pip install matplotlib` and `pip install seaborn` commands.

How to do it...

We first show part of a correlation matrix of the Covid data, and the scatter plots of some key relationships. We then show a heat map of the correlation matrix to visualize the correlations between all variables:

1. Import `matplotlib` and `seaborn`, and load the Covid totals data:

```
>>> import pandas as pd
>>> import numpy as np
>>> import matplotlib.pyplot as plt
>>> import seaborn as sns
>>> covidtotals = pd.read_csv("data/covidtotals.csv",
parse_dates=["lastdate"])
```

2. Generate a correlation matrix.

    View part of the matrix:

```
>>> corr = covidtotals.corr()
>>> corr[['total_cases','total_deaths','total_cases_
pm','total_deaths_pm']]
                      total_cases  total_deaths  total_cases_
pm   total_deaths_pm
total_cases                  1.00          0.93
0.23              0.26
total_deaths                 0.93          1.00
0.20              0.41
total_cases_pm               0.23          0.20
1.00              0.49
total_deaths_pm              0.26          0.41
0.49              1.00
population                   0.34          0.28
-0.04             -0.00
pop_density                 -0.03         -0.03
0.08              0.02
median_age                   0.12          0.17
0.22              0.38
gdp_per_capita               0.13          0.16
0.58              0.37
hosp_beds                   -0.01         -0.01
0.02              0.09
```

3. Show scatter plots of median age and **gross domestic product** (**GDP**) per capita by cases per million.

    Indicate that we want the subplots to share *y* axis values with `sharey=True`:

```
>>> fig, axes = plt.subplots(1,2, sharey=True)
>>> sns.regplot(covidtotals.median_age, covidtotals.
total_cases_pm, ax=axes[0])
>>> sns.regplot(covidtotals.gdp_per_capita, covidtotals.
total_cases_pm, ax=axes[1])
>>> axes[0].set_xlabel("Median Age")
>>> axes[0].set_ylabel("Cases Per Million")
>>> axes[1].set_xlabel("GDP Per Capita")
```

```
>>> axes[1].set_ylabel("")
>>> plt.suptitle("Scatter Plots of Age and GDP with Cases
Per Million")
>>> plt.tight_layout()
>>> fig.subplots_adjust(top=0.92)
>>> plt.show()
```

This results in the following scatter plots:

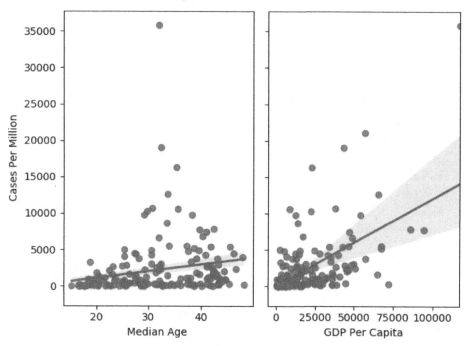

Figure 5.24 – Scatter plots of median age and GDP by cases per million side by side

4. Generate a heat map of the correlation matrix:

```
>>> sns.heatmap(corr, xticklabels=corr.columns,
yticklabels=corr.columns, cmap="coolwarm")
>>> plt.title('Heat Map of Correlation Matrix')
>>> plt.tight_layout()
>>> plt.show()
```

This results in the following heat map:

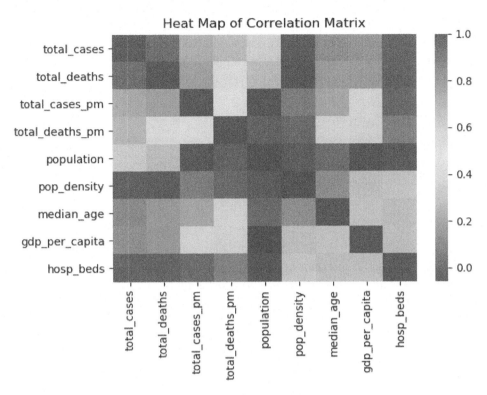

Figure 5.25 – Heat map of Covid data, with strongest correlations in red and peach

Heat maps are a great way to visualize how all key variables in our data frame are correlated with one another.

How it works...

The `corr` method of a data frame generates correlation coefficients of all numeric variables by all other numeric variables. We display part of that matrix in *Step 2*. In *Step 3*, we do scatter plots of median age by cases per million, and GDP per capita by cases per million. These plots give a sense of what it looks like when the correlation is 0.22 (median age and cases per million) and when it is 0.58 (GDP per capita and cases per million). There is not much of a relationship between median age and cases per million. There is more of a relationship between GDP per capita and cases per million.

The heat map provides a visualization of the correlation matrix we created in *Step 2*. All of the red squares are correlations of 1.0 (which is the correlation of the variable with itself). The slightly lighter red squares are between `total_cases` and `total_deaths` (0.93). The peach squares (those with correlations between 0.55 and 0.65) are also interesting. GDP per capita, median age, and hospital beds per 1,000 people are positively correlated with each other, and GDP per capita is positively correlated with cases per million.

There's more...

I find it helpful to always have a correlation matrix or heat map close by when I am doing exploratory analysis or statistical modeling. I understand the data much better when I am able to keep these bivariate relationships in mind.

See also

We go over tools for examining the relationship between two variables in more detail in the *Identifying outliers and unexpected values in bivariate relationships* recipe in *Chapter 4, Identifying Missing Values and Outliers in Subsets of Data*.

6

Cleaning and Exploring Data with Series Operations

We can view the recipes in the first few chapters of this book as, essentially, diagnostic. We imported some raw data and then generated descriptive statistics about key variables. This gave us a sense of how the values for those variables were distributed and helped us identify outliers and unexpected values. We then examined the relationships between variables to look for patterns, and deviations from those patterns, including logical inconsistencies. In short, our primary goal so far has been to figure out what is going on with our data.

The recipes in this chapter demonstrate how to use pandas methods to update series values once we have figured out what needs to be done. Ideally, we need to take the time to carefully examine our data before manipulating the values of our variables. We should have measures of central tendency, indicators of distribution shape and spread, correlations, and visualizations in front of us before we update the variable's values, or before creating new variables based on them. We should also have a good sense of outliers and missing values, understand how they affect summary statistics, and have preliminary plans for imputing new values or otherwise adjusting them.

Having done that, we will be ready to perform some data cleaning tasks. These tasks usually involve working directly with a pandas series object, regardless of whether we are changing values for an existing series or creating a new one. This often involves changing values conditionally, altering only those values that meet specific criteria, or assigning multiple possible values based on existing values for that series, or values for another series.

How we assign such values varies significantly by the series' data type, either for the series to be changed or a criterion series. Querying and cleaning string data bears little resemblance to those tasks containing date or numeric data. With strings, we often need to evaluate whether some string fragment does or does not have a certain value, strip the string of some meaningless characters, or convert the value into a numeric or date value. With dates, we might need to look for invalid or out-of-range dates, or even calculate date intervals.

Fortunately, pandas series have an enormous number of tools for manipulating string, numeric, and date values. We will explore many of the most useful tools in this chapter. Specifically, we will cover the following recipes:

- Getting values from a pandas series
- Showing summary statistics for a pandas series
- Changing series values
- Changing series values conditionally
- Evaluating and cleaning string series data
- Working with dates
- Identifying and cleaning missing data
- Missing value imputation with *k*-nearest neighbor

Let's get started!

Technical requirements

The code and notebooks for this chapter are available on GitHub at `https://github.com/PacktPublishing/Python-Data-Cleaning-Cookbook`

Getting values from a pandas series

A pandas series is a one-dimensional array-like structure that takes a NumPy data type. Each series also has an index; that is, an array of data labels. If an index is not specified when the series is created, it will be the default index of 0 through N-1.

There are several ways to create a pandas series, including from a list, dictionary, NumPy array, or a scalar. In our data cleaning work, we will most frequently be accessing data series that contain columns of data frames, using either attribute access (`dataframename.columnname`) or bracket notation (`dataframename['columnname']`). Attribute access cannot be used to set values for series, but bracket notation will work for all series operations.

In this recipe, we'll explore several ways we can get values from a pandas series. These techniques are very similar to the methods we used to get rows from a pandas DataFrame, which we covered in the *Selecting rows* recipe of *Chapter 3*, *Taking the Measure of Your Data*.

Getting ready

We will be working with data from the **National Longitudinal Survey** (**NLS**) in this recipe – primarily with data about each respondent's overall high school **Grade Point Average** (**GPA**).

> **Data note**
>
> The National Longitudinal Survey of Youth is conducted by the United States Bureau of Labor Statistics. This survey started with a cohort of individuals in 1997 who were born between 1980 and 1985, with annual follow-ups each year until 2017. Survey data is available for public use at `nlsinfo.org`.

How to do it...

For this recipe, we must select series values using the bracket operator and the `loc` and `iloc` accessors. Let's get started:

1. Import `pandas` and the required NLS data:

    ```
    >>> import pandas as pd
    >>> nls97 = pd.read_csv("data/nls97b.csv")
    >>> nls97.set_index("personid", inplace=True)
    ```

2. Create a series from the GPA overall column.

    Show the first few values and associated index labels using `head`. The default number of values shown for `head` is 5. The index for the series is the same as the DataFrame's index, which is `personid`:

    ```
    >>> gpaoverall = nls97.gpaoverall
    >>> type(gpaoverall)
    ```

```
<class 'pandas.core.series.Series'>
>>> gpaoverall.head()
personid
100061    3.06
100139     nan
100284     nan
100292    3.45
100583    2.91
Name: gpaoverall, dtype: float64
>>> gpaoverall.index
Int64Index([100061, 100139, 100284, 100292, 100583,
100833, 100931, 101089,
            101122, 101132,
            ...
            998997, 999031, 999053, 999087, 999103,
999291, 999406, 999543,
            999698, 999963],
           dtype='int64', name='personid', length=8984)
```

3. Select GPA values using the bracket operator.

    Use slicing to create a series with every value from the first value to the fifth.
    Notice that we get the same values that we got with the head method in *step 2*. Not
    including a value to the left of the colon in gpaoverall[:5] means that it must
    start from the beginning. gpaoverall[0:5] will give the same results. Similarly,
    gpaoverall[-5:] shows the values from the fifth to the last position. This
    produces the same results as gpaoverall.tail():

```
>>> gpaoverall[:5]
personid
100061    3.06
100139     nan
100284     nan
100292    3.45
100583    2.91
Name: gpaoverall, dtype: float64
>>> gpaoverall.tail()
personid
999291    3.11
```

```
999406    2.17
999543    nan
999698    nan
999963    3.78
Name: gpaoverall, dtype: float64
>>> gpaoverall[-5:]
personid
999291    3.11
999406    2.17
999543    nan
999698    nan
999963    3.78
Name: gpaoverall, dtype: float64
```

4. Select values using the `loc` accessor.

    We pass an index label (a value for `personid`) to the `loc` accessor to return a scalar. We get a series if we pass a list of index labels, regardless of whether there's one or more. We can even pass a range, separated by a colon. We'll do this here with `gpaoverall.loc[100061:100833]`:

    ```
    >>> gpaoverall.loc[100061]
    3.06
    >>> gpaoverall.loc[[100061]]
    personid
    100061    3.06
    Name: gpaoverall, dtype: float64
    >>> gpaoverall.loc[[100061,100139,100284]]
    personid
    100061    3.06
    100139    nan
    100284    nan
    Name: gpaoverall, dtype: float64
    >>> gpaoverall.loc[100061:100833]
    personid
    100061    3.06
    100139    nan
    100284    nan
    ```

```
100292    3.45
100583    2.91
100833    2.46
Name: gpaoverall, dtype: float64
```

5. Select values using the `iloc` accessor.

    `iloc` differs from `loc` in that it takes a list of row numbers rather than labels. It works similarly to bracket operator slicing. In this step, we pass a one-item list with the value of 0. We then pass a five-item list, `[0,1,2,3,4]`, to return a series containing the first five values. We get the same result if we pass `[:5]` to the accessor:

```
>>> gpaoverall.iloc[[0]]
personid
100061    3.06
Name: gpaoverall, dtype: float64
>>> gpaoverall.iloc[[0,1,2,3,4]]
personid
100061    3.06
100139    nan
100284    nan
100292    3.45
100583    2.91
Name: gpaoverall, dtype: float64
>>> gpaoverall.iloc[:5]
personid
100061    3.06
100139    nan
100284    nan
100292    3.45
100583    2.91
Name: gpaoverall, dtype: float64
>>> gpaoverall.iloc[-5:]
personid
999291    3.11
999406    2.17
999543    nan
```

```
999698      nan
999963      3.78
Name: gpaoverall, dtype: float64
```

Each of these ways of accessing pandas series values – the bracket operator, the `loc` accessor, and the `iloc` accessor – have many use cases, particularly the `loc` accessor.

How it works...

We used the `[]` bracket operator in *step 3* to perform standard Python-like slicing to create a series. This operator allows us to easily select data based on position using a list, or a range of values indicated with slice notation. This notation takes the form of [start:end:step], where 1 is assumed for `step` if no value is provided. When a negative number is used for `start`, it represents the number of rows from the end of the original series.

The `loc` accessor, used in *step 4*, selects data by index labels. Since `personid` is the index for the series, we can pass a list of one or more `personid` values to the `loc` accessor to get a series with those labels and associated GPA values. We can also pass a range of labels to the accessor, which will return a series with GPA values from the index label to the left of the colon and the index label to the right inclusive. So, here, `gpaoverall.loc[100061:100833]` returns a series with GPA values for `personid` between 100061 and 100833, including those two values.

As shown in *step 5*, the `iloc` accessor takes row positions rather than index labels. We can pass either a list of integers or a range using slicing notation.

Showing summary statistics for a pandas series

There are a large number of pandas series methods for generating summary statistics. We can easily get the mean, median, maximum, or minimum values for a series with the `mean`, `median`, `max`, and `min` methods, respectively. The incredibly handy `describe` method will return all of these statistics, as well as several others. We can also get the series value at any percentile using `quantile`. These methods can be used across all values for a series, or just for selected values. This will be demonstrated in this recipe.

Getting ready

We will continue working with the overall GPA column from the NLS.

How to do it...

Let's take a good look at the distribution of the overall GPA for the DataFrame and for the selected rows. To do this, follow these steps:

1. Import pandas and numpy and load the NLS data:

```
>>> import pandas as pd
>>> import numpy as np
>>> nls97 = pd.read_csv("data/nls97b.csv")
>>> nls97.set_index("personid", inplace=True)
```

2. Gather some descriptive statistics:

```
>>> gpaoverall = nls97.gpaoverall
>>> gpaoverall.mean()
2.8184077281812145
>>> gpaoverall.describe()
count    6,004.00
mean         2.82
std          0.62
min          0.10
25%          2.43
50%          2.86
75%          3.26
max          4.17
Name: gpaoverall, dtype: float64
>>> gpaoverall.quantile(np.arange(0.1,1.1,0.1))
0.10    2.02
0.20    2.31
0.30    2.52
0.40    2.70
0.50    2.86
0.60    3.01
0.70    3.17
0.80    3.36
0.90    3.60
1.00    4.17
Name: gpaoverall, dtype: float64
```

3. Show descriptives for a subset of the series:

```
>>> gpaoverall.loc[gpaoverall.between(3,3.5)].head(5)
personid
100061    3.06
100292    3.45
101526    3.37
101527    3.26
102125    3.14
Name: gpaoverall, dtype: float64
>>> gpaoverall.loc[gpaoverall.between(3,3.5)].sum()
1679
>>> gpaoverall.loc[(gpaoverall<2) | (gpaoverall>4)].
sample(5, random_state=2)
personid
932782    1.90
561335    1.82
850001    4.10
292455    1.97
644271    1.97
Name: gpaoverall, dtype: float64
>>> gpaoverall.loc[gpaoverall>gpaoverall.
quantile(0.99)].\
...     agg(['count','min','max'])
count    60.00
min       3.98
max       4.17
Name: gpaoverall, dtype: float64
```

4. Test for a condition across all values.

    Check whether any GPA values are above 4 and if all the values are above or equal to 0. Also, count how many values are missing:

```
>>> (gpaoverall>4).any() # any person has GPA greater
than 4
True
>>> (gpaoverall>=0).all() # all people have GPA greater
than or equal 0
False
```

```
>>> (gpaoverall>=0).sum() # of people with GPA greater
than or equal 0
```
```
6004
```
```
>>> (gpaoverall==0).sum() # of people with GPA equal to 0
```
```
0
```
```
>>> gpaoverall.isnull().sum() # of people with missing
value for GPA
```
```
2980
```

5. Show descriptives for a subset of the series based on values in a different column.

    Show the mean high school GPA for individuals with a wage income in 2016 that's above the 75th percentile, as well as for those with a wage income that's below the 25th percentile:

    ```
    >>> nls97.loc[nls97.wageincome > nls97.wageincome.
    quantile(0.75), 'gpaoverall'].mean()
    ```
    ```
    3.0804171011470256
    ```
    ```
    >>> nls97.loc[nls97.wageincome < nls97.wageincome.
    quantile(0.25), 'gpaoverall'].mean()
    ```
    ```
    2.720143415906124
    ```

6. Show descriptives and frequencies for a series containing categorical data:

    ```
    >>> nls97.maritalstatus.describe()
    ```
    ```
    count          6672
    ```
    ```
    unique            5
    ```
    ```
    top         Married
    ```
    ```
    freq           3066
    ```
    ```
    Name: maritalstatus, dtype: object
    ```
    ```
    >>> nls97.maritalstatus.value_counts()
    ```
    ```
    Married          3066
    ```
    ```
    Never-married    2766
    ```
    ```
    Divorced          663
    ```
    ```
    Separated         154
    ```
    ```
    Widowed            23
    ```
    ```
    Name: maritalstatus, dtype: int64
    ```

Once we have a series, we can use a wide variety of pandas tools to calculate descriptive statistics for all or part of that series.

How it works...

The series `describe` method is quite useful as it gives us a good sense of the central tendency and spread of continuous variables. It is also often helpful to see the value at each decile. We obtained this in *step 2* by passing a list of values ranging from 0.1 to 1.1 to the `quantile` method of the series.

We can use these methods on subsets of a series. In *step 3*, we obtained the count of GPA values between 3 and 3.5. We can also select values based on their relationship to a summary statistic; for example, `gpaoverall>gpaoverall.quantile(0.99)` selects values from the GPA that are greater than the 99th percentile value. We then pass the resulting series to the `agg` method using method chaining, which returns multiple summary statistics (`agg(['count','min','max'])`).

Sometimes, all we need to do is test whether some condition is true across all the values in a series. The any and `all` methods are useful for this. any returns `True` when at least one value in the series satisfies the condition (such as `(gpaoverall>4).any()`). all returns `True` when all the values in the series satisfy the condition. When we chain the test condition with sum (`(gpaoverall>=0).sum()`), we get a count of all the `True` values since pandas interprets `True` values as 1 when performing numeric operations.

`(gpaoverall>4)` is a shorthand for creating a Boolean series with the same index as `gpaoverall`. It has a value of `True` when `gpaoverall` is greater than 4, and `False` otherwise:

```
>>> (gpaoverall>4)
personid
100061    False
100139    False
100284    False
100292    False
100583    False
          ...
999291    False
999406    False
999543    False
999698    False
999963    False
Name: gpaoverall, Length: 8984, dtype: bool
```

We often need to generate summary statistics for a series that has been filtered by another series. We did this in *step 5* by calculating the mean high school GPA for individuals with a wage income that's above the third quartile, as well as for individuals with a wage income that's below the first quartile.

The `describe` method is most useful with continuous variables, such as `gpaoverall;`, but it also provides useful information when used with categorical variables, such as `maritalstatus` (see *step 6*). This returns the count of non-missing values, the number of different values, the category that occurs most frequently, and the frequency of that category.

However, when working with categorical data, the `value_counts` method is more frequently used. It provides the frequency of each category in the series.

There's more...

Working with series is so fundamental to pandas data cleaning tasks that data analysts quickly find that the tools that were used in this recipe are part of their daily data cleaning workflow. Typically, not much time elapses between the initial data import stage and using series methods such as `describe`, `mean`, `sum`, `isnull`, `all`, and `any`.

See also

This chapter is just an introduction to how to generate statistics and test for conditions with series. The recipes in *Chapter 3, Taking the Measure of Your Data*, go into this in more detail. We are also only scratching the surface on aggregating data in this chapter. We'll go through this more thoroughly in *Chapter 7, Fixing Messy Data when Aggregating*.

Changing series values

During the data cleaning process, we often need to change the values in a data series or create a new one. We can change all the values in a series, or just the values in a subset of our data. Most of the techniques we have been using to get values from a series can be used to update series values, though some minor modifications are necessary.

Getting ready

We will work with the overall high school GPA column from the National Longitudinal Survey in this recipe.

How to do it...

We can change the values in a pandas series for all rows, as well as for selected rows. We can update a series with scalars, by performing arithmetic operations on other series, and by using summary statistics. Let's take a look at this:

1. Import pandas and load the NLS data:

```
>>> import pandas as pd
>>> nls97 = pd.read_csv("data/nls97b.csv")
>>> nls97.set_index("personid", inplace=True)
```

2. Edit all the values based on a scalar.

   Multiply gpaoverall by 100:

```
>>> nls97.gpaoverall.head()
personid
100061    3.06
100139     nan
100284     nan
100292    3.45
100583    2.91
Name: gpaoverall, dtype: float64
>>> gpaoverall100 = nls97['gpaoverall'] * 100
>>> gpaoverall100.head()
personid
100061    306.00
100139       nan
100284       nan
100292    345.00
100583    291.00
Name: gpaoverall, dtype: float64
```

3. Set values using index labels.

   Use the loc accessor to specify which values to change by index label:

```
>>> nls97.loc[[100061], 'gpaoverall'] = 3
>>> nls97.loc[[100139,100284,100292],'gpaoverall'] = 0
>>> nls97.gpaoverall.head()
personid
```

```
100061    3.00
100139    0.00
100284    0.00
100292    0.00
100583    2.91
Name: gpaoverall, dtype: float64
```

4. Set values using an operator on more than one series.

Use the + operator to calculate the number of children, which is the sum of children who live at home and children who do not live at home:

```
>>> nls97['childnum'] = nls97.childathome + nls97.childnotathome
>>> nls97.childnum.value_counts().sort_index()
0.00        23
1.00      1364
2.00      1729
3.00      1020
4.00       420
5.00       149
6.00        55
7.00        21
8.00         7
9.00         1
12.00        2
Name: childnum, dtype: int64
```

5. Set the values for a summary statistic using index labels.

Use the `loc` accessor to select `personid` values from 100061 to 100292:

```
>>> nls97.loc[100061:100292,'gpaoverall'] = nls97.gpaoverall.mean()
>>> nls97.gpaoverall.head()
personid
100061    2.82
100139    2.82
100284    2.82
```

```
100292    2.82
100583    2.91
Name: gpaoverall, dtype: float64
```

6. Set the values using position.

    Use the `iloc` accessor to select by position. An integer, or slice notation
    (`start:end:step`), can be used to the left of the comma to indicate the rows
    where the values should be changed. An integer is used to the right of the comma
    to select the column. The `gpaoverall` column is in the 14th position (which is 13
    since the column index is zero-based):

    ```
    >>> nls97.iloc[0, 13] = 2
    >>> nls97.iloc[1:4, 13] = 1
    >>> nls97.gpaoverall.head()
    personid
    100061    2.00
    100139    1.00
    100284    1.00
    100292    1.00
    100583    2.91
    Name: gpaoverall, dtype: float64
    ```

7. Set the GPA values after filtering.

    Change all GPA values over 4 to 4:

    ```
    >>> nls97.gpaoverall.nlargest()
    personid
    312410    4.17
    639701    4.11
    850001    4.10
    279096    4.08
    620216    4.07
    Name: gpaoverall, dtype: float64
    >>> nls97.loc[nls97.gpaoverall>4, 'gpaoverall'] = 4
    >>> nls97.gpaoverall.nlargest()
    personid
    112756    4.00
    ```

```
119784    4.00
160193    4.00
250666    4.00
271961    4.00
Name: gpaoverall, dtype: float64
```

The preceding steps showed us how to update series values with scalars, arithmetic operations, and summary statistics values.

How it works...

The first thing to observe is that, in *step 2*, pandas vectorizes the division by a scalar. It knows that we want to apply the scalar to all rows. `nls97['gpaoverall'] * 100` essentially creates a temporary series with all values set to 100, and with the same index as the `gpaoverall` series. It then multiplies `gpaoverall` by that series of 100 values. This is known as broadcasting.

We can use a lot of what we learned in the first recipe of this chapter, about how to get values from a series, to select particular values to update. The main difference here is that we use the `loc` and `iloc` accessors of the DataFrame (`nls97.loc`) rather than the series (`nls97.gpaoverall.loc`). This is to avoid the dreaded `SettingwithCopyWarning`, which warns us about setting values on a copy of a DataFrame. `nls97.gpaoverall.loc[[100061]] = 3` triggers that warning, while `nls97.loc[[100061], 'gpaoverall'] = 3` does not.

In *step 4*, we saw how pandas handles numeric operations with two or more series. Operations such as addition, subtraction, multiplication, and division are very much like the operations performed on scalars in standard Python, only with vectorization. (This is made possible by pandas' index alignment. Remember that a series in a DataFrame will have the same index.) If you are familiar with NumPy, then you already have a good idea of how this works.

There's more...

It is useful to notice that `nls97.loc[[100061], 'gpaoverall']` returns a series, while `nls97.loc[[100061], ['gpaoverall']]` returns a DataFrame:

```
>>> type(nls97.loc[[100061], 'gpaoverall'])
<class 'pandas.core.series.Series'>
>>> type(nls97.loc[[100061], ['gpaoverall']])
<class 'pandas.core.frame.DataFrame'>
```

If the second argument of the `loc` accessor is a string, it will return a series. If it is a list, even if the list contains only one item, it will return a DataFrame.

For any of the operations we discussed in this recipe, it is good to be mindful of how pandas treats missing values. For example, in *step 3*, if either `childathome` or `childnotathome` is missing, then the operation will return `missing`. We'll discuss how to handle situations like this in the *Identifying and cleaning missing data* recipe in this chapter.

See also

Chapter 3, Taking the Measure of Your Data, goes into greater detail on the use of the `loc` and `iloc` accessors, particularly in the *Selecting rows* and *Selecting and organizing columns* recipes.

Changing series values conditionally

So, changing series values is often more complicated than the previous recipe suggests. We often need to set series values based on the values of one or more other series for that row of data. This is complicated further when we need to set series values based on values from *other* rows; say, a previous value for an individual, or the mean for a subset. We will deal with these complications in this and the next recipe.

Getting ready

We will work with land temperature data and the National Longitudinal Survey data in this recipe.

> **Data note**
>
> The land temperature dataset contains the average temperature readings (in Celsius) in 2019 from over 12,000 stations across the world, though the majority of the stations are in the United States. The raw data was retrieved from the Global Historical Climatology Network integrated database. It has been made available for public use by the United States National Oceanic and Atmospheric Administration at `https://www.ncdc.noaa.gov/data-access/land-based-station-data/land-based-datasets/global-historical-climatology-network-monthly-version-4`.

How to do it...

We will use NumPy's `where` and `select` methods to assign series values based on the values of that series, the values of other series, and summary statistics. We'll then use the `lambda` and `apply` functions to construct more complicated criteria for assignment. Let's get started:

1. Import `pandas` and `numpy`, and then load the NLS and land temperatures data:

```
>>> import pandas as pd
>>> import numpy as np
>>> nls97 = pd.read_csv("data/nls97b.csv")
>>> nls97.set_index("personid", inplace=True)
>>> landtemps = pd.read_csv("data/landtemps2019avgs.csv")
```

2. Use NumPy's `where` function to create a categorical series containing two values.

   First, do a quick check of the distribution of `elevation` values:

```
>>> landtemps.elevation.quantile(np.arange(0.2,1.1,0.2))
0.20        48.00
0.40       190.50
0.60       393.20
0.80     1,066.80
1.00     9,999.00
Name: elevation, dtype: float64
>>> landtemps['elevation_group'] = np.where(landtemps.
elevation>landtemps.elevation.quantile(0.8),'High','Low')
>>> landtemps.elevation_group = landtemps.elevation_
group.astype('category')
>>> landtemps.groupby(['elevation_group'])['elevation'].\
agg(['count','min','max'])
```

elevation_group	count	min	max
High	2409	1,067.00	9,999.00
Low	9686	-350.00	1,066.80

3. Use NumPy's `where` method to create a categorical series containing three values.

Set values above the 80th percentile to `'High'`, values above the median and up to the 80th percentile to `'Medium'`, and the remaining values to `'Low'`:

```
>>> landtemps.elevation.median()
271.3
>>> landtemps['elevation_group'] = np.where(landtemps.
elevation>
...    landtemps.elevation.quantile(0.8),'High',np.
where(landtemps.elevation>
...    landtemps.elevation.median(),'Medium','Low'))
>>> landtemps.elevation_group = landtemps.elevation_
group.astype('category')
>>> landtemps.groupby(['elevation_group'])['elevation'].
agg(['count','min','max'])
```

	count	min	max
elevation_group			
High	2409	1,067.00	9,999.00
Low	6056	-350.00	271.30
Medium	3630	271.40	1,066.80

4. Use NumPy's `select` method to evaluate a list of conditions.

First, set up a list of test conditions and another list for the result. We want individuals with a GPA less than 2 and no degree earned to be in one category, individuals with no degree but with a higher GPA to be in a second category, individuals with a degree but a low GPA in a third category, and the remaining individuals in a fourth category:

```
>>> test = [(nls97.gpaoverall<2) & (nls97.
highestdegree=='0. None'), nls97.highestdegree=='0.
None', nls97.gpaoverall<2]
>>> result = ['1. Low GPA and No Diploma','2. No
Diploma','3. Low GPA']
>>> nls97['hsachieve'] = np.select(test, result, '4. Did
Okay')
>>> nls97[['hsachieve','gpaoverall','highestdegree']].
head()
```

	hsachieve	gpaoverall	highestdegree
personid			
100061	4. Did Okay	3.06	2. High School
100139	4. Did Okay	nan	2. High School

```
100284      2. No Diploma            nan         0. None
100292      4. Did Okay            3.45     4. Bachelors
100583      4. Did Okay            2.91   2. High School
>>> nls97.hsachieve.value_counts().sort_index()
1. Low GPA and No Diploma       95
2. No Diploma                  858
3. Low GPA                     459
4. Did Okay                   7572
Name: hsachieve, dtype: int64
```

5. Use `lambda` to test several columns in one statement.

   The `colenr` columns have the enrollment status in February and October of each year for each person. We want to test whether any of the college enrollment columns have a value of 3. 4-year college. Use `filter` to create a DataFrame of the `colenr` columns. Then, use `apply` to call a `lambda` function that tests the first character of each `colenr` column. (We can just look at the first character and see whether it has a value of 3.) That is then passed to `any` to evaluate whether any (one or more) of the columns has a 3 as its first character. (We only show values for college enrollment between 2000 and 2004 due to space considerations, but we check all the values for the college college enrollment columns between 1997 and 2017.) This can be seen in the following code:

```
>>> nls97.loc[[100292,100583,100139],
'colenrfeb00':'colenroct04'].T
personid                  100292          100583
100139
colenrfeb00   1. Not enrolled   1. Not enrolled   1. Not
enrolled
colenroct00   3. 4-year college   1. Not enrolled   1. Not
enrolled
colenrfeb01   3. 4-year college   1. Not enrolled   1. Not
enrolled
colenroct01   3. 4-year college   3. 4-year college   1. Not
enrolled
colenrfeb02   3. 4-year college   3. 4-year college   1. Not
enrolled
colenroct02   3. 4-year college   1. Not enrolled   1. Not
enrolled
```

```
colenrfeb03    3. 4-year college    1. Not enrolled    1. Not
enrolled

colenroct03    3. 4-year college    1. Not enrolled    1. Not
enrolled

colenrfeb04    3. 4-year college    1. Not enrolled    1. Not
enrolled

colenroct04    1. Not enrolled      1. Not enrolled    1. Not
enrolled

>>> nls97['baenrollment'] = nls97.filter(like="colenr").\
...    apply(lambda x: x.str[0:1]=='3').\
...    any(axis=1)

>>>

>>> nls97.loc[[100292,100583,100139], ['baenrollment']].T
personid         100292    100583    100139
baenrollment     True      True      False

>>> nls97.baenrollment.value_counts()
False    5085
True     3899
Name: baenrollment, dtype: int64
```

6. Create a function that assigns a value based on the value of several series.

   The `getsleepdeprivedreason` function creates a variable that categorizes survey respondents by the possible reasons why they might get fewer than 6 hours of sleep a night. We base this on NLS survey responses about a respondent's employment status, the number of children who live with the respondent, wage income, and highest grade completed:

```
>>> def getsleepdeprivedreason(row):
...    sleepdeprivedreason = "Unknown"
...    if (row.nightlyhrssleep>=6):
...        sleepdeprivedreason = "Not Sleep Deprived"
...    elif (row.nightlyhrssleep>0):
...        if (row.weeksworked16+row.weeksworked17 < 80):
...            if (row.childathome>2):
...                sleepdeprivedreason = "Child Rearing"
...            else:
...                sleepdeprivedreason = "Other Reasons"
...        else:
```

```
...          if (row.wageincome>=62000 or row.
highestgradecompleted>=16):
...             sleepdeprivedreason = "Work Pressure"
...          else:
...             sleepdeprivedreason = "Income Pressure"
...       else:
...          sleepdeprivedreason = "Unknown"
...       return sleepdeprivedreason
...
```

7. Use `apply` to run the function for all rows:

```
>>> nls97['sleepdeprivedreason'] = nls97.
apply(getsleepdeprivedreason, axis=1)
>>> nls97.sleepdeprivedreason = nls97.
sleepdeprivedreason.astype('category')
>>> nls97.sleepdeprivedreason.value_counts()
Not Sleep Deprived      5595
Unknown                 2286
Income Pressure          462
Work Pressure            281
Other Reasons            272
Child Rearing             88
Name: sleepdeprivedreason, dtype: int64
```

The preceding steps demonstrate several techniques we can use to set the values for a series conditionally.

How it works...

If you have used `if-then-else` statements in SQL or Microsoft Excel, then NumPy's `where` should be familiar to you. It follows the form of `where` (test condition, clause if `True`, clause if `False`). In *step 2*, we tested whether the value of elevation for each row is greater than the value at the 80th percentile. If `True`, we return `'High'`. We return `'Low'` otherwise. This is a basic if-then-else construction.

Sometimes, we need to nest a test within a test. We did this in *step 3* to create three elevation groups; high, medium, and low. Instead of a simple statement in the `False` section (after the second comma), we used another `where` statement. This changes it from an `else` clause to an `else if` clause. It takes the form of `where`(test condition, statement if `True`, `where`(test condition, statement if `True`, statement if `False`)).

It is possible to add many more nested `where` statements, though that is not advisable. When we need to evaluate a slightly more complicated test, NumPy's `select` method comes in handy. In *step 4*, we passed a list of tests, as well as a list of results of that test, to `select`. We also provided a default value of `"4. Did Okay"` for any case where none of the tests was `True`. When multiple tests are `True`, the first one that is `True` is used.

Once the logic becomes even more complicated, we can use `apply`. The DataFrame `apply` method can be used to send each row of a DataFrame to a function by specifying `axis=1`. In *step 5*, we used `apply` to call a `lambda` function that tests whether the first character of each college enrollment value is 3. But first, we used the `filter` DataFrame method to select all the college enrollment columns. We explored how to select columns from a DataFrame in *Chapter 3, Taking the Measure of Your Data*.

In *steps 6* and *7*, we created a series that categorizes reasons for being sleep deprived based on weeks worked, the number of children living with the respondent, wage income, and highest grade completed. If the respondent did not work most of 2016 and 2017, and if more than two children lived with them, `sleepdeprivedreason` is set to `"Child Rearing"`. If the respondent did not work most of 2016 and 2017 and two or fewer children lived with them, `sleepdeprivedreason` is set to `"Other Reasons"`. If they worked most of 2016 and 2017, then `sleepdeprivedreason` is `"Work Pressure"` if she had either a high salary or completed 4 years of college, and is `"Income Pressure"` otherwise. Of course, these categories are somewhat contrived, but they do illustrate how to use a function to create a series based on complicated relationships between other series.

You may have noticed that we changed the data type of the new series we created to `category`. The new series was an `object` data type initially. We reduced memory usage by changing the type to `category`.

We used another incredibly useful method in *step 2*, somewhat incidentally. `landtemps. groupby(['elevation_group'])` creates a DataFrame groupby object that we pass to an aggregate (`agg`) function. This gives us a count, min, and max for each `elevation_group`, allowing us to confirm that our group classification works as expected.

There's more...

It has been a long time since I have had a data cleaning project that did not involve a NumPy `where` or `select` statement, nor a `lambda` or `apply` statement. At some point, we need to create or update a series based on values from one or more other series. It is a good idea to get comfortable with these techniques.

Whenever there is a built-in pandas function that does what we need, it is better to use that than `apply`. The great advantage of `apply` is that it is quite generic and flexible, but that is also why it is more resource-intensive than the optimized functions. However, it is a great tool when we want to create a series based on complicated relationships between existing series.

Another way to perform *steps 6 and 7* is to add a `lambda` function to `apply`. This produces the same results:

```
>>> def getsleepdeprivedreason(childathome,
nightlyhrssleep, wageincome, weeksworked16, weeksworked17,
highestgradecompleted):
...     sleepdeprivedreason = "Unknown"
...     if (nightlyhrssleep>=6):
...         sleepdeprivedreason = "Not Sleep Deprived"
...     elif (nightlyhrssleep>0):
...         if (weeksworked16+weeksworked17 < 80):
...             if (childathome>2):
...                 sleepdeprivedreason = "Child Rearing"
...             else:
...                 sleepdeprivedreason = "Other Reasons"
...         else:
...             if (wageincome>=62000 or highestgradecompleted>=16):
...                 sleepdeprivedreason = "Work Pressure"
...             else:
...                 sleepdeprivedreason = "Income Pressure"
...     else:
...         sleepdeprivedreason = "Unknown"
...     return sleepdeprivedreason
...
>>> nls97['sleepdeprivedreason'] = nls97.apply(lambda x:
getsleepdeprivedreason(x.childathome, x.nightlyhrssleep,
x.wageincome, x.weeksworked16, x.weeksworked17,
x.highestgradecompleted), axis=1)
```

See also

We'll go over DataFrame `groupby` objects in detail in *Chapter 7, Fixing Messy Data when Aggregating*. We examined various techniques we can use to select columns from a DataFrame, including `filter`, in *Chapter 3, Taking the Measure of Your Data*.

Evaluating and cleaning string series data

There are many string cleaning methods in Python and pandas. This is a good thing. Given the great variety of data stored in strings, it is important to have a wide range of tools to call upon when performing string evaluation and manipulation: when selecting fragments of a string by position, when checking whether a string contains a pattern, when splitting a string, when testing a string's length, when joining two or more strings, when changing the case of a string, and so on. We'll explore some of the methods that are used most frequently for string evaluation and cleaning in this recipe.

Getting ready

We will work with the National Longitudinal Survey data in this recipe. (The NLS data was actually a little too clean for this recipe. To illustrate working with strings with trailing spaces, I added trailing spaces to the `maritalstatus` column values.)

How to do it...

In this recipe, we will perform some common string evaluation and cleaning tasks. We'll use `contains`, `endswith`, and `findall` to search for patterns, trailing blanks, and more complicated patterns, respectively. We will also create a function for processing string values before assigning values to a new series and then use `replace` for simpler processing. Let's get started:

1. Import `pandas` and `numpy`, and then load the NLS data:

    ```
    >>> import pandas as pd
    >>> import numpy as np
    >>> nls97 = pd.read_csv("data/nls97c.csv")
    >>> nls97.set_index("personid", inplace=True)
    ```

2. Test whether a pattern exists in a string.

    Use `contains` to examine the `govprovidejobs` (whether the government should provide jobs) responses for the "Definitely not" and "Probably not" values. In the `where` call, handle missing values first to make sure that they do not end up in the first `else` clause (the section after the second comma):

    ```
    >>> nls97.govprovidejobs.value_counts()
    2. Probably          617
    3. Probably not      462
    1. Definitely        454
    ```

```
4. Definitely not      300
Name: govprovidejobs, dtype: int64
>>> nls97['govprovidejobsdefprob'] = np.where(nls97.
govprovidejobs.isnull(),
...      np.nan,np.where(nls97.govprovidejobs.str.
contains("not"),"No","Yes"))
>>> pd.crosstab(nls97.govprovidejobs, nls97.
govprovidejobsdefprob)
```

govprovidejobsdefprob	No	Yes
govprovidejobs		
1. Definitely	0	454
2. Probably	0	617
3. Probably not	462	0
4. Definitely not	300	0

3. Handle leading or trailing spaces in a string.

Create an ever-married series. First, examine the values of maritalstatus. Notice that there are two stray values, indicating married. Those two are "Married " with an extra space at the end, unlike the other values of "Married" with no trailing spaces. Use startswith and endswith to test for a leading or trailing space, respectively. Use strip to remove the trailing space before testing for ever-married. strip removes leading and trailing spaces (lstrip removes leading spaces, while rstrip removes trailing spaces, so rstrip would have also worked in this example):

```
>>> nls97.maritalstatus.value_counts()
Married          3064
Never-married    2766
Divorced          663
Separated         154
Widowed            23
Married             2
Name: maritalstatus, dtype: int64
>>> nls97.maritalstatus.str.startswith(' ').any()
False
>>> nls97.maritalstatus.str.endswith(' ').any()
True
```

```
>>> nls97['evermarried'] = np.where(nls97.maritalstatus.
isnull(),np.nan,np.where(nls97.maritalstatus.str.
strip()=="Never-married","No","Yes"))
```

```
>>> pd.crosstab(nls97.maritalstatus, nls97.evermarried)
```

evermarried	No	Yes
maritalstatus		
Divorced	0	663
Married	0	3064
Married	0	2
Never-married	2766	0
Separated	0	154
Widowed	0	23

4. Use isin to compare a string value to a list of values:

```
>>> nls97['receivedba'] = np.where(nls97.highestdegree.
isnull(),np.nan,np.where(nls97.highestdegree.str[0:1].
isin(['4','5','6','7']),"Yes","No"))
```

```
>>> pd.crosstab(nls97.highestdegree, nls97.receivedba)
```

receivedba	No	Yes
highestdegree		
0. None	953	0
1. GED	1146	0
2. High School	3667	0
3. Associates	737	0
4. Bachelors	0	1673
5. Masters	0	603
6. PhD	0	54
7. Professional	0	120

5. Use findall to extract numeric values from a text string.

Use findall to create a list of all numbers in the weeklyhrstv (hours spent each week watching television) string. The "\d+" regular expression that's passed to findall indicates that we just want numbers:

```
>>> pd.concat([nls97.weeklyhrstv.head(),\
...    nls97.weeklyhrstv.str.findall("\d+").head()],
axis=1)
                    weeklyhrstv weeklyhrstv
```

personid		
100061	11 to 20 hours a week	[11, 20]
100139	3 to 10 hours a week	[3, 10]
100284	11 to 20 hours a week	[11, 20]
100292	NaN	NaN
100583	3 to 10 hours a week	[3, 10]

6. Use the list created by `findall` to create a numeric series from the `weeklyhrstv` text.

First, define a function that retrieves the last element in the list created by `findall` for each value of `weeklyhrstv`. The `getnum` function also adjusts that number so that it's closer to the midpoint of the two numbers, where there is more than one number. We then use `apply` to call this function, passing it the list created by `findall` for each value. `crosstab` shows that the new `weeklyhrstvnum` column does what we want it to do:

```
>>> def getnum(numlist):
...     highval = 0
...     if (type(numlist) is list):
...         lastval = int(numlist[-1])
...         if (numlist[0]=='40'):
...             highval = 45
...         elif (lastval==2):
...             highval = 1
...         else:
...             highval = lastval - 5
...     else:
...         highval = np.nan
...     return highval
...
>>> nls97['weeklyhrstvnum'] = nls97.weeklyhrstv.str.\
...     findall("\d+").apply(getnum)
>>>
>>> pd.crosstab(nls97.weeklyhrstv, nls97.weeklyhrstvnum)
weeklyhrstvnum                    1.00    5.00    15.00    25.00
35.00   45.00
weeklyhrstv
```

11 to 20 hours a week 0 0	0	0	1145	0
21 to 30 hours a week 0 0	0	0	0	299
3 to 10 hours a week 0 0	0	3625	0	0
31 to 40 hours a week 116 0	0	0	0	0
Less than 2 hours per week 0 0	1350	0	0	0
More than 40 hours a week 0 176	0	0	0	0

7. Replace the values in a series with alternative values.

The `weeklyhrscomputer` (hours spent each week on a computer) series does not sort nicely with its current values. We can fix this by replacing the values with letters that indicate order. We'll start by creating a list containing the old values and another list containing the new values that we want. We then use the series `replace` method to replace the old values with the new values. Whenever `replace` finds a value from the old values list, it replaces it with a value from the same list position in the new list:

```
>>> comphrsold = ['None','Less than 1 hour a week',
...    '1 to 3 hours a week','4 to 6 hours a week',
...    '7 to 9 hours a week','10 hours or more a week']
>>>
>>> comphrsnew = ['A. None','B. Less than 1 hour a week',
...    'C. 1 to 3 hours a week','D. 4 to 6 hours a week',
...    'E. 7 to 9 hours a week','F. 10 hours or more a
week']
>>>
>>> nls97.weeklyhrscomputer.value_counts().sort_index()
1 to 3 hours a week          733
10 hours or more a week     3669
4 to 6 hours a week          726
7 to 9 hours a week          368
Less than 1 hour a week      296
None                         918
Name: weeklyhrscomputer, dtype: int64
```

```
>>> nls97.weeklyhrscomputer.replace(comphrsold,
comphrsnew, inplace=True)
>>> nls97.weeklyhrscomputer.value_counts().sort_index()
A. None                              918
B. Less than 1 hour a week           296
C. 1 to 3 hours a week               733
D. 4 to 6 hours a week               726
E. 7 to 9 hours a week               368
F. 10 hours or more a week          3669
Name: weeklyhrscomputer, dtype: int64
```

The steps in this recipe demonstrate some of the common string evaluation and manipulation tasks we can perform in pandas.

How it works...

We frequently need to examine a string to see whether a pattern is there. We can use the string `contains` method to do this. If we know exactly where the expected pattern will be, we can use standard slice notation, `[start:stop:step]`, to select text from start through stop-1. (The default value for `step` is 1.) For example, in *step 4*, we got the first character from `highestdegree` with `nls97.highestdegree.str[0:1]`. We then used `isin` to test whether the first string appears in a list of values. (`isin` works for both character and numeric data.)

Sometimes, we need to pull multiple values from a string that satisfy a condition. `findall` is helpful in those situations as it returns a list of all values satisfying the condition. It can be paired with a regular expression when we are looking for something more general than a literal. In *steps 5* and *6*, we were looking for any number.

There's more...

It is important to be deliberate when we're handling missing values when creating a series based on values for another series. Missing values may satisfy the `else` condition in a `where` call when that is not our intention. In *steps 2, 3,* and *4*, we made sure that we handled the missing values appropriately by testing for them at the beginning of the `where` call.

We also need to be careful about case when making string comparisons. For example, "Probably" and "probably" are not equal. One way to get around this is to use the `upper` or `lower` methods when doing comparisons when a potential difference in case is not meaningful. `upper("Probably") == upper("PROBABLY")` is actually True.

Working with dates

Working with dates is rarely straightforward. Data analysts need to successfully parse date values, identify invalid or out-of-range dates, impute dates when they're missing, and calculate time intervals. There are surprising hurdles at each of these steps, but we are halfway there once we've parsed the date value and have a datetime value in pandas. We will start by parsing date values in this recipe before working our way through the other challenges.

Getting ready

We will work with the National Longitudinal Survey and COVID case daily data in this recipe. The COVID daily data contains one row for each reporting day for each country. (The NLS data was actually a little too clean for this purpose. To illustrate working with missing date values, I set one of the values for birth month to missing.)

> **Data note**
>
> Our World in Data provides COVID-19 public use data at `https://ourworldindata.org/coronavirus-source-data`. The data that will be used in this recipe was downloaded on July 18, 2020.

How to do it...

In this recipe, we will convert numeric data into datetime data, first by confirming that the data has valid date values and then by using `fillna` to replace missing dates. We will then calculate some date intervals; that is, the age of respondents for the NLS data and the days since the first COVID case for the COVID daily data. Let's get started:

1. Import `pandas`, `numpy`, and the `datetime` module, and then load the NLS and COVID case daily data:

```
>>> import pandas as pd
>>> import numpy as np
>>> from datetime import datetime
>>> covidcases = pd.read_csv("data/covidcases720.csv")
>>> nls97 = pd.read_csv("data/nls97c.csv")
>>> nls97.set_index("personid", inplace=True)
```

2. Show the birth month and year values.

Notice that there is one missing value for birth month. Other than that, the data that we will use to create the `birthdate` series look pretty clean:

```
>>> nls97[['birthmonth','birthyear']].isnull().sum()
birthmonth    1
birthyear     0
dtype: int64
>>> nls97.birthmonth.value_counts().sort_index()
1      815
2      693
3      760
4      659
5      689
6      720
7      762
8      782
9      839
10     765
11     763
12     736
Name: birthmonth, dtype: int64
>>> nls97.birthyear.value_counts().sort_index()
1980     1691
1981     1874
1982     1841
1983     1807
1984     1771
Name: birthyear, dtype: int64
```

3. Use the series `fillna` method to set a value for the missing birth month.

Pass the average of `birthmonth`, rounded to the nearest integer, to `fillna`. This will replace the missing value for `birthmonth` with the mean of `birthmonth`. Notice that one more person now has a value of 6 for `birthmonth`:

```
>>> nls97.birthmonth.fillna(int(nls97.birthmonth.mean()),
inplace=True)
>>> nls97.birthmonth.value_counts().sort_index()
```

1	815
2	693
3	760
4	659
5	689
6	721
7	762
8	782
9	839
10	765
11	763
12	736

4. Use month and date integers to create a datetime column.

We can pass a dictionary to the pandas to_datetime function. The dictionary needs to contain a key for year, month, and day. Notice that there are no missing values for birthmonth, birthyear, and birthdate:

```
>>> nls97['birthdate'] = pd.to_datetime(dict(year=nls97.
birthyear, month=nls97.birthmonth, day=15))
>>> nls97[['birthmonth','birthyear','birthdate']].head()
          birthmonth  birthyear  birthdate
personid
100061             5       1980  1980-05-15
100139             9       1983  1983-09-15
100284            11       1984  1984-11-15
100292             4       1982  1982-04-15
100583             6       1980  1980-06-15
>>> nls97[['birthmonth','birthyear','birthdate']].
isnull().sum()
birthmonth    0
birthyear     0
birthdate     0
dtype: int64
```

5. Calculate age values using a `datetime` column.

    First, define a function that will calculate age values when given a start date and an end date:

```
>>> def calcage(startdate, enddate):
...     age = enddate.year - startdate.year
...     if (enddate.month<startdate.month or (enddate.
month==startdate.month and enddate.day<startdate.day)):
...       age = age -1
...     return age
...
>>> rundate = pd.to_datetime('2020-07-20')
>>> nls97["age"] = nls97.apply(lambda x: calcage(x.
birthdate, rundate), axis=1)
>>> nls97.loc[100061:100583, ['age','birthdate']]
          age   birthdate
personid
100061    40    1980-05-15
100139    36    1983-09-15
100284    35    1984-11-15
100292    38    1982-04-15
100583    40    1980-06-15
```

6. Convert a string column into a datetime column.

    The `casedate` column is an `object` data type, not a `datetime` data type:

```
>>> covidcases.iloc[:, 0:6].dtypes
iso_code        object
continent       object
location        object
casedate        object
total_cases     float64
new_cases       float64
dtype: object
>>> covidcases.iloc[:, 0:6].sample(2, random_state=1).T
                13482              2445
iso_code        IMN                BRB
continent       Europe   North America
```

location	Isle of Man	Barbados
casedate	2020-06-20	2020-04-28
total_cases	336	80
new_cases	0	1

```
>>> covidcases['casedate'] = pd.to_datetime(covidcases.
casedate, format='%Y-%m-%d')
>>> covidcases.iloc[:, 0:6].dtypes
```

iso_code	object
continent	object
location	object
casedate	datetime64[ns]
total_cases	float64
new_cases	float64
dtype: object	

7. Show descriptive statistics on the `datetime` column:

```
>>> covidcases.casedate.describe()
```

count	29529
unique	195
top	2020-05-23 00:00:00
freq	209
first	2019-12-31 00:00:00
last	2020-07-12 00:00:00
Name: casedate, dtype: object	

8. Create a `timedelta` object to capture a date interval.

For each day, calculate the number of days since the first case was reported for each country. First, create a DataFrame that shows the first day of new cases for each country and then merge it with the full COVID cases data. Then, for each day, calculate the number of days from `firstcasedate` to `casedate`. Notice that one country started reporting data 62 days before its first case:

```
>>> firstcase = covidcases.loc[covidcases.new_
cases>0,['location','casedate']].\
...     sort_values(['location','casedate']).\
...     drop_duplicates(['location'], keep='first').\
...     rename(columns={'casedate':'firstcasedate'})
>>>
```

```
>>> covidcases = pd.merge(covidcases, firstcase, left_
on=['location'], right_on=['location'], how="left")
>>> covidcases['dayssincefirstcase'] = covidcases.
casedate - covidcases.firstcasedate
>>> covidcases.dayssincefirstcase.describe()
count                              29529
mean         56 days 00:15:12.892410
std          47 days 00:35:41.813685
min             -62 days +00:00:00
25%              21 days 00:00:00
50%              57 days 00:00:00
75%              92 days 00:00:00
max             194 days 00:00:00
Name: dayssincefirstcase, dtype: object
```

This recipe showed how it's possible to parse date values and create a datetime series, as well as how to calculate time intervals.

How it works...

The first task when working with dates in pandas is converting them properly into a pandas datetime series. We tackled a couple of the most common issues in *steps 3*, *4*, and 6: missing values, date conversion from integer parts, and date conversion from strings. birthmonth and birthyear are integers in the NLS data. We confirmed that those values are valid values for dates of months and years. If, for example, there were month values of 0 or 20, the conversion to pandas datetime would fail.

Missing values for birthmonth or birthyear will just result in a missing birthdate. We used fillna for the missing value for birthmonth, assigning it to the mean value of birthmonth. In *step 5*, we calculated an age for each person as of July 20, 2020 using the new birthdate column. The calcage function that we created adjusts for individuals whose birth dates come later in the year than July 20.

Data analysts often receive data files containing date values as strings. The to_datetime function is the analyst's key ally when this happens. It is often smart enough to figure out the format of the string date data without us having to specify a format explicitly. However, in *step 6*, we told to_datetime to use the "%Y-%m-%d" format with our data.

Step 7 told us that there were 195 unique days where COVID cases were reported and that the most frequent day is May 23. The first reported day is Dec 31, 2019 and the last is July 12, 2020. This is what we expected.

The first two statements in *step 8* involved techniques (sorting and dropping duplicates) that we will not explore in detail until *Chapter 7*, *Fixing Messy Data when Aggregating*, and *Chapter 8*, *Addressing Data Issues when Combining DataFrames*. All you need to understand here is the objective: creating a DataFrame with one row per `location` (country), and with the date of the first reported COVID case. We did this by only selecting rows from the full data where `new_cases` is greater than 0, before sorting that by `location` and `casedate` and keeping the first row for each `location`. We then changed the name of `casedate` to `firstcasedate` before merging the new `firstcase` DataFrame with the COVID daily cases data.

Since both `casedate` and `firstcasedate` are datetime columns, subtracting the latter from the former will result in a `timedelta` value. This gives us a series that is the number of days before or after the first day of `new_cases` for each reporting day. So, if a country started reporting on COVID cases 3 weeks before its first new case, it would have -21 days for the value of `dayssincefirstcase` for that first day. This is useful if we want to track trends by how long the virus has been obviously present in a country, rather than by date.

See also

Instead of using `sort_values` and `drop_duplicates` in *step 8*, we could have used `groupby` to achieve similar results. We'll explore `groupby` a fair bit in the next *Chapter 7*, *Fixing Messy Data when Aggregating*. This is the first time we have done a merge in this book, but it is far from the last time we will be combining DataFrames. *Chapter 8*, *Addressing Data Issues when Combining DataFrames*, will be devoted to this topic. We'll explore more strategies for handling missing data in the next two recipes.

Identifying and cleaning missing data

We have already explored some strategies for identifying and cleaning missing values, particularly in *Chapter 1*, *Anticipating Data Cleaning Issues when Importing Tabular Data into pandas*. We will polish up on those skills in this recipe. We will do this by exploring a full range of strategies for handling missing data, including using DataFrame means and group means, as well as forward filling with nearby values. In the next recipe, we impute values using *k*-nearest neighbor.

Getting ready

We will continue working with the National Longitudinal Survey data in this recipe.

How to do it...

In this recipe, we will check key demographic and school record columns for missing values. We'll then use several strategies to impute values for missing data: assigning the overall mean for that column, assigning a group mean, and assigning the value of the nearest preceding non-missing value. Let's get started:

1. Import `pandas` and load the NLS data:

```
>>> import pandas as pd
>>> nls97 = pd.read_csv("data/nls97c.csv")
>>> nls97.set_index("personid", inplace=True)
```

2. Set up school record and demographic DataFrames from the NLS data:

```
>>> schoolrecordlist =
['satverbal','satmath','gpaoverall','gpaenglish',
...    'gpamath','gpascience','highestdegree',
'highestgradecompleted']
>>> demolist =
['maritalstatus','childathome','childnotathome',
...    'wageincome','weeklyhrscomputer','weeklyhrstv',
'nightlyhrssleep']
>>> schoolrecord = nls97[schoolrecordlist]
>>> demo = nls97[demolist]
>>> schoolrecord.shape
(8984, 8)
>>> demo.shape
(8984, 7)
```

3. Check data for missing values.

Check the number of missing values for each column in the `schoolrecord` DataFrame. `isnull` returns a Boolean series with `True` when values for that column are missing, and `False` otherwise. When chained with `sum`, a count of `True` values is returned. By setting `axis=1`, we can check the number of missing values for each row. 11 individuals have missing values for all 8 columns, and 946 have missing values for 7 out of 8 columns. Upon taking a look at the data for a few of these individuals, it looks like they mainly have `highestdegree` and no valid values for other columns:

```
>>> schoolrecord.isnull().sum(axis=0)
satverbal                    7578
```

satmath	7577
gpaoverall	2980
gpaenglish	3186
gpamath	3218
gpascience	3300
highestdegree	31
highestgradecompleted	2321

```
dtype: int64
>>> misscnt = schoolrecord.isnull().sum(axis=1)
>>> misscnt.value_counts().sort_index()
```

0	1087
1	312
2	3210
3	1102
4	176
5	101
6	2039
7	946
8	11

```
dtype: int64
>>> schoolrecord.loc[misscnt>=7].head(4).T
```

personid	101705	102061	102648	104627
satverbal	NaN	NaN	NaN	NaN
satmath	NaN	NaN	NaN	NaN
gpaoverall	NaN	NaN	NaN	NaN
gpaenglish	NaN	NaN	NaN	NaN
gpamath	NaN	NaN	NaN	NaN
gpascience	NaN	NaN	NaN	NaN
highestdegree	1. GED	0. None	1. GED	0. None
highestgradecompleted	NaN	NaN	NaN	NaN

4. Remove rows where nearly all the data is missing.

Here, we use the dropna DataFrame method with thresh set to 2. This removes rows with less than two non-missing values (those with seven or eight missing values):

```
>>> schoolrecord = schoolrecord.dropna(thresh=2)
>>> schoolrecord.shape
```

```
(8027, 8)
>>> schoolrecord.isnull().sum(axis=1).value_counts().
sort_index()
0    1087
1     312
2    3210
3    1102
4     176
5     101
6    2039
dtype: int64
```

5. Assign the mean of the GPA values where it's missing:

```
>>> int(schoolrecord.gpaoverall.mean())
2
>>> schoolrecord.gpaoverall.isnull().sum()
2023
>>> schoolrecord.gpaoverall.fillna(int(schoolrecord.
gpaoverall.mean()), inplace=True)
>>> schoolrecord.gpaoverall.isnull().sum()
0
```

6. Use forward fill to replace missing values.

Use the `ffill` option with `fillna` to replace missing values with the nearest non-missing value preceding it in the data:

```
>>> demo.wageincome.head().T
personid
100061     12,500
100139    120,000
100284     58,000
100292        nan
100583     30,000
Name: wageincome, dtype: float64
>>> demo.wageincome.isnull().sum()
3893
```

```
>>> nls97.wageincome.fillna(method='ffill', inplace=True)
>>> demo = nls97[demolist]
>>> demo.wageincome.head().T
personid
100061    12,500
100139   120,000
100284    58,000
100292    58,000
100583    30,000
Name: wageincome, dtype: float64
>>> demo.wageincome.isnull().sum()
0
```

7. Fill missing values with the mean by group.

Create a DataFrame containing the average value of weeks worked in 2017 by the highest degree they've earned. Merge that with the NLS data, then use `fillna` to replace the missing values for weeks worked with the mean for that individual's highest degree earned group:

```
>>> nls97[['highestdegree','weeksworked17']].head()
                highestdegree  weeksworked17
personid
100061        2. High School             48
100139        2. High School             52
100284              0. None              0
100292          4. Bachelors            nan
100583        2. High School             52
>>>
>>> workbydegree = nls97.groupby(['highestdegree'])
['weeksworked17'].mean().\
...      reset_index().
rename(columns={'weeksworked17':'meanweeksworked17'})
>>>
>>> nls97 = nls97.reset_index().\
...      merge(workbydegree, left_on=['highestdegree'],
right_on=['highestdegree'], how='left').set_
index('personid')
```

```
>>>
>>> nls97.weeksworked17.fillna(nls97.meanweeksworked17,
inplace=True)
>>> nls97[['highestdegree','weeksworked17',
'meanweeksworked17']].head()
         highestdegree   weeksworked17
meanweeksworked17
personid
100061    2. High School              48
38
100139    2. High School              52
38
100284           0. None               0
29
100292       4. Bachelors             44
44
100583    2. High School              52
38
```

The preceding steps demonstrated several different approaches we can use to replace missing series values.

How it works...

By shifting the axis when using `isnull`, we can check for missing values column-wise or row-wise. In the latter case, rows with almost all missing data are good candidates for removal. In the former case, where there are particular columns that have missing values but also a fair bit of good data, we can think about imputation strategies.

The very useful `grouby` DataFrame method is used once more in this recipe. By using it in *step 7* to create a DataFrame with a summary statistic by group (in this case, the group mean for weeks worked), we can use those values to improve our data cleaning work. This merge is a little more complicated because, usually, we would lose the index with this kind of merge (we are not merging by the index). We reset the index and then set it again so that it is still available to us in the subsequent statements in that step.

There's more...

We explored several imputation strategies in this recipe, such as setting missing values to the overall mean, setting them to the mean for a particular group, and forward filling values. Which one is appropriate for a given data cleaning task is, of course, determined by your data.

Forward filling makes the most sense with time series data, with the assumption being that the missing value is most likely to be near the value of the immediately preceding time period. But forward filling may also make sense when missing values are rare and spread somewhat randomly throughout the data. When you have reason to believe that the data values for rows near each other have more in common with each other than they do with the overall mean, forward filling might be a better choice than the mean. For this same reason, a group mean might be a better option than both, assuming that the variable of interest varies significantly with group membership.

See also

This discussion leads us to another missing value imputation strategy: using machine learning techniques such as *k*-**nearest neighbor** (**KNN**). The next recipe demonstrates the use of KNN to clean missing data.

Missing value imputation with *K*-nearest neighbor

KNN is a popular machine learning technique because it is intuitive and easy to run and yields good results when there is not a large number of features (variables) and observations. For the same reasons, it is often used to impute missing values. As its name suggests, KNN identifies the *k* observations whose features are most similar to each observation. When used to impute missing values, KNN uses the nearest neighbors to determine what fill values to use.

Getting ready

We will work with the National Longitudinal Survey data again in this recipe, and then try to impute reasonable values for the same school record data that we worked with in the preceding recipe.

You will need scikit-learn to run the code in this recipe. You can install it by entering `pip install sklearn` in a Terminal or Windows PowerShell.

How to do it...

In this recipe, we will use scikit-learn's `KNNImputer` module to fill in missing values for key NLS school record columns. Let's get started:

1. Import `pandas` and scikit-learn's `KNNImputer` module, and then load the NLS data:

```
>>> import pandas as pd
>>> from sklearn.impute import KNNImputer
>>> nls97 = pd.read_csv("data/nls97c.csv")
>>> nls97.set_index("personid", inplace=True)
```

2. Select the NLS school record data:

```
>>> schoolrecordlist =
['satverbal','satmath','gpaoverall','gpaenglish',
...    'gpamath','gpascience','highestgradecompleted']
>>> schoolrecord = nls97[schoolrecordlist]
```

3. Initialize a KNN imputation model and fill in the values:

```
>>> impKNN = KNNImputer(n_neighbors=5)
>>> newvalues = impKNN.fit_transform(schoolrecord)
>>> schoolrecordimp = pd.DataFrame(newvalues,
columns=schoolrecordlist, index=schoolrecord.index)
```

4. View the imputed values:

```
>>> schoolrecord.head().T
```

personid	100061	100139	100284	100292	100583
satverbal	nan	nan	nan	nan	nan
satmath	nan	nan	nan	nan	nan
gpaoverall	3.1	nan	nan	3.5	2.9
gpaenglish	350.0	nan	nan	345.0	283.0
gpamath	280.0	nan	nan	370.0	285.0

gpascience 240.0	315.0	nan	nan	300.0
highestgradecompleted 13.0	13.0	12.0	7.0	nan

```
>>> schoolrecordimp.head().T
```

personid 100583	100061	100139	100284	100292
satverbal 414.0	446.0	412.0	290.8	534.0
satmath 454.0	460.0	470.0	285.2	560.0
gpaoverall 2.9	3.1	2.3	2.5	3.5
gpaenglish 283.0	350.0	232.4	136.0	345.0
gpamath 285.0	280.0	218.0	244.6	370.0
gpascience 240.0	315.0	247.8	258.0	300.0
highestgradecompleted 13.0	13.0	12.0	7.0	9.8

5. Compare the summary statistics:

```
>>> schoolrecord[['gpaoverall','highestgradecompleted']].
agg(['mean','count'])
```

	gpaoverall	highestgradecompleted
mean	2.8	14.1
count	6,004.0	6,663.0

```
>>>
schoolrecordimp[['gpaoverall','highestgradecompleted']].
agg(['mean','count'])
```

	gpaoverall	highestgradecompleted
mean	2.8	13.5
count	8,984.0	8,984.0

This recipe showed us how to use KNN for missing values imputation.

How it works...

Almost all the work in this recipe was done in *step 3*, where we initialized the KNN imputer. The only decision we need to make here is what value the nearest neighbor will have. We chose 5 here, a reasonable value for a DataFrame of this size. Then, we passed the `schoolrecord` DataFrame to the `fit_transform` method, which returns an array of new DataFrame values. The array retains the non-missing values but has imputed values where they were missing. We then loaded the array into a new DataFrame, using the column names and index from the original DataFrame.

We got a good look at the new values in *steps 4* and *5*. All of the missing values have been replaced. There is also little change in the means for `gpaoverall` and `highestgradecompleted`.

There's more...

We are probably asking KNN to do too much work here since a few rows of data have very little information we can use for imputation. We should consider dropping rows from the DataFrame that contain fewer than two or three non-missing values.

See also

KNN is also often used to detect outliers in data. The *Using k-nearest neighbor to find outliers* recipe in *Chapter 4, Identifying Missing Values and Outliers in Subsets of Data*, demonstrates this.

7
Fixing Messy Data when Aggregating

Earlier chapters of this book introduced techniques for generating summary statistics on a whole DataFrame. We used methods such as `describe`, `mean`, and `quantile` to do that. This chapter covers more complicated aggregation tasks: aggregating by categorical variables, and using aggregation to change the structure of DataFrames.

After the initial stages of data cleaning, analysts spend a substantial amount of their time doing what Hadley Wickham has called *splitting-applying-combining*. That is, we subset data by groups, apply some operation to those subsets, and then draw conclusions about a dataset as a whole. In slightly more specific terms, this involves generating descriptive statistics by key categorical variables. For the `nls97` dataset, this might be gender, marital status, and highest degree received. For the COVID-19 data, we might segment the data by country or date.

Often, we need to aggregate data to prepare it for subsequent analysis. Sometimes, the rows of a DataFrame are disaggregated beyond the desired unit of analysis, and some aggregation has to be done before analysis can begin. For example, our DataFrame might have bird sightings by species per day over the course of many years. Since those values jump around, we might decide to smooth that out by working only with the total sightings by species per month, or even per year. Another example is households and car repair expenditures. We might need to summarize those expenditures over a year.

There are several ways to aggregate data using NumPy and pandas, each with particular strengths. We explore the most useful approaches in this chapter; from looping with `itertuples`, to navigating over NumPy arrays, to several techniques using the DataFrame `groupby` method. It is helpful to have a good understanding of the full range of tools available in pandas and NumPy since: almost all data analysis projects require some aggregation; aggregation is among the most consequential steps we take in the data cleaning process; and the best tool for the job is determined more by the attributes of the data than by our personal preferences.

Specifically, the recipes in this chapter examine the following:

- Looping through data with `itertuples` (an anti-pattern)
- Calculating summaries by group with NumPy arrays
- Using `groupby` to organize data by groups
- Using more complicated aggregation functions with `groupby`
- Using user-defined functions and `apply` with `groupby`
- Using `groupby` to change the unit of analysis of a DataFrame

Technical requirements

The code and notebooks for this chapter are available on GitHub at `https://github.com/PacktPublishing/Python-Data-Cleaning-Cookbook`

Looping through data with itertuples (an anti-pattern)

In this recipe, we will iterate over the rows of a DataFrame and generate our own totals for a variable. In subsequent recipes in this chapter we will use NumPy arrays, and then some pandas-specific techniques, for accomplishing the same tasks.

It may seem odd to begin this chapter with a technique that we are often cautioned against using. But I used to do the equivalent of looping every day 30 years ago in SAS, and on select occasions as recently as 7 years ago in R. That is why I still find myself thinking conceptually about iterating over rows of data, sometimes sorted by groups, even though I rarely implement my code in this manner. I think it is good to hold onto that conceptualization, even when using other pandas methods that work for us more efficiently.

I do not want to leave the impression that pandas-specific techniques are always markedly more efficient either. pandas users probably find themselves using `apply` more than they would like, an approach that is only somewhat faster than looping.

Finally, I should add that if your DataFrame has fewer than 10,000 rows then the efficiency gains from using pandas-specific techniques, rather than looping, are likely to be minimal. In that case, analysts should choose the approach that is most intuitive and resistant to errors.

Getting ready

We will work with the COVID-19 case daily data in this recipe. It has one row per day per country, each row having the number of new cases and new deaths for that day. It reflects the totals as of July 18, 2020.

We will also be working with land temperature data from 87 weather stations in Brazil in 2019. Most weather stations had one temperature reading for each month.

Data note

Our World in Data provides Covid-19 public use data at `https://ourworldindata.org/coronavirus-source-data`.

The land temperature data is taken from the *Global Historical Climatology Network* integrated database, which is made available for public use by the United States National Oceanic and Atmospheric Administration at `https://www.ncdc.noaa.gov/data-access/land-based-station-data/land-based-datasets/global-historical-climatology-network-monthly-version-4`. Only data for Brazil in 2019 is used in this recipe.

How to do it...

We will use the `itertuples` DataFrame method to loop over the rows of the COVID-19 daily data and the monthly land temperature data for Brazil. We add logic for handling missing data and unexpected changes in key variable values from one period to the next:

1. Import `pandas` and `numpy`, and load the COVID-19 and land temperature data:

```
>>> import pandas as pd
>>> import numpy as np
>>> coviddaily = pd.read_csv("data/coviddaily720.csv",
parse_dates=["casedate"])
>>> ltbrazil = pd.read_csv("data/ltbrazil.csv")
```

2. Sort data by location and date:

```
>>> coviddaily = coviddaily.sort_
values(['location','casedate'])
```

3. Iterate over rows with `itertuples`.

    Use `itertuples`, which allows us to iterate over all rows as named tuples. Sum new cases over all dates for each country. With each change of country (`location`) append the running total to `rowlist`, and then set the count to `0`: (Note that `rowlist` is a list and we are appending a dictionary to `rowlist` with each change of country. A list of dictionaries is a good place to temporarily store data you might eventually want to convert to a DataFrame.):

```
>>> prevloc = 'ZZZ'
>>> rowlist = []
>>>
>>> for row in coviddaily.itertuples():
...     if (prevloc!=row.location):
...         if (prevloc!='ZZZ'):
...             rowlist.append({'location':prevloc,
    'casecnt':casecnt})
...         casecnt = 0
...         prevloc = row.location
...     casecnt += row.new_cases
...
>>> rowlist.append({'location':prevloc,
'casecnt':casecnt})
>>> len(rowlist)
209
>>> rowlist[0:4]
[{'location': 'Afghanistan', 'casecnt': 34451.0},
{'location': 'Albania', 'casecnt': 3371.0}, {'location':
'Algeria', 'casecnt': 18712.0}, {'location': 'Andorra',
'casecnt': 855.0}]
```

4. Create a DataFrame from the list of summary values, `rowlist`.

    Pass the list we created in the previous step to the pandas `DataFrame` method:

```
>>> covidtotals = pd.DataFrame(rowlist)
>>> covidtotals.head()
```

	location	casecnt
0	Afghanistan	34,451
1	Albania	3,371
2	Algeria	18,712
3	Andorra	855
4	Angola	483

5. Sort the land temperature data.

Also, drop rows with missing values for temperatures:

```
>>> ltbrazil = ltbrazil.sort_values(['station','month'])
>>> ltbrazil = ltbrazil.dropna(subset=['temperature'])
```

6. Exclude rows where there is a large change from one period to the next.

Calculate the average temperature for the year, excluding values for a temperature more than 3°C greater than or less than the temperature for the previous month:

```
>>> prevstation = 'ZZZ'
>>> prevtemp = 0
>>> rowlist = []
>>>
>>> for row in ltbrazil.itertuples():
...     if (prevstation!=row.station):
...         if (prevstation!='ZZZ'):
...             rowlist.append({'station':prevstation,
'avgtemp':tempcnt/stationcnt, 'stationcnt':stationcnt})
...         tempcnt = 0
...         stationcnt = 0
...         prevstation = row.station
...     # choose only rows that are within 3 degrees of the
previous temperature
...     if ((0 <= abs(row.temperature-prevtemp) <= 3) or
(stationcnt==0)):
...         tempcnt += row.temperature
...         stationcnt += 1
...     prevtemp = row.temperature
...
>>> rowlist.append({'station':prevstation,
'avgtemp':tempcnt/stationcnt, 'stationcnt':stationcnt})
```

```
>>> rowlist[0:5]
```
```
[{'station': 'ALTAMIRA', 'avgtemp': 28.310000000000002,
 'stationcnt': 5}, {'station': 'ALTA_FLORESTA_AERO',
 'avgtemp': 29.433636363636367, 'stationcnt': 11},
 {'station': 'ARAXA', 'avgtemp': 21.612499999999997,
 'stationcnt': 4}, {'station': 'BACABAL', 'avgtemp':
 29.75, 'stationcnt': 4}, {'station': 'BAGE', 'avgtemp':
 20.366666666666664, 'stationcnt': 9}]
```

7. Create a DataFrame from the summary values.

    Pass the list we created in the previous step to the pandas `DataFrame` method:

```
>>> ltbrazilavgs = pd.DataFrame(rowlist)
>>> ltbrazilavgs.head()
```

	station	avgtemp	stationcnt
0	ALTAMIRA	28.31	5
1	ALTA_FLORESTA_AERO	29.43	11
2	ARAXA	21.61	4
3	BACABAL	29.75	4
4	BAGE	20.37	9

This gives us a DataFrame with average temperatures for 2019 and the number of observations for each station.

How it works...

After sorting the Covid daily data by `location` and `casedate` in *Step 2*, we loop through our data one row at a time and do a running tally of new cases in *Step 3*. We set that tally back to 0 when we get to a new country, and then resume counting. Notice that we do not actually append our summary of new cases until we get to the next country. This is because there is no way to tell that we are on the last row for any country until we get to the next country. That is not a problem because we append the summary to `rowlist` right before we reset the value to 0. That also means that we need to do something special to output the totals for the last country since there is no next country reached. We do this with a final append after the loop is complete. This is a fairly standard approach to looping through data and outputting totals by group.

The summary DataFrame we create in *Steps 3* and *4* can be created more efficiently, both in terms of the analyst's time and our computer's workload, with other pandas techniques that we cover in this chapter. But that becomes a more difficult call when we need to do more complicated calculations, particularly those that involve comparing values across rows.

Steps 6 and *7* provide an example of this. We want to calculate the average temperature for each station for the year. Most stations have one reading per month. But we are concerned that there might be some outlier values for temperature, defined here by a change of more than 3°C from one month to the next. We want to exclude those readings from the calculation of the mean for each station. It is fairly straightforward to do that while iterating over the data by storing the previous value for temperature (`prevtemp`) and comparing it to the current value.

There's more...

We could have used `iterrows` in *Step 3* rather than `itertuples`, with almost exactly the same syntax. Since we do not need the functionality of `iterrows` here, we use `itertuples`. `itertuples` is easier on system resources than `iterrows`.

The hardest tasks to complete when working with tabular data involve calculations across rows: summing data across rows, basing a calculation on values in a different row, and generating running totals. Such calculations are complicated to implement and resource-intensive, regardless of language. But it is hard to avoid having to do them, particularly when working with panel data. Some values for variables in a given period might be determined by values in a previous period. This is often more complicated than the running totals we have done in this recipe.

For decades, data analysts have tried to address these data-cleaning challenges by looping through rows, carefully inspecting categorical and summary variables for data problems, and then handling the summation accordingly. Although this continues to be the approach that provides the most flexibility, pandas provides a number of data aggregation tools that run more efficiently and are easier to code. The challenge is to match the ability of looping solutions to adjust for invalid, incomplete, or atypical data. We explore these tools later in this chapter.

Calculating summaries by group with NumPy arrays

We can accomplish much of what we did in the previous recipe with `itertuples` using NumPy arrays. We can also use NumPy arrays to get summary values for subsets of our data.

Getting ready

We will work again with the COVID-19 case daily data and the Brazil land temperature data.

How to do it...

We copy DataFrame values to a NumPy array. We then navigate over the array, calculating totals by group and checking for unexpected changes in values:

1. Import `pandas` and `numpy`, and load the Covid and land temperature data:

```
>>> import pandas as pd
>>> import numpy as np
>>> coviddaily = pd.read_csv("data/coviddaily720.csv",
parse_dates=["casedate"])
>>> ltbrazil = pd.read_csv("data/ltbrazil.csv")
```

2. Create a list of locations:

```
>>> loclist = coviddaily.location.unique().tolist()
```

3. Use a NumPy array to calculate sums by location.

   Create a NumPy array of the location and new cases data. We then can iterate over the location list we created in the previous step, and select all new case values (`casevalues[j][1]`) for each location (`casevalues[j][0]`). We then sum the new case values for that location:

```
>>> rowlist = []
>>> casevalues = coviddaily[['location','new_cases']].
to_numpy()
>>>
>>> for locitem in loclist:
...     cases = [casevalues[j][1] for j in
range(len(casevalues))\
```

```
...        if casevalues[j][0]==locitem]
...      rowlist.append(sum(cases))
...
>>> len(rowlist)
209
>>> len(loclist)
209
>>> rowlist[0:5]
[34451.0, 3371.0, 18712.0, 855.0, 483.0]
>>> casetotals = pd.DataFrame(zip(loclist,rowlist),
columns=(['location','casetotals']))
>>> casetotals.head()
        location   casetotals
0   Afghanistan     34,451.00
1       Albania      3,371.00
2       Algeria     18,712.00
3       Andorra        855.00
4        Angola        483.00
```

4. Sort the land temperature data and drop rows with missing values for temperature:

```
>>> ltbrazil = ltbrazil.sort_values(['station','month'])
>>> ltbrazil = ltbrazil.dropna(subset=['temperature'])
```

5. Use a NumPy array to calculate average temperature for the year.

Exclude rows where there is a large change from one period to the next:

```
>>> prevstation = 'ZZZ'
>>> prevtemp = 0
>>> rowlist = []
>>> tempvalues = ltbrazil[['station','temperature']].to_
numpy()
>>>
>>> for j in range(len(tempvalues)):
...     station = tempvalues[j][0]
...     temperature = tempvalues[j][1]
...     if (prevstation!=station):
...       if (prevstation!='ZZZ'):
```

```
...            rowlist.append({'station':prevstation,
'avgtemp':tempcnt/stationcnt, 'stationcnt':stationcnt})
...       tempcnt = 0
...       stationcnt = 0
...       prevstation = station
...    if ((0 <= abs(temperature-prevtemp) <= 3) or
(stationcnt==0)):
...       tempcnt += temperature
...       stationcnt += 1
...    prevtemp = temperature
...
>>> rowlist.append({'station':prevstation,
'avgtemp':tempcnt/stationcnt, 'stationcnt':stationcnt})
>>> rowlist[0:5]
[{'station': 'ALTAMIRA', 'avgtemp': 28.310000000000002,
'stationcnt': 5}, {'station': 'ALTA_FLORESTA_AERO',
'avgtemp': 29.433636363636367, 'stationcnt': 11},
{'station': 'ARAXA', 'avgtemp': 21.612499999999997,
'stationcnt': 4}, {'station': 'BACABAL', 'avgtemp':
29.75, 'stationcnt': 4}, {'station': 'BAGE', 'avgtemp':
20.366666666666664, 'stationcnt': 9}]
```

6. Create a DataFrame of the land temperature averages:

```
>>> ltbrazilavgs = pd.DataFrame(rowlist)
>>> ltbrazilavgs.head()
              station  avgtemp  stationcnt
0            ALTAMIRA    28.31           5
1  ALTA_FLORESTA_AERO    29.43          11
2               ARAXA    21.61           4
3             BACABAL    29.75           4
4                BAGE    20.37           9
```

This gives us a DataFrame with average temperature and number of observations per station. Notice that we get the same results as in the final step of the previous recipe.

How it works...

NumPy arrays can be quite useful when we are working with tabular data but need to do some calculations across rows. This is because accessing items over the equivalent of rows is not really that different from accessing items over the equivalent of columns in an array. For example, `casevalues[5][0]` (the sixth "row" and first "column" of the array) is accessed in the same way as `casevalues[20][1]`. Navigating over a NumPy array is also faster than iterating over a pandas DataFrame.

We take advantage of this in *Step 3*. We get all of the array rows for a given location (`if casevalues[j][0]==locitem`) with a list comprehension. Since we also need the `location` list in the DataFrame we will create of summary values, we use `zip` to combine the two lists.

We start working with the land temperature data in *Step 4*, first sorting it by `station` and `month`, and then dropping rows with missing values for temperature. The logic in *Step 5* is almost identical to the logic in *Step 6* in the previous recipe. The main difference is that we need to refer to the locations of station (`tempvalues[j][0]`) and temperature (`tempvalues[j][1]`) in the array.

There's more...

When you need to iterate over data, NumPy arrays will generally be faster than iterating over a pandas DataFrame with `itertuples` or `iterrows`. Also, if you tried to run the list comprehension in *Step 3* using `itertuples`, which is possible, you would be waiting some time for it to finish. In general, if you want to do a quick summary of values for some segment of your data, using NumPy arrays is a reasonable choice.

See also

The remaining recipes in this chapter rely on the powerful `groupby` method of pandas DataFrames to generate group totals.

Using groupby to organize data by groups

At a certain point in most data analysis projects, we have to generate summary statistics by groups. While this can be done using the approaches in the previous recipe, in most cases the pandas DataFrame `groupby` method is a better choice. If `groupby` can handle an aggregation task—and it usually can—it is likely the most efficient way to accomplish that task. We make good use of `groupby` in the remaining recipes in this chapter. We go over the basics in this recipe.

Getting ready

We will work with the COVID-19 daily data in this recipe.

How to do it...

We will create a pandas groupby DataFrame and use it to generate summary statistics by group:

1. Import pandas and numpy, and load the Covid case daily data:

```
>>> import pandas as pd
>>> import numpy as np
>>> coviddaily = pd.read_csv("data/coviddaily720.csv",
parse_dates=["casedate"])
```

2. Create a pandas groupby DataFrame:

```
>>> countrytots = coviddaily.groupby(['location'])
>>> type(countrytots)
<class 'pandas.core.groupby.generic.DataFrameGroupBy'>
```

3. Create DataFrames for the first and last rows of each country:

```
>>> countrytots.first().iloc[0:5, 0:5]
```

location	iso_code	casedate	continent	new_cases	new_deaths
Afghanistan	AFG	2019-12-31	Asia	0	0
Albania	ALB	2020-03-09	Europe	2	0
Algeria	DZA	2019-12-31	Africa	0	0
Andorra	AND	2020-03-03	Europe	1	0
Angola	AGO	2020-03-22	Africa	2	0

```
>>> countrytots.last().iloc[0:5, 0:5]
```

location	iso_code	casedate	continent	new_cases	new_deaths

Afghanistan 16	AFG	2020-07-12	Asia	85
Albania 4	ALB	2020-07-12	Europe	93
Algeria 16	DZA	2020-07-12	Africa	904
Andorra 0	AND	2020-07-12	Europe	0
Angola 2	AGO	2020-07-12	Africa	25

```
>>> type(countrytots.last())
<class 'pandas.core.frame.DataFrame'>
```

4. Get all the rows for a country:

```
>>> countrytots.get_group('Zimbabwe').iloc[0:5, 0:5]
      iso_code   casedate continent  new_cases  new_
deaths
29099      ZWE 2020-03-21    Africa          1
0
29100      ZWE 2020-03-22    Africa          1
0
29101      ZWE 2020-03-23    Africa          0
0
29102      ZWE 2020-03-24    Africa          0
1
29103      ZWE 2020-03-25    Africa          0
0
```

5. Loop through the groups:

```
>>> for name, group in countrytots:
...    if (name in ['Malta','Kuwait']):
...      print(group.iloc[0:5, 0:5])
...
       iso_code   casedate location continent  new_cases
14707      KWT 2019-12-31   Kuwait      Asia          0
14708      KWT 2020-01-01   Kuwait      Asia          0
14709      KWT 2020-01-02   Kuwait      Asia          0
```

14710	KWT	2020-01-03	Kuwait	Asia	0
14711	KWT	2020-01-04	Kuwait	Asia	0
	iso_code	casedate	location	continent	new_cases
17057	MLT	2020-03-07	Malta	Europe	1
17058	MLT	2020-03-08	Malta	Europe	2
17059	MLT	2020-03-09	Malta	Europe	0
17060	MLT	2020-03-10	Malta	Europe	2
17061	MLT	2020-03-11	Malta	Europe	1

6. Show the number of rows for each country:

```
>>> countrytots.size()
location
Afghanistan      185
Albania          126
Algeria          190
Andorra          121
Angola           113
                 ...
Vietnam          191
Western Sahara    78
Yemen             94
Zambia           116
Zimbabwe         114
Length: 209, dtype: int64
```

7. Show the summary statistics by country:

```
>>> countrytots.new_cases.describe().head()
```

	count	mean	std	min	25%	50%	75%	max
location								
Afghanistan	185	186	257	0	0	37	302	1,063
Albania	126	27	25	0	9	17	36	93
Algeria	190	98	124	0	0	88	150	904
Andorra	121	7	13	0	0	1	9	79
Angola	113	4	9	0	0	1	5	62

```
>>> countrytots.new_cases.sum().head()
location
```

```
Afghanistan    34,451
Albania         3,371
Algeria        18,712
Andorra           855
Angola            483
Name: new_cases, dtype: float64
```

These steps demonstrate how remarkably useful the `groupby` DataFrame object is when we want to generate summary statistics by categorical variables.

How it works...

In *Step 2*, we create a pandas DataFrame `groupby` object using the pandas DataFrame `groupby` method, passing it a column or list of columns for the grouping. Once we have a `groupby` DataFrame, we can generate statistics by group with the same tools that we use to generate summary statistics for the whole DataFrame. `describe`, `mean`, `sum`, and similar methods work on the `groupby` DataFrame—or series created from it—as expected, except the summary is run for each group.

In *Step 3*, we use `first` and `last` to create DataFrames with the first and last occurrence of each group. We use `get_group` to get all the rows for a particular group in *Step 4*. We can also loop over the groups and use `size` to count the number of rows for each group.

In *Step 7*, we create a series `groupby` object from the DataFrame `groupby` object. Using the resulting object's aggregation methods gives us summary statistics for a series by group. One thing is clear about the distribution of `new_cases` from this output: it varies quite a bit by country. For example, we can see right away that the interquartile range is quite different, even for the first five countries.

There's more...

The output from *Step 7* is quite useful. It is worth saving output such as that for each important continuous variable where the distribution is meaningfully different by group.

Pandas `groupby` DataFrames are extraordinarily powerful and easy to use. *Step 7* shows just how easy it is to create the summaries by groups that we created in the first two recipes in this chapter. Unless the DataFrame we are working with is small, or the task involves very complicated calculations across rows, the `groupby` method is a superior choice to looping.

Using more complicated aggregation functions with groupby

In the previous recipe, we created a groupby DataFrame object and used it to run summary statistics by groups. We use chaining in this recipe to create the groups, choose the aggregation variable(s), and select the aggregation function(s), all in one line. We also take advantage of the flexibility of the groupby object, which allows us to choose the aggregation columns and functions in a variety of ways.

Getting ready

We will work with the **National Longitudinal Survey of Youth (NLS)** data in this recipe.

> **Data note**
>
> The **NLS**, administered by the United States Bureau of Labor Statistics, are longitudinal surveys of individuals who were in high school in 1997 when the surveys started. Participants were surveyed each year through 2018. The surveys are available for public use at nlsinfo.org.

How to do it...

We do more complicated aggregations with groupby than we did in the previous recipe, taking advantage of its flexibility:

1. Import pandas and load the NLS data:

    ```
    >>> import pandas as pd
    >>> nls97 = pd.read_csv("data/nls97b.csv")
    >>> nls97.set_index("personid", inplace=True)
    ```

2. Review the structure of the data:

    ```
    >>> nls97.iloc[:,0:7].info()
    <class 'pandas.core.frame.DataFrame'>
    Int64Index: 8984 entries, 100061 to 999963
    Data columns (total 7 columns):
     #   Column                Non-Null Count   Dtype
    ---  ------                --------------   -----
    ```

0	gender	8984 non-null	object
1	birthmonth	8984 non-null	int64
2	birthyear	8984 non-null	int64
3	highestgradecompleted	6663 non-null	float64
4	maritalstatus	6672 non-null	object
5	childathome	4791 non-null	float64
6	childnotathome	4791 non-null	float64

```
dtypes: float64(3), int64(2), object(2)
memory usage: 561.5+ KB
```

3. Review some of the categorical data:

```
>>> catvars = ['gender','maritalstatus','highestdegree']
>>>
>>> for col in catvars:
...     print(col, nls97[col].value_counts().sort_index(),
sep="\n\n", end="\n\n\n")
...
gender
Female    4385
Male      4599
Name: gender, dtype: int64


maritalstatus
Divorced        663
Married         3066
Never-married   2766
Separated       154
Widowed         23
Name: maritalstatus, dtype: int64


highestdegree
0. None         953
1. GED          1146
2. High School  3667
3. Associates   737
4. Bachelors    1673
```

```
5. Masters          603
6. PhD               54
7. Professional     120
Name: highestdegree, dtype: int64
```

4. Review some descriptive statistics:

```
>>> contvars =
['satmath','satverbal','weeksworked06','gpaoverall',
...    'childathome']
>>>
```

```
>>> nls97[contvars].describe()
```

	satmath	satverbal	weeksworked06	gpaoverall
childathome				
count	1,407.0	1,406.0	8,340.0	6,004.0
4,791.0				
mean	500.6	499.7	38.4	2.8
1.9				
std	115.0	112.2	18.9	0.6
1.3				
min	7.0	14.0	0.0	0.1
0.0				
25%	430.0	430.0	27.0	2.4
1.0				
50%	500.0	500.0	51.0	2.9
2.0				
75%	580.0	570.0	52.0	3.3
3.0				
max	800.0	800.0	52.0	4.2
9.0				

5. Look at **Scholastic Assessment Test (SAT)** math scores by gender.

We pass the column name to groupby to group by that column:

```
>>> nls97.groupby('gender')['satmath'].mean()
gender
Female    487
Male      517
Name: satmath, dtype: float64
```

6. Look at the SAT math scores by gender and highest degree earned.

We can pass a list of column names to `groupby` to group by more than one column:

```
>> nls97.groupby(['gender','highestdegree'])['satmath'].
mean()
```

gender	highestdegree	
Female	0. None	333
	1. GED	405
	2. High School	431
	3. Associates	458
	4. Bachelors	502
	5. Masters	508
	6. PhD	575
	7. Professional	599
Male	0. None	540
	1. GED	320
	2. High School	468
	3. Associates	481
	4. Bachelors	542
	5. Masters	574
	6. PhD	621
	7. Professional	588
Name: satmath, dtype: float64		

7. Look at the SAT math and verbal scores by gender and highest degree earned.

We can use a list to summarize values for more than one variable, in this case `satmath` and `satverbal`:

```
>>> nls97.groupby(['gender','highestdegree'])
[['satmath','satverbal']].mean()
```

		satmath	satverbal
gender	highestdegree		
Female	0. None	333	409
	1. GED	405	390
	2. High School	431	444
	3. Associates	458	466
	4. Bachelors	502	506
	5. Masters	508	534

	6. PhD	575	558
	7. Professional	599	587
Male	0. None	540	483
	1. GED	320	360
	2. High School	468	457
	3. Associates	481	462
	4. Bachelors	542	528
	5. Masters	574	545
	6. PhD	621	623
	7. Professional	588	592

8. Add columns for the count, max, and standard deviation.

Use the agg function to return several summary statistics:

```
>>> nls97.groupby(['gender','highestdegree'])
['gpaoverall'].agg(['count','mean','max','std'])
```

		count	mean	max	std
gender	highestdegree				
Female	0. None	148	2.5	4.0	0.7
	1. GED	227	2.3	3.9	0.7
	2. High School	1212	2.8	4.2	0.5
	3. Associates	290	2.9	4.0	0.5
	4. Bachelors	734	3.2	4.1	0.5
	5. Masters	312	3.3	4.1	0.4
	6. PhD	22	3.5	4.0	0.5
	7. Professional	53	3.5	4.1	0.4
Male	0. None	193	2.2	4.0	0.6
	1. GED	345	2.2	4.0	0.6
	2. High School	1436	2.6	4.0	0.5
	3. Associates	236	2.7	3.8	0.5
	4. Bachelors	560	3.1	4.1	0.5
	5. Masters	170	3.3	4.0	0.4
	6. PhD	20	3.4	4.0	0.6
	7. Professional	38	3.4	4.0	0.3

9. Use a dictionary for more complicated aggregations:

```
>>> pd.options.display.float_format = '{:,.1f}'.format
>>> aggdict = {'weeksworked06':['count', 'mean',
'max','std'], 'childathome':['count', 'mean', 'max',
'std']}
>>> nls97.groupby(['highestdegree']).agg(aggdict)
```

	weeksworked06				childathome			
	count	mean	max	std	count	mean	max	std
highestdegree								
0. None	703	29.7	52.0	21.6	439	1.8	8.0	1.6
1. GED	1104	33.2	52.0	20.6	693	1.7	9.0	1.5
2. High School	3368	39.4	52.0	18.6	1961	1.9	7.0	1.3
3. Associates	722	40.7	52.0	17.7	428	2.0	6.0	1.1
4. Bachelors	1642	42.2	52.0	16.1	827	1.9	8.0	1.0
5. Masters	601	42.2	52.0	16.1	333	1.9	5.0	0.9
6. PhD	53	38.2	52.0	18.6	32	2.1	6.0	1.1
7. Professional	117	27.1	52.0	20.4	57	1.8	4.0	0.8

```
>>> nls97.groupby(['maritalstatus']).agg(aggdict)
```

	weeksworked06				childathome			
	count	mean	max	std	count	mean	max	std
maritalstatus								
Divorced	660	37.5	52.0	19.1	524	1.5	5.0	1.2
Married	3033	40.3	52.0	17.9	2563	2.1	8.0	1.1
Never-married	2734	37.2	52.0	19.1	1502	1.6	9.0	1.3
Separated	153	33.8	52.0	20.2	137	1.5	8.0	1.4

```
Widowed                           23 37.1 52.0 19.3              18
1.8 5.0 1.4
```

We display the same summary statistics for weeksworked06 and childathome, but we could have specified different aggregation functions for each using the same syntax as we used in *Step 9*.

How it works...

We first take a look at some summary statistics for key columns in the DataFrame. We get frequencies for the categorical variables in *Step 3*, and some descriptives for the continuous variables in *Step 4*. It is a good idea to have summary values for the DataFrame as a whole in front of us before generating statistics by group.

We are then ready to create summary statistics using groupby. This involves three steps:

1. Creating a groupby DataFrame based on one or more categorical variables
2. Selecting the column(s) to be used for the summary statistics
3. Choosing the aggregation function(s)

We use chaining in this recipe to do all three in one line. So, nls97. groupby('gender')['satmath'].mean() in *Step 5* does three things: nls97. groupby('gender') creates the groupby DataFrame object, ['satmath'] chooses the aggregation column, and mean() is the aggregation function.

We can pass a column name (as in *Step 5*) or a list of column names (as in *Step 6*) to groupby to create groupings by one or more columns. We can select multiple variables for aggregation with a list of those variables, as we do in *Step 7* with [['satmath','satverbal']].

We can chain a specific summary function such as mean, count, or max. Or, we could pass a list to agg to choose multiple aggregation functions, such as with agg(['count','mean','max','std']) in *Step 8*. We can use the familiar pandas and NumPy aggregation functions or a user-defined function, which we explore in the next recipe.

Another important takeaway from *Step 8* is that agg sends the aggregation columns to each function a group at a time. The calculations in each aggregation function are run for each group in the groupby DataFrame. Another way to conceptualize this is that it allows us to run the same functions we are used to running across a whole DataFrame for one group at a time, accomplishing this by automating the process of sending the data for each group to the aggregation functions.

There's more...

We first get a sense of how the categorical and continuous variables in the DataFrame are distributed. Often, we group data to see how a distribution of a continuous variable, such as weeks worked, differs by a categorical variable, such as marital status. Before doing that, it is helpful to have a good idea of how those variables are distributed across the whole dataset.

The `nls97` dataset only has SAT scores for about 1,400 of 8,984 respondents, so we need to be careful when examining SAT scores by different groups. This means that some of the counts by gender and highest degree, especially for PhD recipients, are a little too small to be reliable. There are outliers for SAT math and verbal scores (if we define outliers as 1.5 times the interquartile range above the third quartile or below the first quartile).

We have acceptable counts for weeks worked and number of children living at home for all values of highest degree achieved, and values of marital status except for widowed. The average weeks worked for folks who received a professional degree is unexpected. It is lower than for any other group. A good next step would be to see how persistent this is over the years. (We are just looking at 2006 weeks worked here, but there are 20 years' of data on weeks worked.)

See also

The `nls97` file is panel data masquerading as individual-level data. The panel data structure can be recovered, facilitating analysis over time of areas such as employment and school enrollment. We do this in the recipes in *Chapter 9, Tidying and Reshaping Data*.

Using user-defined functions and apply with groupby

Despite the numerous aggregation functions available in pandas and NumPy, we sometimes have to write our own to get the results we need. In some cases, this requires the use of `apply`.

Getting ready

We will work with the NLS data in this recipe.

How to do it...

We will create our own functions to define the summary statistics we want by group:

1. Import pandas and the NLS data:

```
>>> import pandas as pd
>>> import numpy as np
>>> nls97 = pd.read_csv("data/nls97b.csv")
>>> nls97.set_index("personid", inplace=True)
```

2. Create a function for defining the interquartile range:

```
>>> def iqr(x):
...     return x.quantile(0.75) - x.quantile(0.25)
...
```

3. Run the interquartile range function.

    First, create a dictionary that specifies which aggregation functions to run on each analysis variable:

```
>>> aggdict = {'weeksworked06':['count', 'mean', iqr],
'childathome':['count', 'mean', iqr]}
>>> nls97.groupby(['highestdegree']).agg(aggdict)
```

	weeksworked06			childathome		
	count	mean	iqr	count	mean	iqr
highestdegree						
0. None	703	29.7	47.0	439	1.8	3.0
1. GED	1104	33.2	39.0	693	1.7	3.0
2. High School	3368	39.4	21.0	1961	1.9	2.0
3. Associates	722	40.7	18.0	428	2.0	2.0
4. Bachelors	1642	42.2	14.0	827	1.9	1.0
5. Masters	601	42.2	13.0	333	1.9	1.0
6. PhD	53	38.2	23.0	32	2.1	2.0

```
7. Professional            117 27.1 45.0          57  1.8
1.0
```

4. Define a function to return selected summary statistics as a series:

```
>>> def gettots(x):
...     out = {}
...     out['qr1'] = x.quantile(0.25)
...     out['med'] = x.median()
...     out['qr3'] = x.quantile(0.75)
...     out['count'] = x.count()
...     return pd.Series(out)
...
```

5. Use `apply` to run the function.

    This will create a series with a multi-index based on `highestdegree` values and the desired summary statistics:

```
>>> pd.options.display.float_format = '{:,.0f}'.format
>>> nls97.groupby(['highestdegree'])['weeksworked06'].
apply(gettots)
highestdegree
0. None          qr1          5
                 med         34
                 qr3         52
                 count      703
1. GED           qr1         13
                 med         42
                 qr3         52
                 count    1,104
2. High School   qr1         31
                 med         52
                 qr3         52
                 count    3,368
3. Associates    qr1         34
                 med         52
                 qr3         52
                 count      722
```

```
..... abbreviated to save space .....
Name: weeksworked06, dtype: float64
```

6. Use `reset_index` to use the default index instead of the index created from the groupby DataFrame:

```
>>> nls97.groupby(['highestdegree'])['weeksworked06'].
apply(gettots).reset_index()
```

	highestdegree	level_1	weeksworked06
0	0. None	qr1	5
1	0. None	med	34
2	0. None	qr3	52
3	0. None	count	703
4	1. GED	qr1	13
5	1. GED	med	42
6	1. GED	qr3	52
7	1. GED	count	1,104
8	2. High School	qr1	31
9	2. High School	med	52
10	2. High School	qr3	52
11	2. High School	count	3,368
12	3. Associates	qr1	34
13	3. Associates	med	52
14	3. Associates	qr3	52
15	3. Associates	count	722

```
..... abbreviated to save space .....
```

7. Chain with `unstack` instead to create columns based on the summary variables.

This will create a DataFrame with the `highestdegree` values as the index, and aggregation values in the columns:

```
>>> nlssums = nls97.groupby(['highestdegree'])
['weeksworked06'].apply(gettots).unstack()
>>> nlssums
```

highestdegree	qr1	med	qr3	count
0. None	5	34	52	703
1. GED	13	42	52	1,104

```
2. High School      31    52    52    3,368
3. Associates       34    52    52      722
4. Bachelors        38    52    52    1,642
5. Masters          39    52    52      601
6. PhD              29    50    52       53
7. Professional      4    29    49      117


>>> nlssums.info()
<class 'pandas.core.frame.DataFrame'>
Index: 8 entries, 0. None to 7. Professional
Data columns (total 4 columns):
 #    Column  Non-Null Count   Dtype
---   ------  --------------   -----
 0    qr1     8 non-null       float64
 1    med     8 non-null       float64
 2    qr3     8 non-null       float64
 3    count   8 non-null       float64
dtypes: float64(4)
memory usage: 320.0+ bytes
```

unstack is useful when we want to rotate parts of the index to the columns' axis.

How it works...

We define a very simple function to calculate interquartile ranges by group in *Step 2*. We then include calls to that function in our list of aggregation functions in *Step 3*.

Steps 4 and *5* are a little more complicated. We define a function that calculates the first and third quartiles and median, and counts the number of rows. It returns a series with these values. By combining a groupby DataFrame with apply in *Step 5*, we get the gettots function to return that series for each group.

Step 5 gives us the numbers we want, but maybe not in the best format. If, for example, we want to use the data for another operation—say, a visualization—we need to chain some additional methods. One possibility is to use reset_index. This will replace the multi-index with the default index. Another option is to use unstack. This will create columns from the second level of the index (having qr1, med, qr3, and count values).

There's more...

Interestingly, the interquartile ranges for weeks worked and number of children at home drop substantially as education increases. There seems to be a higher variation in those variables among groups with less education. This should be examined more closely and has implications for statistical testing that assumes common variances across groups.

In *Step 5*, we could have set the groupby method's as_index parameter to False. If we had done so, we would not have had to use reset_index or unstack to deal with the multi-index created. The disadvantage of setting that parameter to False, as you can see in the following code snippet, is that the groupby values are not reflected in the returned DataFrame, either as an index or a column. This is because we use groupby with apply and a user-defined function. When we use as_index=False with an agg function, we get a column with the groupby values (we see a couple of examples of that in the next recipe):

```
>>> nls97.groupby(['highestdegree'], as_index=False)
['weeksworked06'].apply(gettots)
```

	qr1	med	qr3	count
0	5	34	52	703
1	13	42	52	1,104
2	31	52	52	3,368
3	34	52	52	722
4	38	52	52	1,642
5	39	52	52	601
6	29	50	52	53
7	4	29	49	117

See also

We do much more with stack and unstack in *Chapter 9*, *Tidying and Reshaping Data*.

Using groupby to change the unit of analysis of a DataFrame

The DataFrame that we created in the last step of the previous recipe was something of a fortunate by-product of our efforts to generate multiple summary statistics by groups. There are times when we really do need to aggregate data to change the unit of analysis—say, from monthly utility expenses per family to annual utility expenses per family, or from students' grades per course to students' overall **grade point average (GPA)**.

groupby is a good tool for collapsing the unit of analysis, particularly when summary operations are required. When we only need to select unduplicated rows—perhaps the first or last row for each individual over a given interval—then the combination of sort_values and drop_duplicates will do the trick. But we often need to do some calculation across the rows for each group before collapsing. That is when groupby comes in very handy.

Getting ready

We will work with the COVID-19 case daily data, which has one row per country per day. We will also work with the Brazil land temperature data, which has one row per month per weather station.

How to do it...

We will use groupby to create a DataFrame of summary values by group:

1. Import pandas and load the Covid and land temperature data:

```
>>> import pandas as pd
>>> coviddaily = pd.read_csv("data/coviddaily720.csv",
parse_dates=["casedate"])
>>> ltbrazil = pd.read_csv("data/ltbrazil.csv")
```

2. Convert Covid data from one country per day to summaries across all countries by day:

```
>>> coviddailytotals = coviddaily.loc[coviddaily.
casedate.between('2020-02-01','2020-07-12')].\
...    groupby(['casedate'], as_index=False)[['new_
cases','new_deaths']].\
...    sum()
>>>
>>> coviddailytotals.head(10)
     casedate  new_cases  new_deaths
0  2020-02-01      2,120          46
1  2020-02-02      2,608          46
2  2020-02-03      2,818          57
3  2020-02-04      3,243          65
4  2020-02-05      3,897          66
```

5	2020-02-06	3,741	72
6	2020-02-07	3,177	73
7	2020-02-08	3,439	86
8	2020-02-09	2,619	89
9	2020-02-10	2,982	97

3. Create a DataFrame with average temperatures for each station in Brazil.

First, remove rows with missing temperature values, and show some data for a few rows:

```
>>> ltbrazil = ltbrazil.dropna(subset=['temperature'])
>>> ltbrazil.loc[103508:104551,
['station','year','month','temperature','elevation',
'latabs']]
```

	station	year	month	temperature	elevation	latabs
103508	CRUZEIRO_DO_SUL	2019	1	26	194	8
103682	CUIABA	2019	1	29	151	16
103949	SANTAREM_AEROPORTO	2019	1	27	60	2
104051	ALTA_FLORESTA_AERO	2019	1	27	289	10
104551	UBERLANDIA	2019	1	25	943	19

```
>>>
>>> ltbrazilavgs = ltbrazil.groupby(['station'], as_
index=False).\
...    agg({'latabs':'first','elevation':'first',
'temperature':'mean'})
>>>
>>> ltbrazilavgs.head(10)
```

	station	latabs	elevation	temperature
0	ALTAMIRA	3	112	28
1	ALTA_FLORESTA_AERO	10	289	29
2	ARAXA	20	1,004	22
3	BACABAL	4	25	30
4	BAGE	31	242	19

5	BARBALHA	7	409	27
6	BARCELOS	1	34	28
7	BARRA_DO_CORDA	6	153	29
8	BARREIRAS	12	439	27
9	BARTOLOMEU_LISANDRO	22	17	26

Let's take a closer look at how the aggregation functions in these examples work.

How it works...

In *Step 2*, we first select the dates that we want (some countries started reporting COVID-19 cases later than others). We create a DataFrame groupby object based on casedate, choose new_cases and new_deaths as the aggregation variables, and select sum for the aggregation function. This produces a sum for both new_cases and new_deaths for each group (casedate). Depending on your purposes you may not want casedate to be the index, which would happen if we did not set as_index to False.

We often need to use a different aggregation function with different aggregation variables. We might want to take the first (or last) value for one variable, and get the mean of the values of another variable by group. This is what we do in *Step 3*. We do this by passing a dictionary to the agg function, with our aggregation variables as keys and the aggregation function to use as values.

8

Addressing Data Issues When Combining DataFrames

At some point during most data cleaning projects, the analyst will have to combine data from different data tables. This involves either appending data with the same structure to existing data rows or doing a merge to retrieve columns from a different data table. The former is sometimes referred to as combining data vertically, or concatenating, while the latter is referred to as combining data horizontally, or merging.

Merges can be categorized by the amount of duplication of merge-by column values. With one-to-one merges, merge-by column values appear once on each data table. One-to-many merges have unduplicated merge-by column values on one side of the merge and duplicated merge-by column values on the other side. Many-to-many merges have duplicated merge-by column values on both sides. Merging is further complicated by the fact that there is often no perfect correspondence between merge-by values on the data tables; each data table may have values in the merge-by column that are not present in the other data table.

New data issues can be introduced when data is combined. When data is appended, it may have different logical values than the original data, even when the columns have the same names and data types. For merges, whenever merge-by values are missing on one side of a merge, the columns that are added will have missing values. For one-to-one or one-to-many merges, there may be unexpected duplicates in merge-by values, resulting in values for other columns being duplicated unintentionally.

In this chapter, we will combine DataFrames vertically and horizontally and consider strategies for dealing with the data problems that often arise. Specifically, in this chapter, we will cover the following recipes:

- Combining DataFrames vertically
- Doing one-to-one merges
- Doing one-to-one merges by multiple columns
- Doing one-to-many merges
- Doing many-to-many merges
- Developing a merge routine

Technical requirements

The code and notebooks for this chapter are available on GitHub at `https://github.com/PacktPublishing/Python-Data-Cleaning-Cookbook`

Combining DataFrames vertically

There are times when we need to append rows from one data table to another. This will almost always be rows from data tables with similar structures, along with the same columns and data types. For example, we might get a new CSV file containing hospital patient outcomes each month and need to add that to our existing data. Alternatively, we might end up working at a school district central office and receive data from many different schools. We might want to combine this data before conducting analyses.

Even when the data structure across months and across schools (in these examples) is theoretically the same, it may not be in practice. Business practices can change from one period to another. This can be intentional or happen inadvertently due to staff turnover or some external factor. One institution or department might implement practices somewhat differently than another, and some data values might be different for some institutions or missing altogether.

We are likely to come across a change in what seems like similar data when we let our guard down, typically when we start to assume that the new data will look like the old data. I try to remember this whenever I combine data vertically. I will be referring to combining data vertically as *concatenating* or *appending* for the rest of this chapter.

In this recipe, we'll use the pandas `concat` function to append rows from a pandas DataFrame to another DataFrame. We will also do a few common checks on the `concat` operation to confirm that the resulting DataFrame is what we expected.

Getting ready

We will work with land temperature data from several countries in this recipe. This data includes the monthly average temperature, latitude, longitude, and elevation at many weather stations in each country during 2019. The data for each country is contained in a CSV file.

Data note

The data for this recipe has been taken from the *Global Historical Climatology Network* integrated database, which has been made available for public use by the United States National Oceanic and Atmospheric Administration, at `https://www.ncdc.noaa.gov/data-access/land-based-station-data/land-based-datasets/global-historical-climatology-network-monthly-version-4`.

How to do it...

In this recipe, we will combine similarly structured DataFrames vertically, check the values in the concatenated data, and fix missing values. Let's get started:

1. Import `pandas` and `NumPy`, as well as the `os` module:

```
>>> import pandas as pd
>>> import numpy as np
>>> import os
```

2. Load the data from Cameroon and Poland:

```
>>> ltcameroon = pd.read_csv("data/ltcountry/ltcameroon.csv")
>>> ltpoland = pd.read_csv("data/ltcountry/ltpoland.csv")
```

3. Concatenate the Cameroon and Poland data:

```
>>> ltcameroon.shape
(48, 11)
>>> ltpoland.shape
(120, 11)
>>> ltall = pd.concat([ltcameroon, ltpoland])
>>> ltall.country.value_counts()
Poland        120
Cameroon       48
Name: country, dtype: int64
```

4. Concatenate all the country data files.

Loop through all the filenames in the folder that contains the CSV files for each country. Use the `endswith` method to check that the filename has a CSV file extension. Use `read_csv` to create a new DataFrame and print out the number of rows. Use `concat` to append the rows of the new DataFrame to the rows that have already been appended. Finally, display any columns that are missing in the most recent DataFrame, or that are in the most recent DataFrame but not the previous ones. Notice that the `ltoman` DataFrame is missing the `latabs` column:

```
>>> directory = "data/ltcountry"
>>> ltall = pd.DataFrame()
>>>
>>> for filename in os.listdir(directory):
...     if filename.endswith(".csv"):
...         fileloc = os.path.join(directory, filename)
...         # open the next file
...         with open(fileloc) as f:
...             ltnew = pd.read_csv(fileloc)
...             print(filename + " has " + str(ltnew.shape[0])
+ " rows.")
...             ltall = pd.concat([ltall, ltnew])
...             # check for differences in columns
...             columndiff = ltall.columns.symmetric_
difference(ltnew.columns)
...             if (not columndiff.empty):
...                 print("", "Different column names for:",
filename,\
```

```
...              columndiff, "", sep="\n")
...
ltpoland.csv has 120 rows.
ltjapan.csv has 1800 rows.
ltindia.csv has 1056 rows.
ltbrazil.csv has 1104 rows.
ltcameroon.csv has 48 rows.
ltoman.csv has 288 rows.


Different column names for:
ltoman.csv
Index(['latabs'], dtype='object')


ltmexico.csv has 852 rows.
```

5. Show some of the combined data:

```
>>> ltall[['country','station','month','temperature',
'latitude']].sample(5, random_state=1)
```

	country	station	month	temperature	latitude
597	Japan	MIYAKO	4	24	25
937	India	JHARSUGUDA	11	25	22
616	Mexico	TUXPANVER	9	29	21
261	India	MO_AMINI	3	29	11
231	Oman	IBRA	10	29	23

6. Check the values in the concatenated data.

Notice that the values for latabs for Oman are all missing. This is because latabs is missing in the DataFrame for Oman (latabs is the absolute value of the latitude for each station):

```
>>> ltall.country.value_counts().sort_index()
```

Brazil	1104
Cameroon	48
India	1056
Japan	1800
Mexico	852
Oman	288

```
Poland          120
Name: country, dtype: int64
>>>
>>> ltall.groupby(['country']).
agg({'temperature':['min','mean',\
...    'max','count'],'latabs':['min','mean','max','co
unt']})
```

	temperature				latabs			
	min	mean	max	count	min	mean	max	count
country								
Brazil	12	25	34	969	0	14	34	1104
Cameroon	22	27	36	34	4	8	10	48
India	2	26	37	1044	8	21	34	1056
Japan	-7	15	30	1797	24	36	45	1800
Mexico	7	23	34	806	15	22	32	852
Oman	12	28	38	205	nan	nan	nan	0
Poland	-4	10	23	120	50	52	55	120

7. Fix the missing values.

   Set the value of latabs to the value of latitude for Oman. (All of the latitude values for stations in Oman are above the equator and positive. In the Global Historical Climatology Network integrated database, latitude values above the equator are positive, while all the latitude values below the equator are negative). Do this as follows:

```
>>> ltall['latabs'] = np.where(ltall.country=="Oman",
ltall.latitude, ltall.latabs)
>>>
>>> ltall.groupby(['country']).
agg({'temperature':['min','mean',\
...    'max','count'],'latabs':['min','mean','max','co
unt']})
```

	temperature				latabs			
	min	mean	max	count	min	mean	max	count
country								
Brazil	12	25	34	969	0	14	34	1104
Cameroon	22	27	36	34	4	8	10	48

India	2	26	37	1044	8	21	34	1056
Japan	-7	15	30	1797	24	36	45	1800
Mexico	7	23	34	806	15	22	32	852
Oman	12	28	38	205	17	22	26	288
Poland	-4	10	23	120	50	52	55	120

With that, we have combined the data for the seven CSV files we found in the selected folder. We have also confirmed that we have appended the correct number of rows, identified columns that are missing in some files, and fixed missing values.

How it works...

We passed a list of pandas DataFrames to the pandas `concat` function in *step 3*. The rows from the second DataFrame were appended to the bottom of the first DataFrame. If we had listed a third DataFrame, those rows would have been appended to the combined rows of the first two DataFrames. Before concatenating, we used the `shape` attribute to check the number of rows. We confirmed that the concatenated DataFrame contains the expected number of rows for each country.

We could have concatenated data from all the CSV files in the `ltcountry` subfolder by loading each file and then adding it to the list we passed to `concat`. However, this is not always practical. If we want to load and then read more than a few files, we can get Python's `os` module to find the files. In *step 4*, we looked for all the CSV files in a specified folder, loaded each file that was found into memory, and then appended the rows of each file to a DataFrame. We printed the number of rows for each data file we loaded so that we could check those numbers against the totals in the concatenated data later. We also identified any DataFrames with different columns compared to the others. We used `value_counts` in *step 6* to confirm that there was the right number of rows for each country.

The pandas `groupby` method can be used to check column values from each of the original DataFrames. We group by country since that identifies the rows from each of the original DataFrames – all the rows for each DataFrame have the same value for country. (It is helpful to always have a column that identifies the original DataFrames in the concatenated DataFrame, even if that information is not needed for subsequent analysis.) In *step 6*, this helped us notice that there are no values for the `latabs` column for Oman. We replaced the missing values for `latabs` for Oman in *step 7*.

See also

We went over the powerful pandas `groupby` method in some detail in *Chapter 7, Fixing Messy Data when Aggregating.*

We examined NumPy's `where` function in *Chapter 6, Cleaning and Exploring Data with Series Operations.*

Doing one-to-one merges

The remainder of this chapter will explore combining data horizontally; that is, merging columns from a data table with columns from another data table. Borrowing from SQL development, we typically talk about such operations as join operations: left joins, right joins, inner joins, and outer joins. This recipe examines one-to-one merges, where the merge-by values are unduplicated in both files. Subsequent recipes will demonstrate one-to-many merges, where the merge-by values are duplicated on the *right* data table; and many-to-many merges, where merge-by values are duplicated on both the *left and right* data tables.

We often speak of left and right sides of a merge, a convention that we will follow throughout this chapter. But this is of no real consequence, other than for clarity of exposition. We can accomplish exactly the same thing with a merge if A were the left data table and B were the right data table and vice versa.

I am using the expressions merge-by column and merge-by value in this chapter, rather than key column or index column. This avoids possible confusion with pandas index alignment. An index may be used as the merge-by column, but other columns may also be used. I also want to avoid relying on relational database concepts such as primary or foreign keys in this discussion. It is helpful to be aware of which data columns function as primary or foreign keys when we're extracting data from relational systems, and we should take this into account when setting indexes in pandas. But the merging we do for most data cleaning projects often goes beyond these keys.

In the straightforward case of a one-to-one merge, each row in the left data table is matched with one – and only one – row on the right data table, according to the merge-by value. What happens when a merge-by value appears on one, but not the other, data table is determined by the type of join that's specified. The following diagram illustrates the four different types of joins:

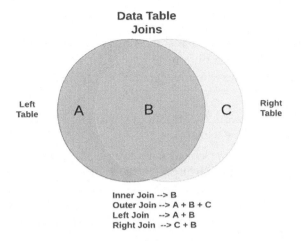

Figure 8.1 – A diagram illustrating the four different types of joins

When two data tables are merged with an inner join, rows are retained when the merge-by values appear in both the left and right data tables. This is the intersection of the left and right data tables, represented by **B** in the preceding diagram. Outer joins return all rows; that is, rows where the merge-by values appear in both data tables, rows where those values appear in the left data table but not the right, and rows where those values appear in the right but not the left – **B**, **A**, and **C**, respectively. This is known as the union. Left joins return rows where the merge-by values are present on the left data table, regardless of whether they are present on the right data table. This is **A** and **B**. Right joins return rows where the merge-by values are present on the right data table, regardless of whether they are present on the left data table.

Missing values may result from outer joins, left joins, or right joins. This is because the returned merged data table will have missing values for columns when the merge-by value is not found. For example, when performing a left join, there may be merge-by values from the left dataset that do not appear on the right dataset. In this case, the columns from the right dataset will all be missing. (I say *may* here because it is possible to do an outer, left, or right join that returns the same results as an inner join because the same merge-by values appear on both sides. Sometimes, a left join is done so that we're certain that all the rows on the left dataset, and only those rows, are returned).

We will look at all four types of joins in this recipe.

Getting ready

We will work with two files from the **National Longitudinal Survey (NLS)**. Both files contain one row per person. One contains employment, educational attainment, and income data, while the other file contains data on the income and educational attainment of the respondents' parents.

> **Data note**
>
> The NLS is conducted by the United States Bureau of Labor Statistics. It is available for public use at `https://www.nlsinfo.org/investigator/pages/search`. The survey started with a cohort of individuals in 1997 who were born between 1980 and 1985, with annual follow-ups each year through 2017. I extracted fewer than 100 variables from the hundreds available from this rich data source.

How to do it...

In this recipe, we will perform left, right, inner, and outer joins on two DataFrames that have one row for each merge-by value. Let's get started:

1. Import `pandas` and load the two NLS DataFrames:

```
>>> import pandas as pd
>>> nls97 = pd.read_csv("data/nls97f.csv")
>>> nls97.set_index("personid", inplace=True)
>>> nls97add = pd.read_csv("data/nls97add.csv")
```

2. Look at some of the NLS data:

```
>>> nls97.head()
            gender  birthmonth  birthyear  ...
colenrfeb17  \
personid                                        ...
100061      Female           5       1980  ...  1. Not
enrolled
100139        Male           9       1983  ...  1. Not
enrolled
100284        Male          11       1984  ...  1. Not
enrolled
100292        Male           4       1982  ...
NaN
```

```
100583        Male              1        1980   ...  1. Not
enrolled
                   colenroct17   originalid
personid
100061    1. Not enrolled          8245
100139    1. Not enrolled          3962
100284    1. Not enrolled          3571
100292                NaN          2979
100583    1. Not enrolled          8511
>>> nls97.shape
(8984, 89)
>>> nls97add.head()
   originalid  motherage  parentincome  fatherhighgrade
motherhighgrade
0            1         26            -3               16
8
1            2         19            -4               17
15
2            3         26         63000               -3
12
3            4         33         11700               12
12
4            5         34            -3               12
12
>>> nls97add.shape
(8984, 5)
```

3. Check that the number of unique values for originalid is equal to the number of rows.

4. We will use originalid for our merge-by column later:

```
>>> nls97.originalid.nunique()==nls97.shape[0]
True
>>> nls97add.originalid.nunique()==nls97add.shape[0]
True
```

5. Create some mismatched IDs.

Unfortunately, the NLS data is a little too clean for our purposes. Due to this, we will mess up a couple of values for `originalid`. `originalid` is the last column in the `nls97` file and the first column in the `nls97add` file:

```
>>> nls97 = nls97.sort_values('originalid')
>>> nls97add = nls97add.sort_values('originalid')
>>> nls97.iloc[0:2, -1] = nls97.originalid+10000
>>> nls97.originalid.head(2)
personid
135335     10001
999406     10002
Name: originalid, dtype: int64
>>> nls97add.iloc[0:2, 0] = nls97add.originalid+20000
>>> nls97add.originalid.head(2)
0     20001
1     20002
Name: originalid, dtype: int64
```

6. Use `join` to perform a left join.

`nls97` is the left DataFrame and `nls97add` is the right DataFrame when we use `join` in this way. Show the values for the mismatched IDs. Notice that the values for the columns from the right DataFrame are all missing when there is no matching ID on that DataFrame (the `orignalid` values `10001` and `10002` appear on the left DataFrame but not on the right DataFrame):

```
>>> nlsnew = nls97.join(nls97add.set_
index(['originalid']))
>>> nlsnew.loc[nlsnew.originalid>9999,
['originalid','gender','birthyear','motherage',
'parentincome']]
        originalid  gender  birthyear  motherage
parentincome
personid
135335      10001  Female       1981        nan
nan
999406      10002    Male       1982        nan
nan
```

7. Perform a left join with `merge`.

The first DataFrame is the left DataFrame, while the second DataFrame is the right DataFrame. Use the `on` parameter to indicate the merge-by column. Set the value of the `how` parameter to `"left"` to do a left join. We get the same results that we get when using `join`, other than with the index:

```
>>> nlsnew = pd.merge(nls97, nls97add, on=['originalid'],
how="left")
```

```
>>> nlsnew.loc[nlsnew.originalid>9999,
['originalid','gender','birthyear','motherage',
'parentincome']]
```

	originalid	gender	birthyear	motherage	parentincome
0	10001	Female	1981	nan	nan
1	10002	Male	1982	nan	nan

8. Perform a right join.

With a right join, the values from the left DataFrame are missing when there is no matching ID on the left DataFrame:

```
>>> nlsnew = pd.merge(nls97, nls97add, on=['originalid'],
how="right")
```

```
>>> nlsnew.loc[nlsnew.originalid>9999,
['originalid','gender','birthyear','motherage',
'parentincome']]
```

	originalid	gender	birthyear	motherage
parentincome				
8982	20001	NaN	nan	26
-3				
8983	20002	NaN	nan	19
-4				

9. Perform an inner join.

None of the mismatched IDs (that have values over `10000`) appear after the inner join. This is because they do not appear on both DataFrames:

```
>>> nlsnew = pd.merge(nls97, nls97add, on=['originalid'],
how="inner")
```

```
>>> nlsnew.loc[nlsnew.originalid>9999,
['originalid','gender','birthyear','motherage',
'parentincome']]
```

```
Empty DataFrame
```

```
Columns: [originalid, gender, birthyear, motherage,
parentincome]
Index: []
```

10. Perform an outer join.

   This retains all the rows, so rows with merge-by values in the left DataFrame but not in the right are retained (`originalid` values `10001` and `10002`), and rows with merge-by values in the right DataFrame but not in the left are also retained (`originalid` values `20001` and `20002`):

```
>>> nlsnew = pd.merge(nls97, nls97add, on=['originalid'],
how="outer")
>>> nlsnew.loc[nlsnew.originalid>9999,
['originalid','gender','birthyear','motherage',
'parentincome']]
        originalid  gender  birthyear  motherage
parentincome
0            10001  Female      1,981        nan
nan
1            10002    Male      1,982        nan
nan
8984         20001     NaN        nan         26
-3
8985         20002     NaN        nan         19
-4
```

11. Create a function to check for ID mismatches.

   The function takes a left and right DataFrame, as well as a merge-by column. It perform an outer join because we want to see which merge-by values are present in either DataFrame, or both of them:

```
>>> def checkmerge(dfleft, dfright, idvar):
...     dfleft['inleft'] = "Y"
...     dfright['inright'] = "Y"
...     dfboth = pd.merge(dfleft[[idvar,'inleft']],\
...         dfright[[idvar,'inright']], on=[idvar],
how="outer")
...     dfboth.fillna('N', inplace=True)
...     print(pd.crosstab(dfboth.inleft, dfboth.inright))
...
```

```
>>> checkmerge(nls97,nls97add, "originalid")
inright   N     Y
inleft
N         0     2
Y         2  8982
```

With that, we have demonstrated how to perform the four types of joins with a one-to-one merge.

How it works...

One-to-one merges are fairly straightforward. The merge-by column(s) only appear once on the left and right DataFrames. However, some merge-by column values may appear on only one DataFrame. This is what makes the type of join important. If all merge-by column values appeared on both DataFrames, then a left join, right join, inner join, or outer join would return the same result. We took a look at the two DataFrames in the first few steps. In *step 3*, we confirmed that the number of unique values for the merge-by column (originalid) is equal to the number of rows in both DataFrames. This tells us that we will be doing a one-to-one merge.

If the merge-by column is the index, then the easiest way to perform a left join is to use the join DataFrame method. We did this in *step 5*. We passed the right DataFrame, after setting the index, to the join method of the left DataFrame. (The index has already been set for the left DataFrame). The same result was returned when we performed a left join using the pandas merge function in *step 6*. We used the how parameter to specify a left join and indicated the merge-by column using on. The value that we passed to on can be any column(s) in the DataFrame.

In *steps 7* to *9*, we performed the right, inner, and outer joins, respectively. This is specified by the how value, which is the only part of the code that is different across these steps.

The simple checkmerge function we created in *step 10* counted the number of rows with merge-by column values on one DataFrame but not the other, and the number of values on both. Passing copies of the two DataFrames to this function tells us that two rows are in the left DataFrame and not in the right, two rows are in the right DataFrame but not the left, and 8,982 rows are in both.

There's more...

You should run a function similar to the `checkmerge` function we created in *step 10* before you do any non-trivial merge – which, in my opinion, is pretty much all merges.

The `merge` function is more flexible than the examples I have used in this recipe suggest. For example, in *step 6*, we did not have to specify the left DataFrame as the first parameter. I could have indicated the left and right DataFrames explicitly, like so:

```
>>> nlsnew = pd.merge(right=nls97add, left=nls97,
on=['originalid'], how="left")
```

We can also specify different merge-by columns for the left and right DataFrames by using `left_on` and `right_on` instead of `on`:

```
>>> nlsnew = pd.merge(nls97, nls97add, left_on=['originalid'],
right_on=['originalid'], how="left")
```

The flexibility of the `merge` function makes it a great tool any time we need to combine data horizontally.

Using multiple merge-by columns

The same logic we used to perform one-to-one merges with one merge-by column applies to merges we perform with multiple merge-by columns. Inner, outer, left, and right joins work the same way when you have two or more merge-by columns. We will demonstrate this in this recipe.

Getting ready

We will work with the NLS data in this recipe, specifically weeks worked and college enrollment from 2000 through 2004. Both the weeks worked and college enrollment files contain one row per person, per year.

How to do it...

We will continue this recipe with one-to-one merges, but this time with multiple merge-by columns on each DataFrame. Let's get started:

1. Import pandas and load the NLS weeks worked and college enrollment data:

```
>>> import pandas as pd
>>> nls97weeksworked = pd.read_csv("data/
nls97weeksworked.csv")
>>> nls97colenr = pd.read_csv("data/nls97colenr.csv")
```

2. Look at some of the NLS weeks worked data:

```
>>> nls97weeksworked.sample(10, random_state=1)
       originalid   year   weeksworked
32923        7199   2003           0.0
14214        4930   2001          52.0
2863         4727   2000          13.0
9746         6502   2001           0.0
2479         4036   2000          28.0
39435        1247   2004          52.0
36416        3481   2004          52.0
6145         8892   2000          19.0
5348         8411   2000           0.0
24193        4371   2002          34.0
>>> nls97weeksworked.shape
(44920, 3)
>>> nls97weeksworked.originalid.nunique()
8984
```

3. Look at some of the NLS college enrollment data:

```
>>> nls97colenr.sample(10, random_state=1)
       originalid   year              colenr
32923        7199   2003   1. Not enrolled
14214        4930   2001   1. Not enrolled
2863         4727   2000                NaN
9746         6502   2001   1. Not enrolled
2479         4036   2000   1. Not enrolled
```

```
39435          1247  2004   3. 4-year college
36416          3481  2004   1. Not enrolled
6145           8892  2000   1. Not enrolled
5348           8411  2000   1. Not enrolled
24193          4371  2002   2. 2-year college
>>> nls97colenr.shape
(44920, 3)
>>> nls97colenr.originalid.nunique()
8984
```

4. Check for unique values in the merge-by columns.

   We get the same number of merge-by column value combinations (44,920) as there are number of rows in both DataFrames:

```
>>> nls97weeksworked.groupby(['originalid','year'])\
...     ['originalid'].count().shape
(44920,)
>>>
>>> nls97colenr.groupby(['originalid','year'])\
...     ['originalid'].count().shape
(44920,)
```

5. Check for mismatches in the merge-by columns:

```
>>> def checkmerge(dfleft, dfright, idvar):
...     dfleft['inleft'] = "Y"
...     dfright['inright'] = "Y"
...     dfboth = pd.merge(dfleft[idvar + ['inleft']],\
...       dfright[idvar + ['inright']], on=idvar,
how="outer")
...     dfboth.fillna('N', inplace=True)
...     print(pd.crosstab(dfboth.inleft, dfboth.inright))
...
>>> checkmerge(nls97weeksworked.copy(),nls97colenr.
copy(), ['originalid','year'])
inright       Y
inleft
Y          44920
```

6. Perform a merge with multiple merge-by columns:

```
>>> nlsworkschool = pd.merge(nls97weeksworked,
nls97colenr, on=['originalid','year'], how="inner")
>>> nlsworkschool.shape
(44920, 4)


>>> nlsworkschool.sample(10, random_state=1)
        originalid  year  weeksworked              colenr
32923         7199  2003            0     1. Not enrolled
14214         4930  2001           52     1. Not enrolled
2863          4727  2000           13                 NaN
9746          6502  2001            0     1. Not enrolled
2479          4036  2000           28     1. Not enrolled
39435         1247  2004           52    3. 4-year college
36416         3481  2004           52     1. Not enrolled
6145          8892  2000           19     1. Not enrolled
5348          8411  2000            0     1. Not enrolled
24193         4371  2002           34    2. 2-year college
```

These steps demonstrate that the syntax for running merges changes very little when there are multiple merge-by columns.

How it works...

Every person in the NLS data has five rows for both the weeks worked and college enrollment DataFrames, with one for each year between 2000 and 2004. In *step 3*, we saw that there is a row even when the colenr value is missing. Both files contain 44,920 rows with 8,984 unique individuals (indicated by originalid). This all makes sense (8,984*5=44,920).

Step 4 confirmed that the combination of columns we will be using for the merge-by columns will not be duplicated, even if individuals are duplicated. Each person has only one row for each year. This means that merging the weeks worked and college enrollment data will be a one-to-one merge. In *step 5*, we checked to see whether there were any individual and year combinations that were in one DataFrame but not the other. There were none.

Finally, we were ready to do the merge in *step 6*. We set the `on` parameter to a list (`['originalid', 'year']`) to tell the merge function to use both columns in the merge. We specified an inner join, even though we would get the same results with any join. This is because the same merge-by values are present in both files.

There's more...

All the logic and potential issues in merging data that we discussed in the previous recipe apply, regardless of whether we are merging with one merge-by column or several. Inner, outer, right, and left joins work the same way. We can still calculate the number of rows that will be returned before doing the merge. However, we still need to check for the number of unique merge-by values and for matches between the DataFrames.

If you have worked with recipes in earlier chapters that used the NLS weeks worked and college enrollment data, you probably noticed that it is structured differently here. In previous recipes, there was one row per person with multiple columns for weeks worked and college enrollment, representing weeks worked and college enrollment for multiple years. For example, `weeksworked01` is the number of weeks worked in 2001. The structure of the weeks worked and college enrollment DataFrames we used in this recipe is considered *tidier* than the NLS DataFrame we used in earlier recipes. We'll learn how to tidy data in *Chapter 9, Tidying and Reshaping Data*.

Doing one-to-many merges

In one-to-many merges, there are unduplicated values for the merge-by column or columns on the left data table and duplicated values for those columns on the right data table. For these merges, we usually do either an inner join or a left join. Which join we use matters when merge-by values are missing on the right data table. When performing a left join, all the rows that would be returned from an inner join will be returned, plus one row for each merge-by value present on the left dataset, but not the right. For those additional rows, values for all the columns on the right dataset will be missing in the resulting merged data. This relatively straightforward fact ends up mattering a fair bit and should be thought through carefully before you code a one-to-many merge.

This is where I start to get nervous, and where I think it makes sense to be a little nervous. When I do workshops on data cleaning, I pause before starting this topic and say, *"do not start a one-to-many merge until you are able to bring a friend with you."*

I am joking, of course… mostly. The point I am trying to make is that something should cause us to pause before doing a non-trivial merge, and one-to-many merges are never trivial. Too much about the structure of our data can change.

Specifically, there are several things we want to know about the two DataFrames we will be merging before starting. First, we should know what columns make sense as merge-by columns on each DataFrame. They do not have to be the same columns. Indeed, one-to-many merges are often used to recapture relationships from an enterprise database system, and they are consistent with the primary keys and foreign keys used, which may have different names. (The primary key on the left data table is often linked to the foreign key on the right data table in a relational database.) Second, we should know what kind of join we will be using and why.

Third, we should know how many rows are on both data tables. Fourth, we should have a good idea of how many rows will be retained based on the type of join, the number of rows in each dataset, and preliminary checks on how many of the merge-by values will match. If all the merge-by values are present on both datasets or if we are doing an inner join, then the number of rows will be equal to the number of rows of the right dataset of a one-to-many merge. But it is often not as straightforward as that. We frequently perform left joins with one-to-many merges. With these types of joins, the number of retained rows will be equal to the number of rows in the right dataset with a matching merge-by value, plus the number of rows in the left dataset with non-matching merge-by values.

This should be clearer once we've worked through the examples in this recipe.

Getting ready

We will be working with data based on weather stations from the *Global Historical Climatology Network* integrated database for this recipe. One of the DataFrames contains one row for each country. The other contains one row for each weather station. There are typically many weather stations for each country.

How to do it...

In this recipe, we will do a one-to-many merge of data for countries, which contains one row per country, and a merge for the weather station data, which contains multiple stations for each country. Let's get started:

1. Import pandas and load the weather station and country data:

```
>>> import pandas as pd
>>> countries = pd.read_csv("data/ltcountries.csv")
>>> locations = pd.read_csv("data/ltlocations.csv")
```

2. Set the index for the weather station (`locations`) and country data.

    Confirm that the merge-by values for the `countries` DataFrame are unique:

```
>>> countries.set_index(['countryid'], inplace=True)
>>> locations.set_index(['countryid'], inplace=True)
>>> countries.head()
```

	country
countryid	
AC	Antigua and Barbuda
AE	United Arab Emirates
AF	Afghanistan
AG	Algeria
AJ	Azerbaijan

```
>>> countries.index.nunique()==countries.shape[0]
True


>>> locations[['locationid','latitude','stnelev']].
head(10)
```

	locationid	latitude	stnelev
countryid			
AC	ACW00011604	58	18
AE	AE000041196	25	34
AE	AEM00041184	26	31
AE	AEM00041194	25	10
AE	AEM00041216	24	3
AE	AEM00041217	24	27
AE	AEM00041218	24	265
AF	AF000040930	35	3,366
AF	AFM00040911	37	378
AF	AFM00040938	34	977

3. Perform a left join of countries and locations using `join`:

```
>>> stations = countries.join(locations)


>>>
stations[['locationid','latitude','stnelev','country']].
head(10)
```

	locationid	latitude	stnelev	
country				
countryid				
AC Barbuda	ACW00011604	58	18	Antigua and
AE Emirates	AE000041196	25	34	United Arab
AE Emirates	AEM00041184	26	31	United Arab
AE Emirates	AEM00041194	25	10	United Arab
AE Emirates	AEM00041216	24	3	United Arab
AE Emirates	AEM00041217	24	27	United Arab
AE Emirates	AEM00041218	24	265	United Arab
AF Afghanistan	AF000040930	35	3,366	
AF Afghanistan	AFM00040911	37	378	
AF Afghanistan	AFM00040938	34	977	

4. Check that the merge-by column matches.

First, reload the DataFrames since we have made some changes. The checkmerge function shows that there are 27,472 rows with merge-by values (from countryid) in both DataFrames and two in countries (the left DataFrame) but not in locations. This indicates that an inner join would return 27,472 rows and a left join would return 27,474 rows. The last statement in the function identifies the countryid values that appear in one DataFrame but not the other:

```
>>> countries = pd.read_csv("data/ltcountries.csv")
>>> locations = pd.read_csv("data/ltlocations.csv")
>>>
>>> def checkmerge(dfleft, dfright, idvar):
...    dfleft['inleft'] = "Y"
...    dfright['inright'] = "Y"
...    dfboth = pd.merge(dfleft[[idvar,'inleft']],\
```

```
...          dfright[[idvar,'inright']], on=[idvar],
how="outer")
...          dfboth.fillna('N', inplace=True)
...          print(pd.crosstab(dfboth.inleft, dfboth.inright))
...          print(dfboth.loc[(dfboth.inleft=='N') | (dfboth.
inright=='N')])
...
>>> checkmerge(countries.copy(), locations.copy(),
"countryid")
inright   N        Y
inleft
N          0        1
Y          2    27472
        countryid inleft inright
9715            LQ      Y       N
13103           ST      Y       N
27474           FO      N       Y
```

5. Show the rows in one file but not the other.

The last statement in the previous step displays the two values of `countryid` in `countries` but not in `locations`, and the one in `locations` but not in `countries`:

```
>>> countries.loc[countries.countryid.isin(["LQ","ST"])]
    countryid                              country
124       LQ  Palmyra Atoll [United States]
195       ST                          Saint Lucia

>>> locations.loc[locations.countryid=="FO"]
       locationid  latitude  longitude  stnelev   station
countryid
7363  FOM00006009        61        -7      102  AKRABERG
FO
```

6. Merge the `locations` and `countries` DataFrames.

    Perform a left join. Also, count the number of missing values for each column, where merge-by values are present in the `countries` data but not in the weather station data:

```
>>> stations = pd.merge(countries, locations,
on=["countryid"], how="left")
```

```
>>>
stations[['locationid','latitude','stnelev','country']].
head(10)
```

	locationid	latitude	stnelev	country
0	ACW00011604	58	18	Antigua and Barbuda
1	AE000041196	25	34	United Arab Emirates
2	AEM00041184	26	31	United Arab Emirates
3	AEM00041194	25	10	United Arab Emirates
4	AEM00041216	24	3	United Arab Emirates
5	AEM00041217	24	27	United Arab Emirates
6	AEM00041218	24	265	United Arab Emirates
7	AF000040930	35	3,366	Afghanistan
8	AFM00040911	37	378	Afghanistan
9	AFM00040938	34	977	Afghanistan

```
>>> stations.shape
```
```
(27474, 7)
```
```
>>> stations.loc[stations.countryid.isin(["LQ","ST"])].
isnull().sum()
```

countryid	0
country	0
locationid	2
latitude	2
longitude	2
stnelev	2
station	2

```
dtype: int64
```

The one-to-many merge returns the expected number of rows and new missing values.

How it works...

In *step 2*, we used the `join` DataFrame method to perform a left join of the `countries` and `locations` DataFrames. This is the easiest way to do a merge. Since the `join` method uses the index of the DataFrames for the merge, we need to set the index first. We then passed the right DataFrame to the `join` method of the left DataFrame.

Although `join` is a little more flexible than this example suggests (you can specify the type of join, for example), I prefer the more verbose pandas `merge` function for all but the simplest of merges. I can be confident when using the `merge` function that all the options I need are available to me. Before we could do the merge, we had to do some checks. We did this in *step 4*. This told us how many rows to expect in the merged DataFrame if we were to do an inner or left join; there would be 27,472 or 27,474 rows, respectively.

We also displayed the rows with merge-by values in one DataFrame but not the other. If we are going to do a left join, we need to decide what to do with the missing values that will result from the right DataFrame. In this case, there were two merge-by values that were not found on the right DataFrame, giving us two missing values for those columns.

There's more...

You may have noticed that in our call to `checkmerge`, we passed copies of the `countries` and `locations` DataFrames:

```
>>> checkmerge(countries.copy(), locations.copy(), "countryid")
```

We use `copy` here because we do not want the `checkmerge` function to make any changes to our original DataFrames.

See also

We discussed join types in detail in the *Doing one-to-one merges* recipe.

Doing many-to-many merges

Many-to-many merges have duplicate merge-by values in both the left and right DataFrames. We should only rarely need to do a many-to-many merge. Even when data comes to us in that form, it is often because we are missing the central file in multiple one-to-many relationships. For example, there are donor, donor contributions, and donor contact information data tables, and the last two files contain multiple rows per donor. However, in this case, we do not have access to the donor file, which has a one-to-many relationship with both the contributions and contact information files. This happens more frequently than you may think. People sometimes give us data with little awareness of the underlying structure. When I do a many-to-many merge, it is typically because I am missing some key information rather than because that was how the database was designed.

Many-to-many merges return the Cartesian product of the merge-by column values. So, if a donor ID appears twice on the donor contact information file and five times on the donor contributions file, then the merge will return 10 rows. The problem here is there will be more rows in the returned data, but this does not make sense analytically. In this example, a many-to-many merge will duplicate the donor contributions, once for each address.

Often, when faced with a potential many-to-many merge situation, the solution is not to do it. Instead, we can recover the implied one-to-many relationships. With the donor example, we could remove all the rows except for the most recent contact information, thus ensuring that there is one row per donor. We could then do a one-to-many merge with the donor contributions file. But we are not always able to avoid doing a many-to-many merge. Sometimes, we must produce an analytical or flat file that keeps all of the data, without regard for duplication. This recipe demonstrates how to do those merges when that is required.

Getting ready

We will work with data based on the Cleveland Museum of Art's collections. We will use two CSV files: one containing each media citation for each item in the collection and another containing the creator(s) of each item.

> **Tip**
> The Cleveland Museum of Art provides an API for public access to this data: `https://openaccess-api.clevelandart.org/`. Much more than the citations and creators data is available in the API.

How to do it...

Follow these steps to complete this recipe:

1. Load pandas and the **Cleveland Museum of Art (CMA)** collections data:

```
>>> import pandas as pd
>>> cmacitations = pd.read_csv("data/cmacitations.csv")
>>> cmacreators = pd.read_csv("data/cmacreators.csv")
```

2. Look at the `citations` data:

```
>>> cmacitations.head(10)
        id
citation
0  92937  Milliken, William M. "The Second Exhibition
of...
1  92937  Glasier, Jessie C. "Museum Gets Prize-Winning
...
2  92937  "Cleveland Museum Acquires Typical Pictures
by...
3  92937  Milliken, William M. "Two Examples of Modern
P...
4  92937  <em>Memorial Exhibition of the Work of George
...
5  92937  The Cleveland Museum of Art. <em>Handbook of
t...
6  92937  Cortissoz, Royal. "Paintings and Prints by
Geo...
7  92937  Isham, Samuel, and Royal Cortissoz. <em>The
Hi...
8  92937  Mather, Frank Jewett, Charles Rufus Morey,
and...
9  92937  "Un Artiste Americain."
<em>L'illustration.</e...
>>> cmacitations.shape
(11642, 2)
>>> cmacitations.id.nunique()
935
```

3. Look at the `creators` data:

```
>>> cmacreators.loc[:,['id','creator','birth_year']].
head(10)
         id                                    creator
birth_year
0    92937               George Bellows (American, 1882-1925)
1882
1    94979   John Singleton Copley (American, 1738-1815)
1738
2   137259              Gustave Courbet (French, 1819-1877)
1819
3   141639   Frederic Edwin Church (American, 1826-1900)
1826
4    93014                  Thomas Cole (American, 1801-1848)
1801
5   110180   Albert Pinkham Ryder (American, 1847-1917)
1847
6   135299              Vincent van Gogh (Dutch, 1853-1890)
1853
7   125249              Vincent van Gogh (Dutch, 1853-1890)
1853
8   126769              Henri Rousseau (French, 1844-1910)
1844
9   135382                Claude Monet (French, 1840-1926)
1840
>>> cmacreators.shape
(737, 8)
>>> cmacreators.id.nunique()
654
```

4. Show duplicates of merge-by values in the `citations` data.

5. There are 174 media citations for collection item 148758:

```
>>> cmacitations.id.value_counts().head(10)
148758    174
122351    116
92937      98
123168     94
```

94979	93
149112	93
124245	87
128842	86
102578	84
93014	79

```
Name: id, dtype: int64
```

6. Show duplicates of the merge-by values in the `creators` data:

```
>>> cmacreators.id.value_counts().head(10)
```

140001	4
149386	4
114537	3
149041	3
93173	3
142752	3
114538	3
146795	3
146797	3
142753	3

```
Name: id, dtype: int64
```

7. Check the merge.

Use the `checkmerge` function we used in the *Doing one-to-many merges* recipe:

```
>>> def checkmerge(dfleft, dfright, idvar):
...     dfleft['inleft'] = "Y"
...     dfright['inright'] = "Y"
...     dfboth = pd.merge(dfleft[[idvar,'inleft']],\
...        dfright[[idvar,'inright']], on=[idvar],
how="outer")
...     dfboth.fillna('N', inplace=True)
...     print(pd.crosstab(dfboth.inleft, dfboth.inright))
...
>>> checkmerge(cmacitations.copy(), cmacreators.copy(),
"id")
inright        N       Y
```

```
inleft
N          0    46
Y       2579  9701
```

8. Show a merge-by value duplicated in both DataFrames:

```
>>> cmacitations.loc[cmacitations.id==124733]
            id
citation
8963   124733   Weigel, J. A. G. <em>Catalog einer Sammlung
vo...
8964   124733   Winkler, Friedrich. <em>Die Zeichnungen
Albrec...
8965   124733   Francis, Henry S. "Drawing of a Dead Blue
Jay ...
8966   124733   Kurz, Otto. <em>Fakes: A Handbook for
Collecto...
8967   124733   Minneapolis Institute of Arts.
<em>Watercolors...
8968   124733   Pilz, Kurt. "Hans Hoffmann: Ein Nürnberger
Dür...
8969   124733   Koschatzky, Walter and Alice Strobl.
<em>Düre...
8970   124733   Johnson, Mark M<em>. Idea to Image:
Preparator...
8971   124733   Kaufmann, Thomas DaCosta. <em>Drawings from
th...
8972   124733   Koreny, Fritz. <em>Albrecht Dürer and the
ani...
8973   124733   Achilles-Syndram, Katrin. <em>Die
Kunstsammlun...
8974   124733   Schoch, Rainer, Katrin Achilles-Syndram,
and B...
8975   124733   DeGrazia, Diane and Carter E. Foster.
<em>Mast...
8976   124733   Dunbar, Burton L., et al. <em>A Corpus of
Draw...
>>> cmacreators.loc[cmacreators.id==124733,
['id','creator','birth_year','title']]
```

```
             id                                      creator
birth_year  \
449   124733          Albrecht Dürer (German, 1471-1528)
1471

450   124733   Hans Hoffmann (German, 1545/50-1591/92)
1545/50


                   title
449   Dead Blue Roller
450   Dead Blue Roller
```

9. Do a many-to-many merge:

```
>>> cma = pd.merge(cmacitations, cmacreators, on=['id'],
how="outer")
>>> cma['citation'] = cma.citation.str[0:20]
>>> cma['creator'] = cma.creator.str[0:20]
>>> cma.loc[cma.id==124733, ['citation','creator','birth_
year']]
                      citation                 creator birth_
year
9457  Weigel, J. A. G. <em  Albrecht Dürer (Germ
1471
9458  Weigel, J. A. G. <em  Hans Hoffmann (Germa
1545/50
9459  Winkler, Friedrich.   Albrecht Dürer (Germ
1471
9460  Winkler, Friedrich.   Hans Hoffmann (Germa
1545/50
9461  Francis, Henry S. "D  Albrecht Dürer (Germ
1471
9462  Francis, Henry S. "D  Hans Hoffmann (Germa
1545/50
9463  Kurz, Otto. <em>Fake  Albrecht Dürer (Germ
1471
9464  Kurz, Otto. <em>Fake  Hans Hoffmann (Germa
1545/50
9465  Minneapolis Institut  Albrecht Dürer (Germ
1471
```

```
9466    Minneapolis Institut    Hans Hoffmann (Germa
1545/50

9467    Pilz, Kurt. "Hans Ho    Albrecht Dürer (Germ
1471

9468    Pilz, Kurt. "Hans Ho    Hans Hoffmann (Germa
1545/50

9469    Koschatzky, Walter a    Albrecht Dürer (Germ
1471

9470    Koschatzky, Walter a    Hans Hoffmann (Germa
1545/50


... last 14 rows removed to save space
```

Now that I have taken you through the messiness of a many-to-many merge, I'll say a little more about how it works.

How it works...

Step 2 told us that there were 11,642 citations for 935 unique IDs. There is a unique ID for each item in the museum's collection. On average, each item has 12 media citations (11,642/935). *Step 3* told us that there are 737 creators over 654 items, so there is only one creator for the overwhelming majority of pieces. But the fact that there are duplicated IDs (our merge-by value) on both the citations and creators DataFrames means that our merge will be a many-to-many merge.

Step 4 gave us a sense of which IDs are duplicated on the citations DataFrame. Some items in the museum's collection have more than 80 citations. It is worth taking a closer look at the citations for those items to see whether they make sense. *Step 5* showed us that even when there is more than one creator, there are rarely more than three. In *step 6*, we saw that most IDs have rows in both the citations file and the creators file, but a fair number have citations rows but no creators rows. We will lose those 2,579 rows if we do an inner join or a right join, but not if we do a left join or an outer join. (This assumes that the citations DataFrame is the left DataFrame and the creators DataFrame is the right one.)

We looked at an ID that is in both DataFrames in *step 7* – one that also has duplicate IDs in both DataFrames. There are 14 rows for this collection item in the citations DataFrame and two in the creators DataFrame. This will result in 28 rows (2 * 14) with that ID in the merged DataFrame. The citations data will be repeated for each row in creators.

This was confirmed when we looked at the results of the merge in *step 8*. We performed an outer join with `id` as the merge-by column. (We also shortened the `citation` and `creator` descriptions to make them easier to view.) When we displayed the rows in the merged file for the same ID we used in *step 7*, we got the 28 rows we were expecting (I removed the last 14 rows of output to save space).

There's more...

It is good to understand what to expect when we do a many-to-many merge because there are times when it cannot be avoided. But even in this case, we can tell that the many-to-many relationship is really just two one-to-many relationships with the data file missing from the one side. There is likely a data table that contains one row per collection item that has a one-to-many relationship with both the `citations` data and the `creators` data. When we do not have access to a file like that, it is probably best to try to reproduce a file with that structure. With this data, we could have created a file containing `id` and maybe `title`, and then done one-to-many merges with the `citations` and `creators` data.

However, there are occasions when we must produce a flat file for subsequent analysis. We might need to do that when we, or a colleague who is getting the cleaned data from us, are using software that cannot handle relational data well. For example, someone in another department might do a lot of data visualization work with Excel. As long as that person knows which analyses require them to remove duplicated rows, a file with a structure like the one we produced in *step 8* might work fine.

Developing a merge routine

I find it helpful to think of merging data as the parking lot of the data cleaning process. Merging data and parking may seem routine, but they are where a disproportionate number of accidents occur. One approach to getting in and out of parking lots without an incident occurring is to use a similar strategy each time you go to a particular lot. It could be that you always go to a relatively low traffic area and you get to that area the same way most of the time.

I think a similar approach can be applied to getting in and out of merges with our data relatively unscathed. If we choose a general approach that works for us 80 to 90 percent of the time, we can focus on what is most important – the data, rather than the techniques for manipulating that data.

In this recipe, I will demonstrate the general approach that works for me, but the particular techniques I will use are not very important. I think it is just helpful to have an approach that you understand well and that you become comfortable using.

Getting ready

We will return to the objectives we focused on in the *Doing one-to-many merges* recipe of this chapter. We want to do a left join of the `countries` data with the `locations` data from the *Global Historical Climatology Network* integrated database.

How to do it...

In this recipe, we will do a left join of the `countries` and `locations` data after checking for merge-by value mismatches. Let's get started:

1. Import `pandas` and load the weather station and country data:

```
>>> import pandas as pd
>>> countries = pd.read_csv("data/ltcountries.csv")
>>> locations = pd.read_csv("data/ltlocations.csv")
```

2. Check the merge-by column matches:

```
>>> def checkmerge(dfleft, dfright, mergebyleft,
 mergebyright):
...     dfleft['inleft'] = "Y"
...     dfright['inright'] = "Y"
...     dfboth = pd.merge(dfleft[[mergebyleft,'inleft']],\
...         dfright[[mergebyright,'inright']], left_
 on=[mergebyleft],\
...         right_on=[mergebyright], how="outer")
...     dfboth.fillna('N', inplace=True)
...     print(pd.crosstab(dfboth.inleft, dfboth.inright))
...     print(dfboth.loc[(dfboth.inleft=='N') | (dfboth.
 inright=='N')].head(20))
...
>>> checkmerge(countries.copy(), locations.copy(),
 "countryid", "countryid")
inright   N        Y
inleft
N         0        1
```

```
Y            2   27472
        countryid inleft inright
9715          LQ     Y       N
13103         ST     Y       N
27474         FO     N       Y
```

3. Merge the country and location data:

```
>>> stations = pd.merge(countries, locations, left_
on=["countryid"], right_on=["countryid"], how="left")

>>>
stations[['locationid','latitude','stnelev','country']].
head(10)
     locationid  latitude  stnelev              country
0   ACW00011604        58       18  Antigua and Barbuda
1   AE000041196        25       34  United Arab Emirates
2   AEM00041184        26       31  United Arab Emirates
3   AEM00041194        25       10  United Arab Emirates
4   AEM00041216        24        3  United Arab Emirates
5   AEM00041217        24       27  United Arab Emirates
6   AEM00041218        24      265  United Arab Emirates
7   AF000040930        35    3,366          Afghanistan
8   AFM00040911        37      378          Afghanistan
9   AFM00040938        34      977          Afghanistan
>>> stations.shape
(27474, 7)
```

Here, we got the expected number of rows from a left join; 27,472 rows with merge-by values in both DataFrames and two rows with merge-by values in the left DataFrame, but not the right.

How it works...

For the overwhelming majority of merges I do, something like the logic used in *steps 2* and *3* works well. We added a fourth argument to the `checkmerge` function we used in the previous recipe. This allows us to specify different merge-by columns for the left and right DataFrames. We do not need to recreate this function every time we do a merge. We can just include it in a module that we import. (We'll go over adding helper functions to modules in the final chapter of this book).

Calling the `checkmerge` function before running a merge gives us enough information so that we know what to expect when running the merge with different join types. We will know how many rows will be returned from an inner, outer, left, or right join. We will also know where the new missing values will be generated before we run the actual merge. Of course, this is a fairly expensive operation, requiring us to run a merge twice each time – one diagnostic outer join followed by whatever join we subsequently choose. But I would argue that it is usually worth it, if for no other reason than that it helps us to stop and think about what we are doing.

Finally, we performed the merge in *step 3*. This is my preferred syntax. I always use the left DataFrame for the first argument and the right DataFrame for the second argument, though `merge` allows us to specify the left and right DataFrames in different ways. I also set values for `left_on` and `right_on`, even if the merge-by column is the same and I could use `on` instead (as we did in the previous recipe). This is so I will not have to change the syntax in cases where the merge-by column is different, and I like it that it makes the merge-by column explicit for both DataFrames.

A somewhat more controversial routine is that I default to a left join, setting the `how` parameter to left initially. I make that my starting assumption and then ask myself if there is any reason to do a different join. The rows in the left DataFrame often represent my unit of analysis (students, patients, customers, and so on) and that I am adding supplemental data (GPA, blood pressure, zip code, and so on). It may be problematic to remove rows from the unit of analysis because the merge-by value is not present on the right DataFrame, as would happen if I did an inner join instead. For example, in the *Doing one-to-one merges* recipe of this chapter, it probably would not have made sense to remove rows from the main NLS data because they do not appear on the supplemental data we have for parents.

See also

We will create modules with useful data cleaning functions in *Chapter 10, User-Defined Functions and Classes to Automate Data Cleaning*.

We have discussed the types of joins in the *Doing one to one merges* recipe in this chapter.

9
Tidying and Reshaping Data

As Leo Tolstoy and Hadley Wickham tell us, all tidy data is fundamentally alike, but all untidy data is messy in its own special way. How many times have we all stared at some rows of data and thought, *"what..... how...... why did they do that?"* This overstates the case somewhat. Although there are many ways that data can be poorly structured, there are limits to human creativity in this regard. It is possible to categorize the most frequent ways in which datasets deviate from normalized or tidy forms.

This was Hadley Wickham's observation in his seminal work on tidy data. We can lean on that work, and our own experiences with oddly structured data, to prepare for the reshaping we have to do. Untidy data often has one or more of the following characteristics: a lack of clarity about merge-by column relationships; data redundancy on the *one* side of one-to-many relationships; data redundancy due to many-to-many relationships; values stored in column names; multiple values stored in one variable value; and data not being structured at the unit of analysis. (Although the last category is not necessarily a case of untidy data, some of the techniques we will review in the next few recipes are applicable to common unit-of-analysis problems.)

We use powerful tools in this chapter to deal with data cleaning challenges like the preceding. Specifically, we'll go over the following:

- Removing duplicated rows

- Fixing many-to-many relationships

- Using `stack` and `melt` to reshape data from a wide to long format

- Melting multiple groups of columns

- Using `unstack` and `pivot` to reshape data from long to wide format

Technical requirements

The code and notebooks for this chapter are available on GitHub at `https://github.com/PacktPublishing/Python-Data-Cleaning-Cookbook`

Removing duplicated rows

There are several reasons why we might have data duplicated at the unit of analysis:

- The existing DataFrame may be the result of a one-to-many merge, and the one side is the unit of analysis.

- The DataFrame is repeated measures or panel data collapsed into a flat file, which is just a special case of the first situation.

- We may be working with an analysis file where multiple one-to-many relationships have been flattened, creating many-to-many relationships.

When the *one* side is the unit of analysis, data on the *many* side may need to be collapsed in some way. For example, if we are analyzing outcomes for a cohort of students at a college, students are the unit of analysis; but we may also have course enrollment data for each student. To prepare the data for analysis, we might need to first count the number of courses, sum the total credits, or calculate the GPA for each student, before ending up with one row per student. To generalize from this example, we often need to aggregate the information on the *many* side before removing duplicated data.

In this recipe, we look at pandas techniques for removing duplicate rows, and consider when we do and don't need to do aggregation during that process. We address duplication in many-to-many relationships in the next recipe.

Getting ready...

We will work with the COVID-19 daily case data in this recipe. It has one row per day per country, each row having the number of new cases and new deaths for that day. There are also demographic data for each country, and running totals for cases and deaths, so the last row for each country provides total cases and total deaths.

> **Note**
>
> *Our World in Data* provides COVID-19 public use data at `https://ourworldindata.org/coronavirus-source-data`. The data used in this recipe was downloaded on July 18, 2020.

How to do it...

We use `drop_duplicates` to remove duplicated demographic data for each country in the COVID daily data. We explore `groupby` as an alternative to `drop_duplicates` when we need to do some aggregation before removing duplicated data:

1. Import `pandas` and the COVID daily cases data:

    ```
    >>> import pandas as pd
    >>> covidcases = pd.read_csv("data/covidcases720.csv")
    ```

2. Create lists for the daily cases and deaths columns, the case total columns, and the demographic columns:

    ```
    >>> dailyvars = ['casedate','new_cases','new_deaths']
    >>> totvars = ['location','total_cases','total_deaths']
    >>> demovars = ['population','population_
    density','median_age',
    ...      'gdp_per_capita','hospital_beds_per_
    thousand','region']
    >>>
    >>> covidcases[dailyvars + totvars + demovars].head(3).T
                              0             1
    2
    casedate         2019-12-31    2020-01-01
    2020-01-02
    new_cases              0.00          0.00
    0.00
    new_deaths             0.00          0.00
    0.00
    ```

location Afghanistan	Afghanistan	Afghanistan
total_cases 0.00	0.00	0.00
total_deaths 0.00	0.00	0.00
population 38,928,341.00	38,928,341.00	38,928,341.00
population_density 54.42	54.42	54.42
median_age 18.60	18.60	18.60
gdp_per_capita 1,803.99	1,803.99	1,803.99
hospital_beds_per_thousand 0.50	0.50	0.50
region South Asia	South Asia	South Asia

3. Create a DataFrame with just the daily data:

```
>>> coviddaily = covidcases[['location'] + dailyvars]
>>> coviddaily.shape
(29529, 4)
>>> coviddaily.head()
     location    casedate   new_cases   new_deaths
0  Afghanistan  2019-12-31       0.00         0.00
1  Afghanistan  2020-01-01       0.00         0.00
2  Afghanistan  2020-01-02       0.00         0.00
3  Afghanistan  2020-01-03       0.00         0.00
4  Afghanistan  2020-01-04       0.00         0.00
```

4. Select one row per country.

Check to see how many countries (location) to expect by getting the number of unique locations. Sort by location and casedate. Then use drop_duplicates to select one row per location, and use the keep parameter to indicate that we want the last row for each country:

```
>>> covidcases.location.nunique()
209
```

```
>>> coviddemo = covidcases[['casedate'] + totvars +
demovars].\
...     sort_values(['location','casedate']).\
...     drop_duplicates(['location'], keep='last').\
...     rename(columns={'casedate':'lastdate'})
>>>
>>> coviddemo.shape
(209, 10)
>>> coviddemo.head(3).T
                                     184               310
500
lastdate                       2020-07-12        2020-07-12
2020-07-12
location                       Afghanistan           Albania
Algeria
total_cases                      34,451.00          3,371.00
18,712.00
total_deaths                      1,010.00             89.00
1,004.00
population                    38,928,341.00      2,877,800.00
43,851,043.00
population_density                   54.42            104.87
17.35
median_age                           18.60             38.00
29.10
gdp_per_capita                    1,803.99         11,803.43
13,913.84
hospital_beds_per_thousand            0.50              2.89
1.90
region                          South Asia    Eastern Europe
North Africa
```

5. Sum the values for each group.

    Use the pandas DataFrame `groupby` method to sum total cases and deaths for
    each country. Also, get the last value for some of the columns that are duplicated
    across all rows for each country: `median_age`, `gdp_per_capita`, `region`, and
    `casedate`. (We select only a few columns from the DataFrame.) Notice that the
    numbers match those from *step 4*:

    ```
    >>> covidtotals = covidcases.groupby(['location'], as_
    index=False).\
    ```

```
...       agg({'new_cases':'sum','new_deaths':'sum','median_
age':'last',
...           'gdp_per_
capita':'last','region':'last','casedate':'last',
...           'population':'last'}).\
...       rename(columns={'new_cases':'total_cases',
...           'new_deaths':'total_
deaths','casedate':'lastdate'})

>>> covidtotals.head(3).T
```

	0	1
2		
location	Afghanistan	Albania
Algeria		
total_cases	34,451.00	3,371.00
18,712.00		
total_deaths	1,010.00	89.00
1,004.00		
median_age	18.60	38.00
29.10		
gdp_per_capita	1,803.99	11,803.43
13,913.84		
region	South Asia	Eastern Europe	North
Africa		
lastdate	2020-07-12	2020-07-12	2020-07-
12		
population	38,928,341.00	2,877,800.00
43,851,043.00		

The choice of `drop_duplicates` or `groupby` to eliminate data redundancy comes down to whether we need to do any aggregation before collapsing the *many* side.

How it works...

The COVID data has one row per country per day, but very little of the data is actually daily data. Only `casedate`, `new_cases`, and `new_deaths` can be considered daily data. The other columns show cumulative cases and deaths, or demographic data. The cumulative data is redundant since we have the actual values for `new_cases` and `new_deaths`. The demographic data has the same values for each country across all days.

There is an implied one-to-many relationship between country (and its associated demographic data) on the *one* side and the daily data on the *many* side. We can recover that structure by creating a DataFrame with the daily data, and another DataFrame with the demographic data. We do that in *steps 3* and *4*. When we need totals across countries we can generate those ourselves, rather than storing redundant data.

The running totals variables are not completely useless, however. We can use them to check our calculations of total cases and total deaths. *Step 5* shows how we can use `groupby` to restructure data when we need to do more than drop duplicates. In this case, we want to summarize `new_cases` and many-to-many relationships `new_deaths` for each country.

There's more...

I can sometimes forget a small detail. When changing the structure of data, the meaning of certain columns can change. In this example, `casedate` becomes the date for the last row for each country. We rename that column `lastdate`.

See also...

We explore `groupby` in more detail in *Chapter 7, Fixing Messy Data when Aggregating*. Hadley Wickham's *Tidy Data* paper is available at `https://vita.had.co.nz/papers/tidy-data.pdf`.

Fixing many-to-many relationships

We sometimes have to work with a data table that was created from a many-to-many merge. This is a merge where merge-by column values are duplicated on both the left and right sides. As we discussed in the previous chapter, many-to-many relationships in a data file often represent multiple one-to-many relationships where the *one* side has been removed. There is a one-to-many relationship between dataset A and dataset B, and also a one-to-many relationship between dataset A and dataset C. The problem we sometimes have is that we receive a data file with B and C merged, but with A excluded.

The best way to work with data structured in this way is to recreate the implied one-to-many relationships, if possible. We do this by first creating a dataset structured like A; that is, how A is likely structured given the many-to-many relationship we see between B and C. The key to being able to do this is in identifying a good merge-by column for the data on both sides of the many-to-many relationship. This column or column(s) will be duplicated in both the B and C datasets, but will be unduplicated in the theoretical A dataset.

The data we use in this recipe is a good example. We have data from the Cleveland Museum of Art on its collections. We have two datasets: a creators file and a media citations file. The creators file has the creator or creators of every item in the museum's collections. There is one row for each creator, so there may be multiple rows for each collection item. The citations file has citations (in newspapers, from news stations, in journals, and so on) for every item. The citations file has a row for each citation, and so often has multiple rows per collection item.

We do not have what we might expect – a collections file with one row (and a unique identifier) for each item in the collection. This leaves us with just the many-to-many relationship between the creators and citations datasets.

I should add that this situation is not the fault of the Cleveland Museum of Art, which generously provides an API that returns collections data as a JSON file. It is possible to extract the data needed from the JSON file to produce a collections DataFrame, in addition to the creators and citations data that I have extracted. But we do not always have access to data like that and it is good to have strategies for when we do not.

Getting ready...

We will work with data on the Cleveland Museum of Art's collections. The CSV file has data on both creators and citations merged by an `id` column that identifies the collection item. There are one or many rows for citations and creators for each item.

> **Note**
>
> The Cleveland Museum of Art provides an API for public access to this data: `https://openaccess-api.clevelandart.org`. Much more than the citations and creators data used in this recipe is available with the API.

How to do it...

We handle many-to-many relationships between DataFrames by recovering the multiple implied one-to-many relationships in the data:

1. Import `pandas` and the museum's `collections` data:

```
>>> import pandas as pd
>>> cma = pd.read_csv("data/cmacollections.csv")
```

2. Show the museum's `collections` data.

    Also show the number of unique `id`, `citation`, and `creator` values:

```
>>> cma.shape
(12326, 9)
>>> cma.head(2).T
```

	0	1
id	92937	92937
citation	Milliken, William	Glasier, Jessie C.
creator	George Bellows (Am	George Bellows (Am
title	Stag at Sharkey's	Stag at Sharkey's
birth_year	1882	1882
death_year	1925	1925
collection	American - Painting	American - Painting
type	Painting	Painting
creation_date	1909	1909

```
>>> cma.id.nunique()
972
>>> cma.drop_duplicates(['id','citation']).id.count()
9758
>>> cma.drop_duplicates(['id','creator']).id.count()
1055
```

3. Show a collection item with duplicated citations and creators.

    Only show the first 14 rows (there are actually 28 in total):

```
>>> cma.set_index(['id'], inplace=True)
>>> cma.loc[124733, ['title','citation','creator','birth_
year']].head(14)
```

	title	citation	creator	birth_year
id				
124733	Dead Blue Roller	Weigel, J. A. G.	Albrecht Dürer(Ge	1471
124733	Dead Blue Roller	Weigel, J. A. G.	Hans Hoffmann(Ger	1545/50
124733	Dead Blue Roller	Winkler, Friedrich	Albrecht Dürer(Ge	1471

```
124733   Dead Blue Roller   Winkler, Friedrich Hans
Hoffmann(Ger     1545/50

124733   Dead Blue Roller   Francis, Henry S.   Albrecht
Dürer(Ge         1471

124733   Dead Blue Roller   Francis, Henry S.   Hans
Hoffmann(Ger     1545/50

124733   Dead Blue Roller   Kurz, Otto. <em>Fa Albrecht
Dürer(Ge         1471

124733   Dead Blue Roller   Kurz, Otto. <em>Fa Hans
Hoffmann(Ger     1545/50

124733   Dead Blue Roller   Minneapolis Instit Albrecht
Dürer(Ge         1471

124733   Dead Blue Roller   Minneapolis Instit Hans
Hoffmann(Ger     1545/50

124733   Dead Blue Roller   Pilz, Kurt. "Hans   Albrecht
Dürer(Ge         1471

124733   Dead Blue Roller   Pilz, Kurt. "Hans   Hans
Hoffmann(Ger     1545/50

124733   Dead Blue Roller   Koschatzky, Walter Albrecht
Dürer(Ge         1471

124733   Dead Blue Roller   Koschatzky, Walter Hans
Hoffmann(Ger     1545/50
```

4. Create a collections DataFrame:

```
>>> collectionsvars = ['title','collection','type']
>>> cmacollections = cma[collectionsvars].\
...     reset_index().\
...     drop_duplicates(['id']).\
...     set_index(['id'])
>>>
>>> cmacollections.shape
(972, 3)
>>> cmacollections.head()
                                        title
collection      type
id
92937                     Stag at Sharkey's   American -
Painting  Painting
94979                      Nathaniel Hurd   American -
Painting  Painting
```

```
137259          Mme L... (Laure Borreau)  Mod Euro -
Painting    Painting
141639          Twilight in the Wilderness    American -
Painting    Painting
93014    View of Schroon Mountain, Esse    American -
Painting    Painting
>>> cmacollections.loc[124733]
title          Dead Blue Roller
collection          DR - German
type               Drawing
Name: 124733, dtype: object
```

5. Create a citations DataFrame:

This will just have the id and the citation:

```
>>> cmacitations = cma[['citation']].\
...     reset_index().\
...     drop_duplicates(['id','citation']).\
...     set_index(['id'])
>>>
>>> cmacitations.loc[124733]
                citation
id
124733  Weigel, J. A. G. <
124733  Winkler, Friedrich
124733  Francis, Henry S.
124733  Kurz, Otto. <em>Fa
124733  Minneapolis Instit
124733  Pilz, Kurt. "Hans
124733  Koschatzky, Walter
124733  Johnson, Mark M<em
124733  Kaufmann, Thomas D
124733  Koreny, Fritz. <em
124733  Achilles-Syndram,
124733  Schoch, Rainer, Ka
124733  DeGrazia, Diane an
124733  Dunbar, Burton L.,
```

6. Create a creators DataFrame:

```
>>> creatorsvars = ['creator','birth_year','death_year']
>>>
>>> cmacreators = cma[creatorsvars].\
...     reset_index().\
...     drop_duplicates(['id','creator']).\
...     set_index(['id'])
>>>
>>> cmacreators.loc[124733]
                creator birth_year death_year
id
124733  Albrecht Dürer (Ge     1471      1528
124733  Hans Hoffmann (Ger  1545/50   1591/92
```

7. Count the number of collection items with a creator born after 1950.

    First, convert the `birth_year` values from string to numeric. Then create a DataFrame with just young artists. Finally, merge that DataFrame with the collections DataFrame to create a flag for collection items that have at least one creator born after 1950:

```
>>> cmacreators['birth_year'] = cmacreators.birth_year.
str.findall("\d+").str[0].astype(float)
>>> youngartists = cmacreators.loc[cmacreators.birth_
year>1950, ['creator']].assign(creatorbornafter1950='Y')
>>> youngartists.shape[0]==youngartists.index.nunique()
True
>>> youngartists
                creator creatorbornafter1950
id
371392  Belkis Ayón (Cuban              Y
162624  Robert Gober (Amer              Y
172588  Rachel Harrison (A              Y
169335  Pae White (America              Y
169862  Fred Wilson (Ameri              Y
312739  Liu Jing (Chinese,              Y
293323  Zeng Xiaojun (Chin              Y
```

```
172539  Fidencio Fifield-P                          Y
>>> cmacollections = pd.merge(cmacollections,
youngartists, left_on=['id'], right_on=['id'],
how='left')
>>> cmacollections.creatorbornafter1950.fillna("N",
inplace=True)
>>> cmacollections.shape
(972, 5)
>>> cmacollections.creatorbornafter1950.value_counts()
N       964
Y         8
Name: creatorbornafter1950, dtype: int64
```

We now we have three DataFrames – collection items (cmacollections), citations (cmacitations), and creators (cmacreators) – instead of one. cmacollections has a one-to-many relationship with both cmacitations and cmacreators.

How it works...

If you mainly work directly with enterprise data, you probably rarely see a file with this kind of structure, but many of us are not so lucky. If we requested data from the museum on both the media citations and creators of their collections, it would not be completely surprising to get a data file similar to this one, with duplicated data for citations and creators. But the presence of what looks like a unique identifier of collection items gives us some hope of recovering the one-to-many relationships between a collection item and its citations, and a collection item and its creators.

Step 2 shows that there are 972 unique id values. This suggests that there are probably only 972 collection items represented in the 12,326 rows of the DataFrame. There are 9,758 unique id and citation pairs, or about 10 citations per collection item on average. There are 1,055 id and creator pairs.

Step 3 shows the duplication of collection item values such as title. The number of rows returned is equal to the Cartesian product of the merge-by values on the left and ride side of the merge. For the *Dead Blue Roller* item, there are 14 citations (we only show half of them in *step 3*) and 2 creators. The row for each creator is duplicated 14 times; once for each citation. There are very few use cases for which it makes sense to leave the data in this state.

Our North Star to guide us in getting this data into better shape is the `id` column. We use it to create a collections DataFrame in *step 4*. We keep only one row for each value of `id`, and get other columns associated with a collection item, rather than a citation or creator – `title`, `collection`, and `type` (since `id` is the index we need to first reset the index before dropping duplicates).

We follow the same procedure to create `citations` and `creators` DataFrames in *steps 5* and *6*. We use `drop_duplicates` to keep unique combinations of `id` and `citation`, and unique combinations of `id` and `creator`, respectively. This gives us the expected number of rows in the example case: 14 `citations` rows and 2 `creators` rows.

Step 7 demonstrates how we can now work with these DataFrames to construct new columns and do analysis. We want the number of collection items that have at least one creator born after 1950. The unit of analysis is the collection items, but we need information from the creators DataFrame for the calculation. Since the relationship between `cmacollections` and `cmacreators` is one-to-many, we make sure that we are only retrieving one row per `id` in the creators DataFrame, even if more than one creator for an item was born after 1950:

```
youngartists.shape[0]==youngartists.index.nunique()
```

There's more...

The duplication that occurs with many-to-many merges is most problematic when we are working with quantitative data. If the original file had the assessed value of each item in the collection, it would be duplicated in much the same way as `title` is duplicated. Any descriptive statistics we generated on the assessed value would be off by a fair bit. For example, if the *Dead Blue Roller* item had an assessed value of $1,000,000, we would get $28,000,000 when summarizing the assessed value, since there are 28 duplicated values.

This shows the importance of normalized and tidy data. If there were an assessed value column, we would have included it in the `cmacollections` DataFrame we created in *step 4*. This value would be unduplicated and we would be able to generate summary statistics for collections.

I find it helpful to always return to the unit of analysis, which overlaps with the tidy data concept, but is different in some ways. The approach in *step 7* would have been very different if we were just interested in the number of creators born after 1950, instead of the number of collection items with a creator born after 1950. In that case, the unit of analysis would be the creator and we would just use the creators DataFrame.

See also...

We examine many-to-many merges in the *Doing many-to-many merges* recipe in *Chapter 8, Addressing Data Issues when Combining DataFrames.*

We demonstrate a very different way to work with data structured in this way in *Chapter 10, User Defined Functions and Classes to Automate Data Cleaning*, in the *Classes that handle non-tabular data structures* recipe.

Using stack and melt to reshape data from wide to long format

One type of untidiness that Wickham identified is variable values embedded in column names. Although this rarely happens with enterprise or relational data, it is fairly common with analytical or survey data. Variable names might have suffixes that indicate a time period, such as a month or year. Another case is that similar variables on a survey might have similar names, such as `familymember1age`, `familymember2age`, and so on, because that is convenient and consistent with the survey designers' understanding of the variable.

One reason why this messiness happens relatively frequently with survey data is that there can be multiple units of analysis on one survey instrument. An example is the United States decennial census, which asks both household and person questions. Survey data is also sometimes made up of repeated measures or panel data, but nonetheless often has only one row per respondent. When this is the case, new measurements or responses are stored in new columns rather than new rows, and the column names will be similar to column names for responses from earlier periods, except for a change in suffix.

The United States **National Longitudinal Survey of Youth (NLS)** is a good example of this. It is panel data, where each individual is surveyed each year. However, there is just one row of data per respondent in the analysis file provided. Responses to questions such as the number of weeks worked in a given year are placed in new columns. Tidying the NLS data means converting columns such as `weeksworked00` through `weeksworked04` (for weeks worked in 2000 through 2004) to just one column for weeks worked, another column for year, and five rows for each person (one for each year) rather than one.

Amazingly, pandas has several functions that make transformations like this relatively easy: `stack`, `melt`, and `wide_to_long`. We use `stack` and `melt` in this recipe, and explore `wide_to_long` in the next.

Getting ready...

We will work with the NLS data on the number of weeks worked and college enrollment status for each year. The DataFrame has one row per survey respondent.

> **Note**
>
> The NLS is conducted by the United States Bureau of Labor Statistics. It is available for public use at `https://www.nlsinfo.org/ investigator/pages/search`. The survey started with a cohort of individuals in 1997 who were born between 1980 and 1985, with annual follow-ups each year through 2017.

How to do it...

We will use `stack` and `melt` to transform the NLS' weeks worked data from wide to long, pulling out year values from the column names as we do so:

1. Import `pandas` and the NLS data:

```
>>> import pandas as pd
>>> nls97 = pd.read_csv("data/nls97f.csv")
```

2. View some of the values for the number of weeks worked.

First, set the index:

```
>>> nls97.set_index(['originalid'], inplace=True)
>>>
>>> weeksworkedcols = ['weeksworked00','weeksworked01','w
eeksworked02',
...     'weeksworked03','weeksworked04']
>>> nls97[weeksworkedcols].head(2).T
originalid      8245   3962
weeksworked00     46      5
weeksworked01     52     49
weeksworked02     52     52
weeksworked03     48     52
weeksworked04     52     52
>>> nls97.shape
(8984, 89)
```

3. Use stack to transform the data from wide to long.

First, select only the weeksworked## columns. Use stack to move each column name in the original DataFrame into the index and move the weeksworked## values into the associated row. Reset the index so that the weeksworked## column names become the values for the level_0 column (which we rename year), and the weeksworked## values become the values for the 0 column (which we rename weeksworked):

```
>>> weeksworked = nls97[weeksworkedcols].\
...      stack(dropna=False).\
...      reset_index().\
...      rename(columns={'level_1':'year',0:'weeksworked'})
>>>
>>> weeksworked.head(10)
     originalid           year   weeksworked
0         8245   weeksworked00            46
1         8245   weeksworked01            52
2         8245   weeksworked02            52
3         8245   weeksworked03            48
4         8245   weeksworked04            52
5         3962   weeksworked00             5
6         3962   weeksworked01            49
7         3962   weeksworked02            52
8         3962   weeksworked03            52
9         3962   weeksworked04            52
```

4. Fix the year values.

Get the last digits of the year values, convert them to integers, and add 2000:

```
>>> weeksworked['year'] = weeksworked.year.str[-2:].
astype(int)+2000
>>> weeksworked.head(10)
     originalid   year   weeksworked
0         8245   2000            46
1         8245   2001            52
2         8245   2002            52
3         8245   2003            48
4         8245   2004            52
```

5	3962	2000	5
6	3962	2001	49
7	3962	2002	52
8	3962	2003	52
9	3962	2004	52

```
>>> weeksworked.shape
(44920, 3)
```

5. Alternatively, use `melt` to transform the data from wide to long.

First, reset the index and select the `originalid` and `weeksworked##` columns. Use the `id_vars` and `value_vars` parameters of `melt` to specify `originalid` as the ID variable and the `weeksworked##` columns as the columns to be rotated, or *melted*. Use the `var_name` and `value_name` parameters to rename the columns to `year` and `weeksworked` respectively. The column names in `value_vars` become the values for the new `year` column (which we convert to an integer using the original suffix). The values for the `value_vars` columns are assigned to the new `weeksworked` column for the associated row:

```
>>> weeksworked = nls97.reset_index().\
...    loc[:,['originalid'] + weeksworkedcols].\
...      melt(id_vars=['originalid'], value_
vars=weeksworkedcols,
...        var_name='year', value_name='weeksworked')
>>>
>>> weeksworked['year'] = weeksworked.year.str[-2:].
astype(int)+2000
>>> weeksworked.set_index(['originalid'], inplace=True)
>>> weeksworked.loc[[8245,3962]]
            year  weeksworked
originalid
8245        2000     46
8245        2001     52
8245        2002     52
8245        2003     48
8245        2004     52
3962        2000     5
3962        2001     49
3962        2002     52
```

3962	2003	52
3962	2004	52

6. Reshape the college enrollment columns with `melt`.

   This works the same way as the `melt` function for the weeks worked columns:

   ```
   >>> colenrcols =
   ['colenroct00','colenroct01','colenroct02',
   ...    'colenroct03','colenroct04']
   >>>
   >>> colenr = nls97.reset_index().\
   ...    loc[:,['originalid'] + colenrcols].\
   ...    melt(id_vars=['originalid'], value_vars=colenrcols,
   ...        var_name='year', value_name='colenr')
   >>>
   >>> colenr['year'] = colenr.year.str[-2:].
   astype(int)+2000
   >>> colenr.set_index(['originalid'], inplace=True)
   >>> colenr.loc[[8245,3962]]
                  year          colenr
   originalid
   8245          2000  1. Not enrolled
   8245          2001  1. Not enrolled
   8245          2002  1. Not enrolled
   8245          2003  1. Not enrolled
   8245          2004  1. Not enrolled
   3962          2000  1. Not enrolled
   3962          2001  1. Not enrolled
   3962          2002  1. Not enrolled
   3962          2003  1. Not enrolled
   3962          2004  1. Not enrolled
   ```

7. Merge the weeks worked and college enrollment data:

   ```
   >>> workschool = pd.merge(weeksworked, colenr,
   on=['originalid','year'], how="inner")
   >>> workschool.shape
   (44920, 4)
   >>> workschool.loc[[8245,3962]]
   ```

	year	weeksworked	colenr
originalid			
8245	2000	46	1. Not enrolled
8245	2001	52	1. Not enrolled
8245	2002	52	1. Not enrolled
8245	2003	48	1. Not enrolled
8245	2004	52	1. Not enrolled
3962	2000	5	1. Not enrolled
3962	2001	49	1. Not enrolled
3962	2002	52	1. Not enrolled
3962	2003	52	1. Not enrolled
3962	2004	52	1. Not enrolled

This gives us one DataFrame from the melting of both the weeks worked and the college enrollment columns.

How it works...

We can use `stack` or `melt` to reshape data from wide to long form, but `melt` provides more flexibility. `stack` will move all of the column names into the index. We see in *step 4* that we get the expected number of rows after stacking, `44920`, which is 5*8,984, the number of rows in the initial data.

With `melt`, we can rotate the column names and values based on an ID variable other than the index. We do this with the `id_vars` parameter. We specify which variables to melt by using the `value_vars` parameter.

In *step 6*, we also reshape the college enrollment columns. To create one DataFrame with the reshaped weeks worked and college enrollment data, we merge the two DataFrames we created in *steps 5* and *6*. We will see in the next recipe how to accomplish what we did in *steps 5* through *7* in one step.

Melting multiple groups of columns

When we needed to melt multiple groups of columns in the previous recipe, we used `melt` twice and then merged the resulting DataFrames. That worked fine, but we can accomplish the same tasks in one step with the `wide_to_long` function. `wide_to_long` has more functionality than `melt`, but is a bit more complicated to use.

Getting ready...

We will work with the weeks worked and college enrollment data from the NLS in this recipe.

How to do it...

We will transform multiple groups of columns at once using `wide_to_long`:

1. Import `pandas` and load the NLS data:

```
>>> import pandas as pd
>>> nls97 = pd.read_csv("data/nls97f.csv")
>>> nls97.set_index('personid', inplace=True)
```

2. View some of the weeks worked and college enrollment data:

```
>>> weeksworkedcols = ['weeksworked00','weeksworked01','w
eeksworked02',
...     'weeksworked03','weeksworked04']
>>> colenrcols =
['colenroct00','colenroct01','colenroct02',
...     'colenroct03','colenroct04']
>>>
>>> nls97.loc[nls97.originalid.isin([1,2]),
...     ['originalid'] + weeksworkedcols + colenrcols].T
```

personid	135335	999406
originalid	1	2
weeksworked00	53	51
weeksworked01	52	52
weeksworked02	NaN	44
weeksworked03	42	45
weeksworked04	52	52
colenroct00	3. 4-year college	3. 4-year college
colenroct01	3. 4-year college	2. 2-year college
colenroct02	3. 4-year college	3. 4-year college
colenroct03	1. Not enrolled	3. 4-year college
colenroct04	1. Not enrolled	3. 4-year college

3. Run the `wide_to_long` function.

Pass a list to `stubnames` to indicate the column groups wanted. (All columns starting with the same characters as each item in the list will be selected for melting.) Use the `i` parameter to indicate the ID variable (`originalid`), and use the `j` parameter to name the column (`year`) that is based on the column suffixes – 00, 01, and so on:

```
>>> workschool = pd.wide_to_long(nls97[['originalid'] +
weeksworkedcols

...    + colenrcols],
stubnames=['weeksworked','colenroct'],

...    i=['originalid'], j='year').reset_index()

>>>

>>> workschool['year'] = workschool.year+2000
>>> workschool = workschool.sort_
values(['originalid','year'])
>>> workschool.set_index(['originalid'], inplace=True)
>>> workschool.head(10)
```

originalid	year	weeksworked	colenroct
1	2000	53	3. 4-year college
1	2001	52	3. 4-year college
1	2002	nan	3. 4-year college
1	2003	42	1. Not enrolled
1	2004	52	1. Not enrolled
2	2000	51	3. 4-year college
2	2001	52	2. 2-year college
2	2002	44	3. 4-year college
2	2003	45	3. 4-year college
2	2004	52	3. 4-year college

`wide_to_long` accomplishes in one step what it took us several steps to accomplish in the previous recipe using `melt`.

How it works...

The `wide_to_long` function does almost all of the work for us, though it takes more effort to set it up than for `stack` or `melt`. We need to provide the function with the characters (`weeksworked` and `colenroct` in this case) of the column groups. Since our variables are named with suffixes indicating the year, `wide_to_long` translates the suffixes into values that make sense and melts them into the column that is named with the `j` parameter. It's almost magic!

There's more...

The suffixes of the `stubnames` columns in this recipe are the same: 00 through 04. But that does not have to be the case. When suffixes are present for one column group, but not for another, the values for the latter column group for that suffix will be missing. We can see that if we exclude `weeksworked03` from the DataFrame and add `weeksworked05`:

```
>>> weeksworkedcols = ['weeksworked00','weeksworked01','weeksw
orked02',
...    'weeksworked04','weeksworked05']
>>>
>>> workschool = pd.wide_to_long(nls97[['originalid'] +
weeksworkedcols
...    + colenrcols], stubnames=['weeksworked','colenroct'],
...    i=['originalid'], j='year').reset_index()
>>>
>>> workschool['year'] = workschool.year+2000
>>> workschool = workschool.sort_values(['originalid','year'])
>>> workschool.set_index(['originalid'], inplace=True)
>>> workschool.head(12)
            year  weeksworked          colenroct
originalid
1           2000           53  3. 4-year college
1           2001           52  3. 4-year college
1           2002          nan  3. 4-year college
1           2003          nan     1. Not enrolled
1           2004           52     1. Not enrolled
1           2005           53                 NaN
2           2000           51  3. 4-year college
2           2001           52  2. 2-year college
```

2	2002	44	3. 4-year college
2	2003	nan	3. 4-year college
2	2004	52	3. 4-year college
2	2005	53	NaN

The weeksworked values for 2003 are now missing, as are the colenroct values for 2005. (The weeksworked value for 2002 for originalid 1 was already missing.)

Using unstack and pivot to reshape data from long to wide

Sometimes, we actually have to move data from a tidy to an untidy structure. This is often because we need to prepare the data for analysis with software packages that do not handle relational data well, or because we are submitting data to some external authority that has requested it in an untidy format. unstack and pivot can be helpful when we need to reshape data from long to wide format. unstack does the opposite of what we did with stack, and pivot does the opposite of melt.

Getting ready...

We continue to work with the NLS data on weeks worked and college enrollment in this recipe.

How to do it...

We use unstack and pivot to return the melted NLS DataFrame to its original state:

1. Import pandas and load the stacked and melted NLS data:

```
>>> import pandas as pd
>>> nls97 = pd.read_csv("data/nls97f.csv")
>>> nls97.set_index(['originalid'], inplace=True)
```

2. Stack the data again.

This repeats the stack operation from an earlier recipe in this chapter:

```
>>> weeksworkedcols = ['weeksworked00','weeksworked01',
...     'weeksworked02','weeksworked03','weeksworked04']
>>> weeksworkedstacked = nls97[weeksworkedcols].\
...     stack(dropna=False)
```

```
>>> weeksworkedstacked.loc[[1,2]]
originalid
1              weeksworked00       53
               weeksworked01       52
               weeksworked02       nan
               weeksworked03       42
               weeksworked04       52
2              weeksworked00       51
               weeksworked01       52
               weeksworked02       44
               weeksworked03       45
               weeksworked04       52
dtype: float64
```

3. Melt the data again.

This repeats the `melt` operation from an earlier recipe in this chapter:

```
>>> weeksworkedmelted = nls97.reset_index().\
...    loc[:,['originalid'] + weeksworkedcols].\
...    melt(id_vars=['originalid'], value_
vars=weeksworkedcols,
...        var_name='year', value_name='weeksworked')
>>>
>>> weeksworkedmelted.loc[weeksworkedmelted.originalid.
isin([1,2])].\
...     sort_values(['originalid','year'])
```

	originalid	year	weeksworked
377	1	weeksworked00	53
9361	1	weeksworked01	52
18345	1	weeksworked02	nan
27329	1	weeksworked03	42
36313	1	weeksworked04	52
8980	2	weeksworked00	51
17964	2	weeksworked01	52
26948	2	weeksworked02	44
35932	2	weeksworked03	45
44916	2	weeksworked04	52

4. Use `unstack` to convert the stacked data from long to wide:

```
>>> weeksworked = weeksworkedstacked.unstack()
>>> weeksworked.loc[[1,2]]
weeksworked00   weeksworked01   weeksworked02
weeksworked03   weeksworked04
originalid
1               53              52              nan
42                      52
2               51              52              44
45                      52
```

5. Use `pivot` to convert the melted data from long to wide.

    `pivot` is slightly more complicated than `unstack`. We need to pass arguments
    to do the reverse of `melt`, telling `pivot` the column to use for the column
    name suffixes (`year`) and where to grab the values to be unmelted (from the
    `weeksworked` columns, in this case):

```
>>> weeksworked = weeksworkedmelted.
pivot(index='originalid', \
...     columns='year', values=['weeksworked']).reset_
index()
>>>
>>> weeksworked.columns = ['originalid'] + \
...     [col[1] for col in weeksworked.columns[1:]]
>>>
>>> weeksworked.loc[weeksworked.originalid.isin([1,2])].T
                0  1
originalid      1  2
weeksworked00   53 51
weeksworked01   52 52
weeksworked02   nan 44
weeksworked03   42 45
weeksworked04   52 52
```

This returns the NLS data back to its original untidy form.

How it works...

We first do a `stack` and a `melt` in *steps 2 and 3* respectively. This rotates the DataFrames from wide to long format. We then unstack (*step 4*) and pivot (*step 5*) those data frames to rotate them back from long to wide.

`unstack` uses the multi-index that is created by the `stack` to figure out how to rotate the data.

The `pivot` function needs for us to indicate the index column (`originalid`), the column whose values will be appended to the column names (`year`), and the name of the columns with the values to be unmelted (`weeksworked`). Pivot will return multilevel column names. We fix that by pulling from the second level with `[col[1] for col in weeksworked.columns[1:]]`.

10

User-Defined Functions and Classes to Automate Data Cleaning

There are a number of great reasons to write code that is reusable. When we step back from the particular data cleaning problem at hand and consider its relationship to very similar problems, we can actually improve our understanding of the key issues involved. We are also more likely to address a task systematically when we set our sights more on solving it for the long term than on the before-lunch solution. This has the additional benefit of helping us to disentangle the substantive issues from the mechanics of data manipulation.

We will create several modules to accomplish routine data cleaning tasks in this chapter. The functions and classes in these modules are examples of code that can be reused across DataFrames, or for one DataFrame over an extended period of time. These functions handle many of the tasks we discussed in the first nine chapters, but in a manner that allows us to reuse our code.

Specifically, the recipes in this chapter cover the following:

- Functions for getting a first look at our data
- Functions for displaying summary statistics and frequencies
- Functions for identifying outliers and unexpected values
- Functions for aggregating or combining data
- Classes that contain the logic for updating series values
- Classes that handle non-tabular data structures

Technical requirements

The code and notebooks for this chapter are available on GitHub at `https://github.com/PacktPublishing/Python-Data-Cleaning-Cookbook`

Functions for getting a first look at our data

The first few steps we take after we import our data into a pandas DataFrame are pretty much the same regardless of the characteristics of the data. We almost always want to know the number of columns and rows and the column data types, and see the first few rows. We also might want to view the index and check whether there is a unique identifier for DataFrame rows. These discrete, easily repeatable tasks are good candidates for a collection of functions we can organize into a module.

In this recipe, we will create a module with functions that give us a good first look at any pandas DataFrame. A module is simply a collection of Python code that we can import into another Python program. Modules are easy to reuse because they can be referenced by any program with access to the folder where the module is saved.

Getting ready...

We create two files in this recipe: one with a function we will use to look at our data and another to call that function. Let's call the file with the function we will use `basicdescriptives.py` and place it in a subfolder called `helperfunctions`.

We work with the **National Longitudinal Survey** (**NLS**) data in this recipe.

> **Note**
>
> The NLS is conducted by the United States Bureau of Labor Statistics.
> It is available for public use at `https://www.nlsinfo.org/`
> `investigator/pages/search`. The survey started with a cohort
> of individuals in 1997 who were born between 1980 and 1985, with annual
> follow-ups each year through 2017.

How to do it...

We will create a function to take an initial look at a DataFrame.

1. Create the `basicdescriptives.py` file with the function we want.

    The `getfirstlook` function will return a dictionary with summary
    information on a DataFrame. Save the file in the `helperfunctions` subfolder
    as `basicdescriptives.py`. (You can also just download the code from the
    GitHub repository). Also, create a function (`displaydict`) to pretty up the
    display of a dictionary:

    ```
    >>> import pandas as pd
    >>> def getfirstlook(df, nrows=5, uniqueids=None):
    ...     out = {}
    ...     out['head'] = df.head(nrows)
    ...     out['dtypes'] = df.dtypes
    ...     out['nrows'] = df.shape[0]
    ...     out['ncols'] = df.shape[1]
    ...     out['index'] = df.index
    ...     if (uniqueids is not None):
    ...         out['uniqueids'] = df[uniqueids].nunique()
    ...     return out

    >>> def displaydict(dicttodisplay):
    ...     print(*(': '.join(map(str, x)) \
    ...         for x in dicttodisplay.items()), sep='\n\n')
    ```

2. Create a separate file, `firstlook.py`, to call the `getfirstlook` function.

    Import the pandas, os, and sys libraries, and load the NLS data:

    ```
    >>> import pandas as pd
    >>> import os
    ```

```
>>> import sys
>>> nls97 = pd.read_csv("data/nls97f.csv")
```

3. Import the `basicdescriptives` module.

    First, append the `helperfunctions` subfolder to the Python path. We can then import `basicdescriptives`. We use the same name as the name of the file to import the module. We create an alias, bd, to make it easier to access the functions in the module later. (We can use `importlib`, commented out here, if we need to reload `basicdescriptives` because we have made some changes in the code in that module).

    ```
    >>> sys.path.append(os.getcwd() + "/helperfunctions")
    >>> import basicdescriptives as bd
    >>> # import importlib
    >>> # importlib.reload(bd)
    ```

4. Take a first look at the NLS data.

    We can just pass the DataFrame to the `getfirstlook` function in the `basicdescriptives` module to get a quick summary of the NLS data. The `displaydict` function gives us prettier printing of the dictionary:

    ```
    >>> dfinfo = bd.getfirstlook(nls97)
    >>> bd.displaydict(dfinfo)
    head:           gender   birthmonth  ...        colenroct17
    originalid
    personid                         ...
    100061      Female             5  ...  1. Not enrolled
    8245
    100139        Male             9  ...  1. Not enrolled
    3962
    100284        Male            11  ...  1. Not enrolled
    3571
    100292        Male             4  ...              NaN
    2979
    100583        Male             1  ...  1. Not enrolled
    8511

    [5 rows x 89 columns]

    dtypes: gender                         object
    ```

birthmonth	int64
birthyear	int64
highestgradecompleted	float64
maritalstatus	object
	...
colenrfeb16	object
colenroct16	object
colenrfeb17	object
colenroct17	object
originalid	int64

```
Length: 89, dtype: object
nrows: 8984
ncols: 89
index: Int64Index([100061, 100139, 100284, 100292,
100583, 100833, 100931,
                ...
        999543, 999698, 999963],
        dtype='int64', name='personid', length=8984)
```

5. Pass values to the `nrows` and `uniqueids` parameters of `getfirstlook`.

The two parameters default to values of 5 and `None`, unless we provide values:

```
>>> dfinfo = bd.getfirstlook(nls97,2,'originalid')
>>> bd.displaydict(dfinfo)
head:           gender  birthmonth  ...      colenroct17
originalid
personid                        ...
100061     Female        5  ...  1. Not enrolled
8245
100139       Male        9  ...  1. Not enrolled
3962

[2 rows x 89 columns]

dtypes: gender                      object
```

birthmonth	int64
birthyear	int64
highestgradecompleted	float64

```
maritalstatus                   object
                                 ...
colenrfeb16                     object
colenroct16                     object
colenrfeb17                     object
colenroct17                     object
originalid                       int64
Length: 89, dtype: object
nrows: 8984
ncols: 89
index: Int64Index([100061, 100139, 100284, 100292,
100583, 100833, 100931,
             ...
        999543, 999698, 999963],
        dtype='int64', name='personid', length=8984)

uniqueids: 8984
```

6. Work with some of the returned dictionary keys and values.

    We can also display selected key values from the dictionary returned from `getfirstlook`. Show the number of rows and data types, and check to see whether each row has a `uniqueid` instance (`dfinfo['nrows']` == `dfinfo['uniqueids']`):

    ```
    >>> dfinfo['nrows']
    8984


    >>> dfinfo['dtypes']
    gender                      object
    birthmonth                   int64
    birthyear                    int64
    highestgradecompleted      float64
    maritalstatus               object
                                 ...
    colenrfeb16                 object
    colenroct16                 object
    colenrfeb17                 object
    ```

```
colenroct17                    object
originalid                      int64
Length: 89, dtype: object
>>> dfinfo['nrows'] == dfinfo['uniqueids']
True
```

Let's take a closer look at how the function works and how we call it.

How it works...

Almost all of the action in this recipe is in the getfirstlook function, which we look at in *step 1*. We place the getfirstlook function in a separate file that we name basicdescriptives.py, which we can import as a module with that name (minus the extension).

We could have typed the function into the file we were using and called it from there. By putting it in a module instead, we can call it from any file that has access to the folder where the module is saved. When we import the basicdescriptives module in *step 3*, we load all of the code in basicdescriptives, allowing us to call all functions in that module.

The getfirstlook function returns a dictionary with useful information about the DataFrame that is passed to it. We see the first five rows, the number of columns and rows, the data types, and the index. By passing a value to the uniqueid parameter, we also get the number of unique values for the column.

By adding keyword parameters (nrows and uniqueid) with default values, we improve the flexibility of getfirstlook, without increasing the amount of effort it takes to call the function when we do not need the extra functionality. In the first call, in *step 4*, we do not pass values for nrows or uniqueid, sticking with the default values. In *step 5*, we indicate that we only want two rows displayed and that we want to examine unique values for originalid.

There's more...

The point of this recipe, and the ones that follow it, is not to provide code that you can download and run on your own data, though you are certainly welcome to do that. I am mainly trying to demonstrate how you can collect your favorite approaches to data cleaning in handy modules, and how this allows easy code reuse. The specific code here is just a serving suggestion, if you will.

Whenever we use a combination of positional and keyword parameters, the positional parameters must go first.

Functions for displaying summary statistics and frequencies

During the first few days of working with a DataFrame, we try to get a good sense of the distribution of continuous variables and counts for categorical variables. We also often do counts by selected groups. Although pandas and NumPy have many built-in methods for these purposes – describe, mean, valuecounts, crosstab, and so on – data analysts often have preferences for how they work with these tools. If, for example, an analyst finds that she usually needs to see more percentiles than those generated by describe, she can use her own function instead. We will create user-defined functions for displaying summary statistics and frequencies in this recipe.

Getting ready

We will be working with the basicdescriptives module again in this recipe. All of the functions we will define are saved in that module. We continue to work with the NLS data.

How to do it...

We will use functions we create to generate summary statistics and counts:

1. Create the gettots function in the basicdescriptives module.

    The function takes a pandas DataFrame and creates a dictionary with selected summary statistics. It returns a pandas DataFrame:

    ```
    >>> def gettots(df):
    ...     out = {}
    ...     out['min'] = df.min()
    ...     out['per15'] = df.quantile(0.15)
    ...     out['qr1'] = df.quantile(0.25)
    ...     out['med'] = df.median()
    ...     out['qr3'] = df.quantile(0.75)
    ...     out['per85'] = df.quantile(0.85)
    ...     out['max'] = df.max()
    ...     out['count'] = df.count()
    ...     out['mean'] = df.mean()
    ...     out['iqr'] = out['qr3']-out['qr1']
    ...     return pd.DataFrame(out)
    ```

2. Import the `pandas`, `os`, and `sys` libraries.

Do this from a different file, which you can call `taking_measure.py`:

```
>>> import pandas as pd
>>> import os
>>> import sys
>>> nls97 = pd.read_csv("data/nls97f.csv")
>>> nls97.set_index('personid', inplace=True)
```

3. Import the `basicdescriptives` module:

```
>>> sys.path.append(os.getcwd() + "/helperfunctions")
>>> import basicdescriptives as bd
```

4. Show summary statistics for continuous variables.

Use the `gettots` function from the `basicdescriptives` module that we created in *step 1*:

```
>>> bd.gettots(nls97[['satverbal','satmath']]).T
```

	satverbal	satmath
min	14.00000	7.000000
per15	390.00000	390.000000
qr1	430.00000	430.000000
med	500.00000	500.000000
qr3	570.00000	580.000000
per85	620.00000	621.000000
max	800.00000	800.000000
count	1406.00000	1407.000000
mean	499.72404	500.590618
iqr	140.00000	150.000000

```
>>> bd.gettots(nls97.filter(like="weeksworked"))
```

	min	per15	qr1	...	count	mean	iqr
weeksworked00	0.0	0.0	5.0	...	8603	26.417761	45.0
weeksworked01	0.0	0.0	10.0	...	8564	29.784096	41.0
weeksworked02	0.0	0.0	13.0	...	8556	31.805400	39.0

weeksworked03 38.0	0.0	0.0	14.0	... 8490	33.469611
weeksworked04 34.0	0.0	1.0	18.0	... 8458	35.104635
...					
weeksworked15 19.0	0.0	0.0	33.0	... 7389	39.605630
weeksworked16 30.0	0.0	0.0	23.0	... 7068	39.127476
weeksworked17 15.0	0.0	0.0	37.0	... 6670	39.016642

5. Create a function to count missing values by columns and rows.

The getmissings function will take a DataFrame and a parameter for showing percentages or counts. Return two series, one with the missing values for each column and the other with missing values by row. Save the function in the basicdescriptives module:

```
>>> def getmissings(df, byrowperc=False):
...     return df.isnull().sum(),\
...         df.isnull().sum(axis=1).value_
counts(normalize=byrowperc).sort_index()
```

6. Call the getmissings function.

Call it first with byrowperc (the second parameter) set to True. This will show the percentage of rows with the associated number of missing values. For example, the missingbyrows value shows that 73.9% of rows have 0 missing values for weeksworked16 and weeksworked17. Call it again, leaving byrowperc at its default value of False, to get counts instead:

```
>>> missingsbycols, missingsbyrows =
bd.getmissings(nls97[['weeksworked16','weeksworked17']],
True)
>>> missingsbycols
weeksworked16     1916
weeksworked17     2314
dtype: int64
>>> missingsbyrows
0     0.739203
1     0.050757
```

```
2        0.210040
dtype: float64
>>> missingsbycols, missingsbyrows =
bd.getmissings(nls97[['weeksworked16','weeksworked17']])
>>> missingsbyrows
0      6641
1       456
2      1887
dtype: int64
```

7. Create a function to calculate frequencies for all categorical variables.

The `makefreqs` function loops through all columns with the category data type in the passed DataFrame, running `value_counts` on each one. The frequencies are saved to the file indicated by `outfile`:

```
>>> def makefreqs(df, outfile):
...      freqout = open(outfile, 'w')
...      for col in df.select_dtypes(include=["category"]):
...          print(col, "----------------------",
"frequencies",
...          df[col].value_counts().sort_
index(),"percentages",
...          df[col].value_counts(normalize=True).sort_
index(),
...          sep="\n\n", end="\n\n\n", file=freqout)
...      freqout.close()
```

8. Call the `makefreqs` function.

First change data type of each object column to category. This call runs `value_counts` on category data columns in the NLS data frame and saves the frequencies to `nlsfreqs.txt` in the `views` subfolder of the current folder.

```
>>> nls97.loc[:, nls97.dtypes == 'object'] = \
...      nls97.select_dtypes(['object']). \
...      apply(lambda x: x.astype('category'))
>>> bd.makefreqs(nls97, "views/nlsfreqs.txt")
```

9. Create a function to get counts by groups.

    The `getcnts` function counts the number of rows for each combination of column values in `cats`, a list of column names. It also counts the number of rows for each combination of column values excluding the final column in `cats`. This provides a total across all values of the final column. (The next step shows what this looks like).

    ```
    >>> def getcnts(df, cats, rowsel=None):
    ...     tots = cats[:-1]
    ...     catcnt = df.groupby(cats).size().reset_
    index(name='catcnt')
    ...     totcnt = df.groupby(tots).size().reset_
    index(name='totcnt')
    ...     percs = pd.merge(catcnt, totcnt, left_on=tots,
    ...        right_on=tots, how="left")
    ...     percs['percent'] = percs.catcnt / percs.totcnt
    ...     if (rowsel is not None):
    ...        percs = percs.loc[eval("percs." + rowsel)]
    ...     return percs
    ```

10. Pass the marital status, gender, and college enrollment columns to the `getcnts` function.

    This returns a DataFrame with counts for each column value combination, as well as counts for all combinations excluding the last column. This is used to calculate percentages within groups. For example, 393 respondents were divorced and female and 317 of those (or 81%) were not enrolled in college in October of 2000:

    ```
    >>> bd.getcnts(nls97,
    ['maritalstatus','gender','colenroct00'])
    ```

	maritalstatus	gender	colenroct00	catcnt	totcnt	percent
0	Divorced	Female	1. Not enrolled	317	393	0.806616
1	Divorced	Female	2. 2-year college	35	393	0.089059
2	Divorced	Female	3. 4-year college	41	393	0.104326
3	Divorced	Male	1. Not enrolled	238	270	0.881481
4	Divorced	Male	2. 2-year college	15	270	0.055556

. .	. . .	. . .	. . .	. . .
. . .	. . .			

25	Widowed	Female	2. 2-year college	1
19	0.052632			
26	Widowed	Female	3. 4-year college	2
19	0.105263			
27	Widowed	Male	1. Not enrolled	3
4	0.750000			
28	Widowed	Male	2. 2-year college	0
4	0.000000			
29	Widowed	Male	3. 4-year college	1
4	0.250000			

11. Use the `rowsel` parameter of `getcnts` to limit the output to specific rows:

```
>>> bd.getcnts(nls97,
['maritalstatus','gender','colenroct00'], "colenroct00.
str[0:1]=='1'")
```

	maritalstatus	gender	colenroct00	catcnt
totcnt	percent			
0	Divorced	Female	1. Not enrolled	317
393	0.806616			
3	Divorced	Male	1. Not enrolled	238
270	0.881481			
6	Married	Female	1. Not enrolled	1168
1636	0.713936			
9	Married	Male	1. Not enrolled	1094
1430	0.765035			
12	Never-married	Female	1. Not enrolled	1094
1307	0.837031			
15	Never-married	Male	1. Not enrolled	1268
1459	0.869088			
18	Separated	Female	1. Not enrolled	66
79	0.835443			
21	Separated	Male	1. Not enrolled	67
75	0.893333			
24	Widowed	Female	1. Not enrolled	16
19	0.842105			
27	Widowed	Male	1. Not enrolled	3
4	0.750000			

These steps demonstrate how to create functions and use them to generate summary statistics and frequencies.

How it works...

In *step 1*, we create a function that calculates descriptive statistics for all columns in a DataFrame, returning those results in a summary DataFrame. Most of the statistics can be generated with the `describe` method, but we add a few statistics – the 15th percentile, the 85th percentile, and the interquartile range. We call that function twice in *step 4*, the first time for the SAT verbal and math scores and the second time for all weeks worked columns.

Steps 5 and 6 create and call a function that shows the number of missing values for each column in the passed DataFrame. It also counts missing values for each row, displaying the frequency of missing values. The frequency of missing values by row can also be displayed as a percentage of all rows by passing a value of `True` to the `byrowperc` parameter.

Steps 7 and 8 produce a text file with frequencies for all categorical variables in the passed DataFrame. We just loop through all columns with the category data type and run `value_counts`. Since often the output is long, we save it to a file. It is also good to have frequencies saved somewhere for later reference.

The `getcnts` function we create in *step 9* and call in *steps 10 and 11* is a tad idiosyncratic. pandas has a very useful `crosstab` function, which I use frequently. But I often need a no-fuss way to look at group counts and percentages for subgroups within groups. The `getcnts` function does that.

There's more...

A function can be very helpful even when it does not do very much. There is not much code in the `getmissings` function, but I check for missing values so frequently that the small time-savings are significant cumulatively. It also reminds me to check for missing values by column and by row.

See also...

We explore pandas' tools for generating summary statistics and frequencies in *Chapter 3, Taking the Measure of Your Data*.

Functions for identifying outliers and unexpected values

If I had to pick one data cleaning area where I find reusable code most beneficial, it would be in the identification of outliers and unexpected values. This is because our prior assumptions often lead us to the central tendency of a distribution, rather than to the extremes. Quickly – think of a cat. Unless you were thinking about a particular cat in your life, an image of a generic feline between 8 and 10 pounds probably came to mind; not one that is 6 pounds or 22 pounds.

We often need to be more deliberate to elevate extreme values to consciousness. This is where having a standard set of diagnostic functions to run on our data is very helpful. We can run these functions even if nothing in particular triggers us to run them. This recipe provides examples of functions that we can use regularly to identify outliers and unexpected values.

Getting ready

We will create two files in this recipe, one with the functions we will use to check for outliers and another with the code we will use to call those functions. Let's call the file with the functions we will use `outliers.py`, and place it in a subfolder called `helperfunctions`.

You will need the `matplotlib` and `scipy` libraries, in addition to pandas, to run the code in this recipe. You can install `matplotlib` and `scipy` by entering `pip install matplotlib` and `pip install scipy` in a Terminal client or in Windows PowerShell. You will also need the `pprint` utility, which you can install with `pip install pprint`.

We will work with the NLS and COVI-19 data in this recipe. The Covid data has one row per country, with cumulative cases and deaths for that country.

> **Note**
>
> Our World in Data provides Covid-19 public use data at `https://ourworldindata.org/coronavirus-source-data`. The data used in this recipe were downloaded on July 18, 2020.

How to do it...

We create and call functions to check the distribution of variables, list extreme values, and visualize a distribution:

1. Import the `pandas`, `os`, `sys`, and `pprint` libraries.

    Also, load the NLS and Covid data:

    ```
    >>> import pandas as pd
    >>> import os
    >>> import sys
    >>> import pprint
    >>> nls97 = pd.read_csv("data/nls97f.csv")
    >>> nls97.set_index('personid', inplace=True)
    >>> covidtotals = pd.read_csv("data/covidtotals720.csv")
    ```

2. Create a function to show some important properties of a distribution.

    The `getdistprops` function takes a series and generates measures of central tendency, shape, and spread. The function returns a dictionary with these measures. It also handles situations where the Shapiro test for normality does not return a value. It will not add keys for `normstat` and `normpvalue` when that happens. Save the function in a file named `outliers.py` in the `helperfunctions` subfolder of the current directory. (Also load the `pandas`, `matplotlib`, `scipy`, and `math` libraries we will need for this and other functions in this module.)

    ```
    >>> import pandas as pd
    >>> import matplotlib.pyplot as plt
    >>> import scipy.stats as scistat
    >>> import math
    >>>
    >>> def getdistprops(seriestotest):
    ...     out = {}
    ...     normstat, normpvalue = scistat.
    shapiro(seriestotest)
    ...     if (not math.isnan(normstat)):
    ...         out['normstat'] = normstat
    ...         if (normpvalue>=0.05):
    ...             out['normpvalue'] = str(round(normpvalue, 2)) +
    ": Accept Normal"
    ...         elif (normpvalue<0.05):
    ```

```
...          out['normpvalue'] = str(round(normpvalue, 2)) +
": Reject Normal"
...       out['mean'] = seriestotest.mean()
...       out['median'] = seriestotest.median()
...       out['std'] = seriestotest.std()
...       out['kurtosis'] = seriestotest.kurtosis()
...       out['skew'] = seriestotest.skew()
...       out['count'] = seriestotest.count()
...       return out
```

3. Pass the total cases per million in population series to the `getdistprops` function.

The `skew` and `kurtosis` values suggest that the distribution of `total_cases_pm` has significantly positive skew and fatter tails than a normally distributed variable. The Shapiro test of normality (`normpvalue`) confirms this. (Use `pprint` to improve the display of the dictionary returned by `getdistprops`).

```
>>> dist = ol.getdistprops(covidtotals.total_cases_pm)
>>> pprint.pprint(dist)
{'count': 209,
 'kurtosis': 26.137524276840452,
 'mean': 2297.0221435406693,
 'median': 868.866,
 'normpvalue': '0.0: Reject Normal',
 'normstat': 0.5617035627365112,
 'skew': 4.284484653881833,
 'std': 4039.840202653782}
```

4. Create a function to list the outliers in a DataFrame.

The `getoutliers` function iterates over all columns in `sumvars`. It determines outlier thresholds for those columns, setting them at 1.5 times the interquartile range (the distance between the first and third quartile) below the first quartile or above the third quartile. It then selects all rows with values above the high threshold or below the low threshold. It adds columns that indicate the variable examined (`varname`) for outliers and the threshold levels. It also includes columns in the `othervars` list in the DataFrame it returns:

```
>>> def getoutliers(dfin, sumvars, othervars):
...       dfin = dfin[sumvars + othervars]
```

```
...      dfout = pd.DataFrame(columns=dfin.columns,
data=None)
...      dfsums = dfin[sumvars]
...      for col in dfsums.columns:
...          thirdq, firstq = dfsums[col].quantile(0.75),\
...              dfsums[col].quantile(0.25)
...          interquartilerange = 1.5*(thirdq-firstq)
...          outlierhigh, outlierlow =
interquartilerange+thirdq,\
...              firstq-interquartilerange
...          df = dfin.loc[(dfin[col]>outlierhigh) | \
...              (dfin[col]<outlierlow)]
...          df = df.assign(varname = col, threshlow =
outlierlow,\
...              threshhigh = outlierhigh)
...          dfout = pd.concat([dfout, df])
...      return dfout
```

5. Call the `getoutlier` function.

   Pass a list of columns to check for outliers (`sumvars`) and another list of columns to include in the returned DataFrame (`othervars`). Show the count of outliers for each variable and view the outliers for SAT math:

```
>>> sumvars = ['satmath','wageincome']
>>> othervars =
['originalid','highestdegree','gender','maritalstatus']
>>> outliers = ol.getoutliers(nls97, sumvars, othervars)
>>> outliers.varname.value_counts(sort=False)
satmath            10
wageincome        260
Name: varname, dtype: int64
>>> outliers.loc[outliers.varname=='satmath', othervars +
sumvars]
```

	originalid	highestdegree	...	satmath	wageincome
223058	6696	0. None	...	46.0	30000.0
267254	1622	2. High School	...	48.0	100000.0
291029	7088	2. High School	...	51.0	NaN
337438	159	2. High School	...	200.0	NaN

399109	3883	2. High School	...	36.0	NaN
448463	326	4. Bachelors	...	47.0	NaN
738290	7705	0. None	...	7.0	NaN
748274	3394	4. Bachelors	...	42.0	NaN
799095	535	5. Masters	...	59.0	120000.0
955430	2547	2. High School	...	200.0	NaN

```
[10 rows x 6 columns]
>>> outliers.to_excel("views/nlsoutliers.xlsx")
```

6. Create a function to generate histograms and boxplots.

The makeplot function takes a series, title, and label for the x-axis. The default plot is set as a histogram:

```
>>> def makeplot(seriestoplot, title, xlabel,
plottype="hist"):
...     if (plottype=="hist"):
...         plt.hist(seriestoplot)
...         plt.axvline(seriestoplot.mean(), color='red',\
...           linestyle='dashed', linewidth=1)
...         plt.xlabel(xlabel)
...         plt.ylabel("Frequency")
...     elif (plottype=="box"):
...         plt.boxplot(seriestoplot.dropna(),
labels=[xlabel])
...     plt.title(title)
...     plt.show()
```

7. Call the makeplot function to create a histogram:

```
>>> ol.makeplot(nls97.satmath, "Histogram of SAT Math",
"SAT Math")
```

This generates the following histogram:

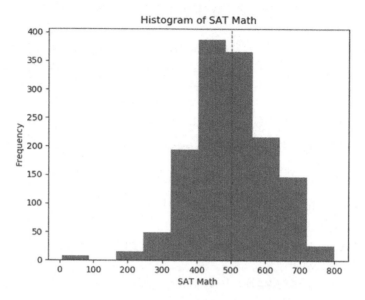

Figure 10.1 – Frequencies of SAT math values

8. Use the `makeplot` function to create a boxplot:

```
>>> ol.makeplot(nls97.satmath, "Boxplot of SAT Math",
"SAT Math", "box")
```

This generates the following boxplot:

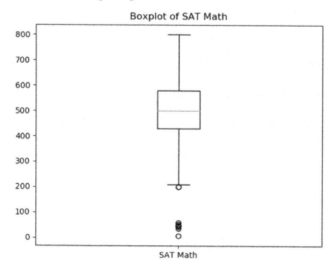

Figure 10.2 – Show the median, interquartile range, and outlier thresholds with a boxplot

The preceding steps show how we can develop reusable code to check for outliers and unexpected values.

How it works...

We start by getting the key attributes of a distribution, including the mean, median, standard deviation, skew, and kurtosis. We do this by passing a series to the getdistprop function in *step 3*, getting back a dictionary with these measures.

The function in *step 4* selects rows where one of the columns in sumvars has a value that is an outlier. It also includes the values for the columns in othervars and the threshold amounts in the DataFrame it returns.

We create a function in *step 6* that makes it easier to create a simple histogram or boxplot. The functionality of matplotlib is great, but it can take a minute to remind ourselves of the syntax when we just want to create a simple histogram or boxplot. We can avoid that by defining a function with a few routine parameters: series, title, and x-label. We call that function in *steps 7 and 8*.

There's more...

We do not want to do too much work with a continuous variable before getting a good sense of how its values are distributed; what are the central tendency and shape of the distribution? If we run something like the functions in this recipe for key continuous variables, we would be off to a good start.

The relatively painless portability of Python modules makes this pretty easy to do. If we wanted to use the outliers module that we use in this example, we would just need to save the outliers.py file to a folder that our program can access, add that folder to the Python path, and import it.

Usually, when we are inspecting an extreme value, we want to have a better idea of the context of other variables that might explain why the value is extreme. For example, a height of 178 centimeters is not an outlier for an adult male, but it definitely is for a 9-year old. The DataFrame produced in *steps 4 and 5* provides us with both the outlier values and other data that might be relevant. Saving the data to an Excel file makes it easy to inspect outlier rows later or share that data with others.

See also

We go into a fair bit of detail on detecting outliers and unexpected values in *Chapter 4, Identifying Missing Values and Outliers in Subsets of Data*. We examine histograms, boxplots, and many other visualizations in *Chapter 5, Using Visualizations for the Identification of Unexpected Values*.

Functions for aggregating or combining data

Most data analysis projects require some reshaping of data. We may need to aggregate by group or combine data vertically or horizontally. We have to do similar tasks each time we prepare our data for this reshaping. We can routinize some of these tasks with functions, improving both the reliability of our code and our efficiency in getting the work done. We sometimes need to check for mismatches in merge-by columns before doing a merge, check for unexpected changes in values in panel data from one period to the next before aggregating, or concatenate a number of files at once and verify that data has been combined accurately.

These are just a few examples of the kind of data aggregation and combining tasks that might lend themselves to a more generalized coding solution. In this recipe, we define functions that can help with these tasks.

Getting ready

We will work with the Covid daily data in this recipe. This data comprises new cases and new deaths for each country by day. We will also work with land temperatures data for several countries in 2019. The data for each country is in a separate file and has one row per weather station in that country for each month.

> **Note**
>
> The land temperatures data is taken from the Global Historical Climatology Network integrated database, which is made available for public use by the United States National Oceanic and Atmospheric Administration at https://www.ncdc.noaa.gov/data-access/land-based-station-data/land-based-datasets/global-historical-climatology-network-monthly-version-4.

How to do it...

We will use functions to aggregate data, combine data vertically, and check
merge-by values:

1. Import the pandas, os, and sys libraries:

    ```
    >>> import pandas as pd
    >>> import os
    >>> import sys
    ```

2. Create a function (adjmeans) to aggregate values by period for a group.

    Sort the values in the passed DataFrame by group (byvar) and then period.
    Convert the DataFrame values to a NumPy array. Loop through the values, do
    a running tally of the var column, and set the running tally back to 0 when you
    reach a new value for byvar. Before aggregating, check for extreme changes in
    values from one period to the next. The changeexclude parameter indicates the
    size of a change from one period to the next that should be considered extreme.
    The excludetype parameter indicates whether the changeexclude value is an
    absolute amount or a percentage of the var column's mean. Save the function in a
    file called combineagg.py in the helperfunctions subfolder:

    ```
    >>> def adjmeans(df, byvar, var, period,
      changeexclude=None, excludetype=None):
    ...     df = df.sort_values([byvar, period])
    ...     df = df.dropna(subset=[var])
    ...     # iterate using numpy arrays
    ...     prevbyvar = 'ZZZ'
    ...     prevvarvalue = 0
    ...     rowlist = []
    ...     varvalues = df[[byvar, var]].values
    ...     # convert exclusion ratio to absolute number
    ...     if (excludetype=="ratio" and changeexclude is not
      None):
    ...         changeexclude = df[var].mean()*changeexclude
    ...     # loop through variable values
    ...     for j in range(len(varvalues)):
    ...         byvar = varvalues[j][0]
    ...         varvalue = varvalues[j][1]
    ```

```
...         if (prevbyvar!=byvar):
...            if (prevbyvar!='ZZZ'):
...               rowlist.append({'byvar':prevbyvar,
'avgvar':varsum/byvarcnt,\
...                  'sumvar':varsum, 'byvarcnt':byvarcnt})
...            varsum = 0
...            byvarcnt = 0
...            prevbyvar = byvar
...         # exclude extreme changes in variable value
...         if ((changeexclude is None) or (0 <=
abs(varvalue-prevvarvalue) \
...            <= changeexclude) or (byvarcnt==0)):
...            varsum += varvalue
...            byvarcnt += 1
...         prevvarvalue = varvalue
...      rowlist.append({'byvar':prevbyvar, 'avgvar':varsum/
byvarcnt, \
...         'sumvar':varsum, 'byvarcnt':byvarcnt})
...      return pd.DataFrame(rowlist)
```

3. Import the `combineagg` module:

```
>>> sys.path.append(os.getcwd() + "/helperfunctions")
>>> import combineagg as ca
```

4. Load the DataFrames:

```
>>> coviddaily = pd.read_csv("data/coviddaily720.csv")
>>> ltbrazil = pd.read_csv("data/ltbrazil.csv")
>>> countries = pd.read_csv("data/ltcountries.csv")
>>> locations = pd.read_csv("data/ltlocations.csv")
```

5. Call the `adjmeans` function to summarize panel data by group and time period.

    Indicate that we want a summary of new_cases by `location`:

```
>>> ca.adjmeans(coviddaily, 'location','new_
cases','casedate')
          byvar         avgvar      sumvar   byvarcnt
0       Afghanistan   186.221622   34451.0        185
```

1	Albania	26.753968	3371.0	126
2	Algeria	98.484211	18712.0	190
3	Andorra	7.066116	855.0	121
4	Angola	4.274336	483.0	113
..	...	...	...	...
204	Vietnam	1.937173	370.0	191
205	Western Sahara	6.653846	519.0	78
206	Yemen	14.776596	1389.0	94
207	Zambia	16.336207	1895.0	116
208	Zimbabwe	8.614035	982.0	114

```
[209 rows x 4 columns]
```

6. Call the `adjmeans` function again, this time excluding values where `new_cases` go up or down by more than 150 from one day to the next. Notice some reduction in the counts for some countries:

```
>>> ca.adjmeans(coviddaily, 'location','new_
cases','casedate', 150)
```

	byvar	avgvar	sumvar	byvarcnt
0	Afghanistan	141.968750	22715.0	160
1	Albania	26.753968	3371.0	126
2	Algeria	94.133690	17603.0	187
3	Andorra	7.066116	855.0	121
4	Angola	4.274336	483.0	113
..	...	...	...	...
204	Vietnam	1.937173	370.0	191
205	Western Sahara	2.186667	164.0	75
206	Yemen	14.776596	1389.0	94
207	Zambia	11.190909	1231.0	110
208	Zimbabwe	8.614035	982.0	114

```
[209 rows x 4 columns]
```

7. Create a function to check values for merge-by columns on one file but not another.

The `checkmerge` function does an outer join of two DataFrames passed to it, using the third and fourth parameters for the merge-by columns for the first and second DataFrame respectively. It then does a crosstab that shows the number of rows with merge-by values in both DataFrames and those in one DataFrame but not the other. It also shows up to 20 rows of data for merge-by values found in just one file:

```
>>> def checkmerge(dfleft, dfright, mergebyleft,
mergebyright):
...    dfleft['inleft'] = "Y"
...    dfright['inright'] = "Y"
...    dfboth = pd.merge(dfleft[[mergebyleft,'inleft']],\
        dfright[[mergebyright,'inright']], left_
on=[mergebyleft],\
...       right_on=[mergebyright], how="outer")
...    dfboth.fillna('N', inplace=True)
...    print(pd.crosstab(dfboth.inleft, dfboth.inright))
...    print(dfboth.loc[(dfboth.inleft=='N') | (dfboth.
inright=='N')].head(20))
```

8. Call the `checkmerge` function.

Check a merge between the `countries` land temperatures DataFrame (which has one row per country) and the `locations` DataFrame (which has one row for each weather station in each country). The crosstab shows that 27,472 merge-by column values are in both DataFrames, two are in the `countries` file and not in the `locations` file, and one is in the `locations` file but not the `countries` file:

```
>>> ca.checkmerge(countries.copy(), locations.copy(),\
...    "countryid", "countryid")
inright  N       Y
inleft
N        0       1
Y        2   27472
        countryid inleft inright
9715          LQ      Y       N
13103         ST      Y       N
27474         FO      N       Y
```

9. Create a function that concatenates all CSV files in a folder.

This function loops through all of the filenames in the specified folder. It uses the endswith method to check that the filename has a CSV file extension. It then loads the DataFrame and prints out the number of rows. Finally, it uses concat to append the rows of the new DataFrame to the rows already appended. If column names on a file are different, it prints those column names:

```python
>>> def addfiles(directory):
...     dfout = pd.DataFrame()
...     columnsmatched = True
...     # loop through the files
...     for filename in os.listdir(directory):
...         if filename.endswith(".csv"):
...             fileloc = os.path.join(directory, filename)
...             # open the next file
...             with open(fileloc) as f:
...                 dfnew = pd.read_csv(fileloc)
...                 print(filename + " has " + str(dfnew.
shape[0]) + " rows.")
...                 dfout = pd.concat([dfout, dfnew])
...                 # check if current file has any different
columns
...                 columndiff = dfout.columns.symmetric_
difference(dfnew.columns)
...                 if (not columndiff.empty):
...                     print("", "Different column names for:",
                        filename,\
...                         columndiff, "", sep="\n")
...                     columnsmatched = False
...     print("Columns Matched:", columnsmatched)
...     return dfout
```

10. Use the `addfiles` function to concatenate all of the `countries` land temperatures files.

It looks like the file for Oman (`ltoman`) is slightly different. It does not have the `latabs` column. Notice that the counts for each country in the combined DataFrame match the number of rows for each country file:

```
>>> landtemps = ca.addfiles("data/ltcountry")
ltpoland.csv has 120 rows.
ltjapan.csv has 1800 rows.
ltindia.csv has 1056 rows.
ltbrazil.csv has 1104 rows.
ltcameroon.csv has 48 rows.
ltoman.csv has 288 rows.

Different column names for:
ltoman.csv
Index(['latabs'], dtype='object')

ltmexico.csv has 852 rows.
Columns Matched: False
>>> landtemps.country.value_counts()
Japan        1800
Brazil       1104
India        1056
Mexico        852
Oman          288
Poland        120
Cameroon       48
Name: country, dtype: int64
```

The preceding steps demonstrate how we can systematize some of our messy data reshaping work. I am sure you can think of a number of other functions that might be helpful.

How it works...

You may have noticed that in the adjmeans function we define in *step 2*, we actually do not append our summary of the var column values until we get to the next byvar column value. This is because there is no way to tell that we are on the last row for any byvar value until we get to the next byvar value. That is not a problem because we append the summary to rowlist right before we reset the value to 0. This also means that we need to do something special to output the totals for the last byvar value since no next byvar value is reached. We do this with a final append after the loop is complete.

In *step 5*, we call the adjmeans function we defined in *step 2*. Since we do not set a value for the changeexclude parameter, the function will include all values in the aggregation. This will give us the same results as we would get using groupby with an aggregation function. When we pass an argument to changeexclude, however, we determine which rows to exclude from the aggregation. In *step 6*, the fifth argument in the call to adjmeans indicates that we should exclude new cases values that are more than 150 cases higher or lower than the value for the previous day.

The function in *step 9* works well when the data files to be concatenated have the same, or nearly the same, structure. We print an alert when the column names are different, as *step 10* shows. The latabs column is not in the Oman file. This means that in the concatenated file, latabs will be missing for all of the rows for Oman.

There's more...

The adjmeans function does a fairly straightforward check of each new value to be aggregated before including it in the total. But we could imagine much more complicated checks. We could even have made a call to another function within the adjmeans function where we are deciding whether to include the row.

See also

We examine combining DataFrames vertically and horizontally in *Chapter 8, Addressing Data Issues when Combining DataFrames*.

Classes that contain the logic for updating series values

We sometimes work with a particular dataset for an extended period of time, occasionally years. The data might be updated regularly, for a new month or year, or with additional individuals, but the data structure might be fairly stable. If that dataset also has a large number of columns, we might be able to improve the reliability and readability of our code by implementing classes.

When we create classes, we define the attributes and methods of objects. When I use classes for my data cleaning work, I tend to conceptualize a class as representing my unit of analysis. So, if my unit of analysis is a student, then I have a student class. Each instance of a student created by that class might have birth date and gender attributes and a course registration method. I might also create a subclass for alumni that inherits methods and attributes from the student class.

Data cleaning for the NLS DataFrame could be implemented nicely with classes. The dataset has been stable for 20 years, both in terms of the variables and the allowable values for each variable. We explore how to create a respondent class for NLS survey responses in this recipe.

Getting ready

You will need to create a `helperfunctions` subfolder in your current directory to run the code in this recipe. We will save the file (`respondent.py`) for our new class in that subfolder.

How to do it...

We will define a respondent class to create several new series based on the NLS data:

1. Import the `pandas`, `os`, `sys`, and `pprint` libraries.

    We store this code in a different file than we will save the respondent class. Let's call this file `class_cleaning.py`. We will instantiate respondent objects from this file:

    ```
    >>> import pandas as pd
    >>> import os
    >>> import sys
    >>> import pprint
    ```

2. Create a respondent class and save it to `respondent.py` in the `helperfunctions` subfolder.

    When we call our class (instantiate a class object), the `__init__` method runs automatically. (There is a double underscore before and after `init`). The `__init__` method has `self` as the first parameter, as any instance method does. The `__init__` method of this class also has a `respdict` parameter, which expects a dictionary of values from the NLS data. In later steps, we will instantiate a respondent object once for each row of data in the NLS DataFrame.

    The `__init__` method assigns the passed `respdict` value to `self.respdict` to create an instance variable that we can reference in other methods. Finally, we increment a counter, `respondentcnt`. We will be able to use this later to confirm the number of instances of `respondent` that we created. We also import the `math` and `datetime` modules because we will need them later. (Notice that class names are capitalized by convention).

    ```
    >>> import math
    >>> import datetime as dt
    >>>
    >>> class Respondent:
    ...     respondentcnt = 0


    ...     def __init__(self, respdict):
    ...         self.respdict = respdict
    ...         Respondent.respondentcnt+=1
    ```

3. Add a method for counting the number of children.

    This is a very simple method that just adds the number of children living with the respondent to the number of children not living with the respondent, to get the total number of children. It uses the `childathome` and `childnotathome` key values in the `self.respdict` dictionary:

    ```
    >>> def childnum(self):
    ...     return self.respdict['childathome'] + self.
    respdict['childnotathome']
    ```

4. Add a method for calculating average weeks worked across the 20 years of the survey.

Use dictionary comprehension to create a dictionary (`workdict`) of the weeks worked keys that do not have missing values. Sum the values in `workdict` and divide that by the length of `workdict`:

```
>>> def avgweeksworked(self):
...     workdict = {k: v for k, v in self.respdict.items() \
...         if k.startswith('weeksworked') and not math.isnan(v)}
...     nweeks = len(workdict)
...     if (nweeks>0):
...         avgww = sum(workdict.values())/nweeks
...     else:
...         avgww = 0
...     return avgww
```

5. Add a method for calculating age as of a given date.

This method takes a date string (`bydatestring`) to use for the end date of the age calculation. We use the `datetime` module to convert the `date` string to a `datetime` object, `bydate`. We subtract the birth year value in `self.respdict` from the year of `bydate`, subtracting 1 from that calculation if the birth date has not happened yet that year. (We only have birth month and birth year in the NLS data, so we choose 15 as a midpoint).

```
>>> def ageby(self, bydatestring):
...     bydate = dt.datetime.strptime(bydatestring, '%Y%m%d')
...     birthyear = self.respdict['birthyear']
...     birthmonth = self.respdict['birthmonth']
...     age = bydate.year - birthyear
...     if (bydate.month<birthmonth or (bydate.month==birthmonth \
...         and bydate.day<15)):
...         age = age -1
...     return age
```

6. Add a method to create a flag if the respondent ever enrolled at a 4-year college.

Use dictionary comprehension to check whether any college enrollment values are at a 4-year college:

```
>>> def baenrollment(self):
...     colenrdict = {k: v for k, v in self.respdict.
items() \
...         if k.startswith('colenr') and v=="3. 4-year
college"}
...     if (len(colenrdict)>0):
...         return "Y"
...     else:
...         return "N"
```

7. Import the respondent class.

Now we are ready to instantiate some Respondent objects! Let's do that from the class_cleaning.py file we started in *step 1*. We start by importing the respondent class. (This step assumes that respondent.py is in the helperfunctions subfolder).

```
>>> sys.path.append(os.getcwd() + "/helperfunctions")
>>> import respondent as rp
```

8. Load the NLS data and create a list of dictionaries.

Use the to_dict method to create the list of dictionaries (nls97list). Each row from the DataFrame will be a dictionary with column names as keys. Show part of the first dictionary (the first row):

```
>>> nls97 = pd.read_csv("data/nls97f.csv")
>>> nls97list = nls97.to_dict('records')
>>> nls97.shape
(8984, 89)
>>> len(nls97list)
8984
>>> pprint.pprint(nls97list[0:1])
[{'birthmonth': 5,
  'birthyear': 1980,
  'childathome': 4.0,
```

```
'childnotathome': 0.0,
'colenrfeb00': '1. Not enrolled',
'colenrfeb01': '1. Not enrolled',
...
'weeksworked16': 48.0,
'weeksworked17': 48.0}]
```

9. Loop through the list, creating a `respondent` instance each time.

    We pass each dictionary to the respondent class, `rp.Respondent(respdict)`.
    Once we have created a respondent object (`resp`), we can then use all of the instance
    methods to get the values we need. We create a new dictionary with those values
    returned by instance methods. We then append that dictionary to `analysisdict`:

```
>>> analysislist = []
>>>
>>> for respdict in nls97list:
...     resp = rp.Respondent(respdict)
...     newdict = dict(originalid=respdict['originalid'],
...         childnum=resp.childnum(),
...         avgweeksworked=resp.avgweeksworked(),
...         age=resp.ageby('20201015'),
...         baenrollment=resp.baenrollment())
...     analysislist.append(newdict)
```

10. Pass the dictionary to the pandas `DataFrame` method.

    First, check the number of items in `analysislist` and the number of
    instances created:

```
>>> len(analysislist)
8984
>>> resp.respondentcnt
8984
>>> pprint.pprint(analysislist[0:2])
[{'age': 40,
  'avgweeksworked': 49.05555555555556,
  'baenrollment': 'Y',
  'childnum': 4.0,
  'originalid': 8245},
```

```
{'age': 37,
 'avgweeksworked': 49.388888888888886,
 'baenrollment': 'N',
 'childnum': 2.0,
 'originalid': 3962}]
>>> analysis = pd.DataFrame(analysislist)
>>> analysis.head(2)
   originalid  childnum  avgweeksworked  age baenrollment
0        8245       4.0       49.055556   40            Y
1        3962       2.0       49.388889   37            N
```

These steps demonstrated how to create a class in Python, how to pass data to a class, how to create an instance of a class, and how to call the methods of the class to update variable values.

How it works...

The key work in this recipe is done in *step 2*. It creates the respondent class and sets us up well for the remaining steps. We pass a dictionary with the values for each row to the class's __init__ method. The __init__ method assigns that dictionary to an instance variable that will be available to all of the class's methods (self.respdict = respdict).

Steps 3 through 6 use that dictionary to calculate number of children, average weeks worked per year, age, and college enrollment. *Steps 4 and 6* show how helpful dictionary comprehensions are when we need to test for the same value over many keys. The dictionary comprehensions select the relevant keys, weeksworked##, colenroct##, and colenrfeb##, and allow us to inspect the values of those keys. This is incredibly useful when we have data that is untidy in this way, as survey data often is.

In *step 8*, we create a list of dictionaries with the to_dict method. It has the expected number of list items, 8,984, the same as the number of rows in the DataFrame. We use pprint to show what the dictionary looks like for the first list item. The dictionary has keys for the column names and values for the column values.

We iterate over the list in *step 9*, creating a new respondent object and passing the list item. We call the methods to get the values we want, except for originalid, which we can pull directly from the dictionary. We create a dictionary (newdict) with those values, which we append to a list (analysislist).

In *step 10*, we create a pandas DataFrame from the list (`analysislist`) we created in *step 9*. We do this by passing the list to the pandas `DataFrame` method.

There's more...

We pass dictionaries to the class rather than data rows, which is also a possibility. We do this because navigating a NumPy array is more efficient than looping over a DataFrame with `itertuples` or `iterrows`. We do not lose much of the functionality needed for our class when we work with dictionaries rather than DataFrame rows. We are still able to use functions such as `sum` and `mean` and count the number of values meeting certain criteria.

It is hard to avoid having to iterate over data with this conceptualization of a respondent class. This respondent class is consistent with our understanding of the unit of analysis, the survey respondent. That is also, unsurprisingly, how the data comes to us. But iterating over data one row at a time is resource-intensive, even with more efficient NumPy arrays.

I would argue, however, that you gain more than you lose by constructing a class like this one when working with data with many columns and with a structure that does not change much over time. The most important advantage is that it matches our intuition about the data and focuses our work on understanding the data for each respondent. I also think we find that when we construct the class well we do far fewer passes through the data than we otherwise might.

See also

We examine navigating over DataFrame rows and NumPy arrays in *Chapter 7, Fixing Messy Data when Aggregating*.

This was a very quick introduction to working with classes in Python. If you would like to learn more about object-oriented programming in Python, I would recommend *Python 3 Object-Oriented Programming, Third Edition* by Dusty Phillips.

Classes that handle non-tabular data structures

Data scientists increasingly receive non-tabular data, often in the form of JSON or XML files. The flexibility of JSON and XML allows organizations to capture complicated relationships between data items in one file. A one-to-many relationship stored in two tables in an enterprise data system can be represented well in JSON by a parent node for the one side and child nodes for data on the many side.

When we receive JSON data we often start by trying to normalize it. Indeed, we do that in a couple of recipes in this book. We try to recover the one-to-one and one-to-many relationships in the data obfuscated by the flexibility of JSON. But there is another way to work with such data, one that has many advantages.

Instead of normalizing the data, we can create a class that instantiates objects at the appropriate unit of analysis, and use the methods of the class to navigate the many side of one-to-many relationships. For example, if we get a JSON file that has student nodes and then multiple child nodes for each course taken by a student, we would usually normalize that data by creating a student file and a course file, with student ID as the merge-by column on both files. An alternative, which we explore in this recipe, would be to leave the data as it is, create a student class, and create methods that do calculations on the child nodes, such as calculating total credits taken.

Let's try that with this recipe, using data from the Cleveland Museum of Art, which has collection items, one or more nodes for media citations for each item, and one or more nodes for each creator of the item.

Getting ready

This recipe assumes you have the `requests` and `pprint` libraries. If they are not installed, you can install them with `pip`. From the Terminal, or PowerShell (in Windows), enter `pip install requests` and `pip install pprint`.

I show here the structure of the JSON file that is created when using the `collections` API of the Cleveland Museum of Art. (I have abbreviated the JSON file to save space.)

```
{
"id": 165157,
"title": "Fulton and Nostrand",
"creation_date": "1958",
"citations": [
  {
    "citation": "Annual Exhibition: Sculpture, Paintings,
Watercolors, Drawings,
    "page_number": "Unpaginated, [8],[12]",
    "url": null
  },
  {
    "citation": "\"Moscow to See Modern U.S. Art,\"<em> New York
Times</em> (May 31, 1959).",
```

```
    "page_number": "P. 60",
    "url": null
  }]
"creators": [
    {
      "description": "Jacob Lawrence (American, 1917-2000)",
      "role": "artist",
      "birth_year": "1917",
      "death_year": "2000"
    }
  ]
}
```

> **Note**
>
> The Cleveland Museum of Art provides an API for public access to this data:
> `https://openaccess-api.clevelandart.org/`. Much more
> than the citations and creators data used in this recipe is available with the API.

How to do it...

We create a collection item class that summarizes the data we need on creators and
media citations:

1. Import the pandas, json, pprint, and requests libraries.

    Let's first create a file that we will use to instantiate collection item objects and call
    it class_cleaning_json.py:

    ```
    >>> import pandas as pd
    >>> import json
    >>> import pprint
    >>> import requests
    ```

2. Create a `Collectionitem` class.

We pass a dictionary for each collection item to the `__init__` method of the class, which runs automatically when an instance of the class is created. We assign the collection item dictionary to an instance variable. Save the class as `collectionitem.py` in the `helperfunctions` folder:

```
>>> class Collectionitem:
...     collectionitemcnt = 0

...     def __init__(self, colldict):
...         self.colldict = colldict
...         Collectionitem.collectionitemcnt+=1
```

3. Create a method to get the birth year of the first creator for each collection item.

Remember that collection items can have multiple creators. This means that the `creators` key has one or more list items as values, and these items are themselves dictionaries. To get the birth year of the first creator, then, we need `['creators'] [0] ['birth_year']`. We also need to allow for the birth year key to be missing, so we test for that first:

```
>>> def birthyearcreator1(self):
...     if ("birth_year" in self.colldict['creators'] [0]):
...         byear = self.colldict['creators'] [0] ['birth_
year']
...     else:
...         byear = "Unknown"
...     return byear
```

4. Create a method to get the birth years for all creators.

Use list comprehension to loop through all the creators items. This will return the birth years as a list:

```
>>> def birthyearsall(self):
...     byearlist = [item.get('birth_year') for item in \
...         self.colldict['creators']]
...     return byearlist
```

5. Create a method to count the number of creators:

```
>>> def ncreators(self):
...     return len(self.colldict['creators'])
```

6. Create a method to count the number of media citations:

```
>>> def ncitations(self):
...     return len(self.colldict['citations'])
```

7. Import the `collectionitem` module.

    We do this from the `class_cleaning_json.py` file we created in *step 1*:

```
>>> sys.path.append(os.getcwd() + "/helperfunctions")
>>> import collectionitem as ci
```

8. Load the art museum's collections data.

    This returns a list of dictionaries:

```
>>> response = requests.get("https://openaccess-api.
clevelandart.org/api/artworks/?african_american_artists")
>>> camcollections = json.loads(response.text)
>>> camcollections = camcollections['data']
```

9. Loop through the `camcollections` list.

    Create a collection item instance for each item in `camcollections`. Pass each item, which is a dictionary of collections, creators, and citation keys, to the class. Call the methods we have just created and assign the values they return to a new dictionary (`newdict`). Append that dictionary to a list (`analysislist`). (Some of the values can be pulled directly from the dictionary, such as with `title=colldict['title']`, since we do not need to change the value in any way).

```
>>> analysislist = []
>>>
>>> for colldict in camcollections:
...     coll = ci.Collectionitem(colldict)
...     newdict = dict(id=colldict['id'],
...         title=colldict['title'],
...         type=colldict['type'],
```

```
...        creationdate=colldict['creation_date'],
...        ncreators=coll.ncreators(),
...        ncitations=coll.ncitations(),
...        birthyearsall=coll.birthyearsall(),
...        birthyear=coll.birthyearcreator1())
...     analysislist.append(newdict)
```

10. Create an analysis DataFrame with the new list of dictionaries.

Confirm that we are getting the correct counts, and print the dictionary for the first item:

```
>>> len(camcollections)
789
>>> len(analysislist)
789
>>> pprint.pprint(analysislist[0:1])
[{'birthyear': '1917',
  'birthyearsall': ['1917'],
  'creationdate': '1958',
  'id': 165157,
  'ncitations': 24,
  'ncreators': 1,
  'title': 'Fulton and Nostrand',
  'type': 'Painting'}]
>>> analysis = pd.DataFrame(analysislist)
>>> analysis.birthyearsall.value_counts().head()
[1951]          262
[1953]          118
[1961, None]    105
[1886]           34
[1935]           17
Name: birthyearsall, dtype: int64
>>> analysis.head(2)
        id              title  ...  birthyearsall
birthyear
```

```
0   165157   Fulton and Nostrand   ...        [1917]
1917

1   163769         Go Down Death   ...        [1899]
1899


[2 rows x 8 columns]
```

These steps give a sense of how we can use classes to handle non-tabular data.

How it works...

This recipe demonstrated how to work directly with a JSON file, or any file with implied one-to-many or many-to-many relationships. We created a class at the unit of analysis (a collection item, in this case) and then created methods to summarize multiple nodes of data for each collection item.

The methods we created in *steps 3 through 6* are satisfyingly straightforward. When we first look at the structure of the data, displayed in the *Getting ready* section of this recipe, it is hard not to feel that it will be really difficult to clean. It looks like anything goes. But it turns out to have a fairly reliable structure. We can count on one or more child nodes for `creators` and `citations`. Each `creators` and `citations` node also has child nodes, which are key and value pairs. These keys are not always present, so we need to first check to see whether they are present before trying to grab their values. We do this in *step 3*.

There's more...

I go into some detail about the advantages of working directly with JSON files in *Chapter 2, Anticipating Data Cleaning Issues when Importing HTML and JSON into pandas*. I think the museum's collections data is a good example of why we might want to stick with JSON if we can. The structure of the data actually makes sense, even if it is in a very different form. There is always a danger when we try to normalize it that we will miss some aspects of its structure.

Other Books You May Enjoy

If you enjoyed this book, you may be interested in these other books by Packt:

Practical Data Analysis Using Jupyter Notebook

Marc Wintjen

ISBN: 978-1-83882-603-1

- Understand the importance of data literacy and how to communicate effectively using data
- Find out how to use Python packages such as NumPy, pandas, Matplotlib, and the Natural Language Toolkit (NLTK) for data analysis
- Wrangle data and create DataFrames using pandas
- Produce charts and data visualizations using time-series datasets
- Discover relationships and how to join data together using SQL
- Use NLP techniques to work with unstructured data to create sentiment analysis models
- Discover patterns in real-world datasets that provide accurate insights

Hands-On Exploratory Data Analysis with Python

Suresh Kumar Mukhiya, Usman Ahmed

ISBN: 978-1-78953-725-3

- Import, clean, and explore data to perform preliminary analysis using powerful Python packages
- Identify and transform erroneous data using different data wrangling techniques
- Explore the use of multiple regression to describe non-linear relationships
- Discover hypothesis testing and explore techniques of time-series analysis
- Understand and interpret results obtained from graphical analysis
- Build, train, and optimize predictive models to estimate results
- Perform complex EDA techniques on open source datasets

Leave a review - let other readers know what you think

Please share your thoughts on this book with others by leaving a review on the site that you bought it from. If you purchased the book from Amazon, please leave us an honest review on this book's Amazon page. This is vital so that other potential readers can see and use your unbiased opinion to make purchasing decisions, we can understand what our customers think about our products, and our authors can see your feedback on the title that they have worked with Packt to create. It will only take a few minutes of your time, but is valuable to other potential customers, our authors, and Packt. Thank you!

Index